American Torture from
the Philippines to Iraq

American Torture from the Philippines to Iraq

A Recurring Nightmare

WILLIAM L. D'AMBRUOSO

OXFORD
UNIVERSITY PRESS

OXFORD
UNIVERSITY PRESS

Oxford University Press is a department of the University of Oxford. It furthers
the University's objective of excellence in research, scholarship, and education
by publishing worldwide. Oxford is a registered trade mark of Oxford University
Press in the UK and certain other countries.

Published in the United States of America by Oxford University Press
198 Madison Avenue, New York, NY 10016, United States of America.

© Oxford University Press 2022

Library of Congress Control Number: 2021947725
ISBN 978-0-19-757032-6

DOI: 10.1093/oso/9780197570326.001.0001

1 3 5 7 9 8 6 4 2

Printed by Integrated Books International, United States of America

Contents

Acknowledgements

I have accumulated no shortage of debts in writing this book. What follows is only a partial list.

Many of my mentors and colleagues at the University of Washington, my graduate school alma mater, deserve special mention. Beth Kier was the project's first and most consistent champion. Her early encouragement, persistent enthusiasm, and vision proved invaluable. Jon Mercer's detailed comments on several underdeveloped drafts, along with plenty of discussion time, improved my work and made graduate school life more enjoyable. I puzzled through the project's ideas with Jamie Mayerfeld, who helped me outline the limits of my arguments and take seriously the ethical implications. Chris Adolph and Jim Caporaso showed me how my approach was more compatible with other perspectives than I had realized. Beth and Jon's University of Washington International Security Colloquium (UWISC) was a fantastic atmosphere for trying out ideas, and the UWISC regulars provided excellent feedback when I presented on parts of the project. Following my presentation, a lengthy discussion with Stephan Hamberg helped me clarify the book's central claims. Many other colleagues at UW, too numerous to name, had a hand in moving the project forward.

I owe special thanks to archivists at the National Archives, the National Security Archives, and the U.S. Army Heritage and Education Center, as well as the kind hosts that put me up in Washington, D.C., and Carlisle, PA, for many days. Marlea Leljedal and Christopher Einolf sent me materials that I had previously overlooked.

My colleagues at Bates College, where I taught after UW, cheered on my writing progress, and some of the feedback during my job talk there carried over into the final product. Leslie Hill and Stephen Engel showed me how feminist theorizing complemented my explanations. Jim Richter, Jason Scheideman, and Jiyoung Ko kept my mind on international politics, and Nina Hagel fueled me with words of encouragement, professional advice, and baked goods.

The book's post-dissertation life got a much-needed boost when Nimah Mazaheri told me to send him the manuscript, refused to take "not yet" for an answer, and gave me detailed comments. Nimah's advice on this and other projects, plus his generosity as an informal mentor, continues to inspire me. Chris Heurlin's assembled student group at Bowdoin, MIT's Security Studies Working Group, and Harvard's Political Violence Working Group provided additional chances to present and hear back from smart and engaged participants. Annual APSA, MPSA, ISA, and NEPSA meetings left me grateful for discussants' and participants' insights.

This book's finishing touches were completed while on a fellowship funded by the Stanton Foundation at the Harvard Kennedy School's Belfer Center for Science and International Affairs. A presentation for the International Security Program's seminar series, well-led by Steve Miller and Steve Walt and administered by Susan Lynch, gave me a chance to receive some last-minute suggestions. A follow-up exchange with Averell Schmidt helped me amend the concluding chapter.

I am grateful for Angela Chnapko, Alexcee Bechthold, Saloni Vohra, and their colleagues at Oxford University Press and Newgen Publishing. Two excellent anonymous readers' comments improved the manuscript substantially and limited future embarrassments.

My mother and step-father provided encouragement, as did my sisters. My father was a source of inspiration. My mother-in-law and her husband were also in my corner. It was not just verbal support, either; grandparents grandparented the kids so that I could sneak in extra researching and writing time.

The breadth of my debt to my wife Abby is difficult to capture—from crucial emotional support to writing help to taking the lead on parenting at key moments. She is also jealous of my time and energy in all the best ways, and I'm thankful for how she keeps me grounded in family. My children, August and Greta, have shown admirable patience with me. They help me believe that the future is bright and the world worth improving.

1

Torture and the Norm against It

Undying Rivals

"Unthinkable." This is how observers repeatedly described the post-2001 U.S. torture program during the war on terror. "I am willing to think the unthinkable," one prominent legal commentator proudly announced in his 2002 book arguing that interrogators should pursue "torture warrants" to give what he considered necessary work the legal cover that a nation of laws demands. That same year, the Central Intelligence Agency scrambled to put together a secret interrogation program that included severe sleep deprivation, confinement in small spaces, forced standing, and choking by water, i.e., waterboarding. After the release of photos showing U.S. soldiers abusing prisoners at the Abu Ghraib prison in Iraq in 2004, another well-known lawyer and commentator discussed "thinking the unthinkable" en route to claiming that torture should, in essence, be (to borrow a phrase from the 1990s abortion debate in the United States), "safe, legal, and rare." Critics of torture also used the word. "[T]he unthinkable is not only being thought, but openly considered," reported one columnist as part of an argument that torture should never be permitted. "Torture used to be unthinkable," lamented another.[1] The term has also made its way into the titles of scholarly works and movies.[2]

The label "unthinkable" sometimes serves as a synonym for "unspeakable," referring to the gruesome nature of the act. McCarthy (2004) writes that "even reading or thinking about such practices may make the teeth clench and the stomach churn." It also suggests a perceived mismatch between American moral commitments and torture. Both international and domestic norms proscribe torture. That is, there exists a collective expectation that torture is wrong. Deeply held norms can lend the acts they proscribe an "unthinking" quality—violating such taboos does not, or should not, even come to mind (Price and Tennenwald 1996). Critics of the torture program also frequently point out that the United States has a history of treating prisoners well. After the truth of the post-2001 program set in, it prompted a reevaluation. As legal

American Torture from the Philippines to Iraq. William L. d'Ambruoso, Oxford University Press. © Oxford University Press 2022. DOI: 10.1093/oso/9780197570326.003.0001

scholars such as Luban (2007, 1425) observed, "Torture used to be incompatible with American values." The United States used to punish torturers, sometimes with death (Begala 2009).

While I will contend that the U.S. record of detainee abuse is far from spotless, and the norm against torture is not as robust as it could be, observers of war-on-terror torture were somewhat justified in their surprise. After all, for torture to reach all the way to the twenty-first century in the United States, it had to be remarkably resilient. Torture had to survive the intellectual assault from European Enlightenment authors like Beccaria, who argued persuasively that torture for judicial purposes would generate lots of false confessions. It had to find a way around the founding documents of the United States, which, with strong influence from European thinkers and experience, expressly prohibit cruel and unusual punishment in the Eighth Amendment to the Constitution. Torture persisted despite being prohibited in the American Civil War's Lieber Code, a forerunner to modern laws of war. It managed to continue beyond the Geneva Conventions from the first half of the twentieth century and the Convention against Torture of 1984. Torture has also endured less legalistic admonishment. The U.S. government's own State Department has been a leading whistleblower for torture and other cruel treatment abroad, with reports so comprehensive that scholars have used them to construct torture variables for quantitative analysis.[3] "The norm against torture," writes Andrew Linklater (2007, 113), "has been thought to be the pre-eminent manifestation of a global commitment to civilized norms."[4] This book asks the following: Why has torture recurred, and in particular why have torture and the norm against it persisted in tandem like undying rivals for over a century?

Torture and liberalism make for especially strange bedfellows. Luban (2007) argues that most forms of torture, for punishment or humiliation, make no sense in combination with the liberal value of popular sovereignty, because the people would be trying to impress themselves with a show of absolute control. Luban believes that the incompatibility between torture for intelligence and liberalism is less fundamental, and he discusses at length why even the promise of limited, rare torture exclusively for intelligence in high-stakes cases would unravel. His argument understates the case. Even torture for intelligence is essentially illiberal because it treats individuals as means rather than ends. Michael Ignatieff writes that "torture should remain anathema to a liberal democracy and should never be regulated, countenanced, or covertly accepted in a war on terror. For torture, when committed by a state, expresses the state's ultimate view that human beings are expendable" (quoted in Lukes 2005, 4).

While liberal states have not tortured as much as their illiberal counterparts, they have done their share. In fact, they have invented their own "liberal" methods. Darius Rejali (2007) explains how international and domestic monitoring of detainee treatment has forced liberal states to develop and perpetuate "stealth torture" methods that leave no trace and help the perpetrator escape detection. Any given "enhanced interrogation" technique from the war on terror is more likely to be a descendent of American slavery or British military punishment than fascist or Communist coercion. These techniques lived on through the twentieth century, in British and French colonies, as well as in American counterinsurgencies and interrogation manuals. The U.S. war on terror brought liberal-democratic torture to this century.

The case of the war on terror is particularly crucial for arguing that torture has been persistent, because many of the background conditions that carried detainee abuse through the twentieth century are no longer in effect. Old-fashioned colonialism is mostly done, and liberal democracies' rejections of the horrors of torture may even have had a hand in colonialism's demise (Merom 2003). The Cold War is over, and with it the counterrevolutionary torture that clandestine U.S. bureaucracies helped to develop and spread. The three main empirical cases of this book—the Philippine-American War (1899–1902), the CIA from its founding to the Vietnam War, and the post-2001 war on terror—correspond with imperialism, the Cold War, and post–Cold War conflict, respectively. My strategy is to extract from these cases the common factors that have allowed torture to persist across the varied contexts.

The hypocrisy of liberal torture would not surprise most international relations scholars, especially realists and rational choice theorists who expect states to say and do things in pursuit of self-gain, even if their words and deeds are mutually inconsistent.[5] However, there are (at least) five instrumental reasons for avoiding interrogational torture. First, torture is a questionable method for gathering intelligence. Perhaps the most persistent critique of interrogational torture is its flimsy connection to truth: victims are likely to say anything, including false statements, to stop the suffering.[6] Torture "tests endurance rather than veracity" (Langbein 2004, 73). Second, torture can fuel the enemy's recruitment efforts, giving life to terrorist and insurgent groups.[7] Third, torture may deter the enemy from surrendering, prolonging wars and causing more casualties on both sides.[8] Fourth, torture can produce extreme stress in the interrogator (Risen 2014). Fifth, torture runs counter to the "hearts and minds" campaigns that many modern counterinsurgency strategists advocate (U.S. Army 2006). Torture does not easily lend itself to straightforward, utility-maximizing explanations. Why have states persisted in practicing it? More broadly, why would states do something that is both odious and of dubious instrumental value?

If the reader buys the foregoing argument that torture for intelligence carries great risks and little promise, then the significance of the puzzle is clear. Torture that does not work has no redeeming ethical qualities and is therefore a horrendous mistake. Knowing why and how it occurs can have implications for its eradication. And although the puzzle specifies torture for intelligence, people turn to torture for many reasons—punishment, forced confession, revenge, social control, sadistic glee—but it often begins with superiors' approval of interrogational torture. Once states approve torture, it is notoriously difficult to regulate (Rejali 2007, 454–58). Understanding why states approve torture for intelligence can have implications for preventing other types of torture as well.

Even a reader who is skeptical of torture's supposed inefficacy has reason to seek explanations. Liberal states' use of torture is still puzzling on ideological grounds. Moreover, even if torture reliably yields valuable information, this does not imply that it was chosen for rational reasons. The choice still needs explanation.

The puzzle is also significant because it provides a more complete picture of self-proclaimed liberal democracies. Torture by liberal democracies has evoked deep questions and debates about who these liberal states are and what values they should uphold; it can lead to heated confrontations over identity. (Even apologists for torture use the language of definition: after the press showed pictures of torture at Abu Ghraib prison in Iraq, President George W. Bush, whose approval of coercive interrogation techniques is partly responsible for the abuse, stated, "This is not the America I know" [Klein 2009].) A clearer picture of why liberal democracies torture could have implications for who liberal democracies are.

Summary of the Argument

I argue that the norm against torture has two features that can help explain why violation of the norm occurs. First, the norm against torture may contribute to the belief that torture works. By categorizing certain behavior as appropriate, norms also define what is inappropriate. Some policymakers and soldiers believe (not always unreasonably) that in the nasty world of international politics, cheaters—those who are willing to break the rules—have an advantage, especially in security matters. "Bad" deeds become "good" because they appear effective. Rule-following becomes naïve and dangerous. Torture, a practice condemned in international laws and norms at least by name, appears sufficiently harsh to take on the worst of the worst in international politics. I call this the Cheaters Win argument.

Second, despite universal condemnation, the antitorture norm is—and has been—insufficiently robust. In particular, the norm lacks what Jeffrey Legro (1997) calls "specificity," or the ability to separate norm-compliant behavior from violations. The problem is inherent in torture itself. For example, it is impossible to specify exactly how many hours must pass before forced standing becomes torture. As a result of torture's blurry definition, torturers can justify their actions by favorable comparison ("The other side does worse"), modifiers ("torture lite"), euphemisms ("enhanced interrogation"), and flat-out denial ("This isn't torture"). They can also redefine torture to exclude their own acts. In short, lack of specificity leads to justifications and redefinitions, which in turn enable transgressions. I refer to this as the Lack of Specificity explanation.

At first blush, these two explanations appear to be in conflict: if the torture norm lacks specificity, then maybe it isn't lending torture an aura of effectiveness, because it isn't defining torture as clearly inappropriate. However, an actor sufficiently motivated to be both moral and effective can make the explanations complementary in practice: he or she could understand "torture lite" or "enhanced interrogation techniques" as sufficiently harsh to be effective, but far enough down the sliding scale from the most overtly brutal abuses to be morally and legally permissible.

Both of these explanations fall squarely in the constructivist school of international relations. Constructivists take norms seriously. My second explanation echoes a fairly conventional hypothesis: more robust norms entail more compliance. I am arguing that, along the specificity dimension, the torture norm is not as robust as some observers have believed, and compliance has suffered as a result. The first explanation pushes constructivism a bit further. Constructivists believe that norms can have "constitutive" effects; that is, they can define interests, roles, and identities. For proscriptive norms, this usually means that the norms help states define themselves as moral and civilized by avoiding the behavior that the norm condemns. I am turning this typical scenario on its head by suggesting that for some actors, proscriptive norms define what is off-limits—and therefore effective—in international politics.

Plan for the Book

Chapter 2 discusses the answered and unanswered questions regarding liberal democracies' use of torture. I show why the stealth techniques favored by democracies deserve the label "torture." I give a very brief history of democratic torture. The chapter then considers some of the available explanations for the recurrence of torture. First, perhaps torture occurs when actors perceive that they have permission, even a mandate, from significant segments of the population to do so. Alternatively, public monitoring might be insufficient, and torture sufficiently surreptitious, to weaken the restraining effects of democracy. Second, torture may be a rational response to desperate situations. Third, revenge and racism can lead to torture. Fourth, pro-torture advocacy can pervade organizational cultures. Most of these alternatives are distinct from, but still compatible with, my central claims, and I find some evidence for them in the empirical chapters.

While the alternatives make meaningful contributions to our understanding of the recurrence of torture, they leave important questions unanswered. If torturers are responding to popular demand, then why is torture so often done in secret? And when it is exposed, why do torturers frequently play down their acts rather than try to deny that such acts occurred at all? If civilian and military leaders are desperate, why turn to torturers rather than other interrogation specialists, especially in instances in which the latter have more experience (e.g., during the war on terror)? If racism or revenge explains torture, why does torture so often occur as part of a search for intelligence?

Chapter 3, in which I present my explanations, provides some answers to these questions. The torture norm's specificity problem clarifies why torturers frequently try to sell their acts as legitimate rather than deny that those acts occurred. Moreover, the promise—a false promise, in my view—that certain torture techniques will be harsh enough to work but mild enough to be sold as legal and ethical explains why interrogators are repeatedly attracted to torture as an interrogation tool. The chapter then details the methodology. I use in-depth case studies, focusing on important moments in each case when key actors made torture more likely. The chapter concludes with a discussion of case selection.

In chapter 4, I explain the U.S. use of torture in the Philippine-American War, which was an offshoot of the Spanish-American War in 1898. The Philippines was a Spanish colony that Spain essentially forfeited to the United States after it lost the war. Filipino leaders had been led to believe that their independence was imminent, and when the United States did not grant it, war broke out. The U.S. Army won the war, in part through the use of brutal tactics, including free-fire zones and village burning. American soldiers and Filipino allies also used torture, most famously the "water cure."

To my knowledge, civilian politicians and top generals never explicitly advocated torture of Filipino insurgents. Rather, consistent with the Cheaters Win explanation, some soldiers (up to midlevel officers) believed that interrogations required stern measures that represented the extent of the laws of war at that time and went beyond the standards with which most Americans were comfortable. Political elites such as Theodore Roosevelt (as influential civilian, vice president, and president) and high-level officers pushed for more unrestrained methods of war-fighting in general, and this attitude created a context in which the occurrence of torture was unsurprising. As for the Lack of Specificity argument, the hearings, trials, and letters exchanged toward the end of the war are filled with quibbling over what exactly constitutes torture and whether techniques like pumping and choking by water should count. Torturers also justified themselves by going on about how much more terrible the enemy was and how mild the American tactics were by contrast. These justifications would have been impossible if torture were clearly separate from less brutal acts.

I also examine alternative explanations for torture during the Philippine-American War. I find some evidence that torture and other severe tactics were timed with an eye on U.S. domestic politics. With President William McKinley running for reelection, the Republicans and some of their allies in uniform had been pretending that the war was well in hand in the lead-up to the 1900 elections. For this reason, some civilians and officers waited to enact harsh measures until after the elections, lest it complicate the story they were selling. Other soldiers may have heard about the anticipated changes and gotten a head start, but the evidence for this is not ironclad, and the gradual increase in torture is only somewhat consistent with an argument based on election timing. The degree of desperation also does not appear to affect the timing of torture and other cruel tactics in the war, at least at the strategic level. Some of the most brutal conduct by the U.S. military occurred when the war was actually all but over, from mid-1901 to 1902.

Chapter 5 traces the Central Intelligence Agency's development and use of torture from the origins of the agency to the Vietnam War, as well as the U.S. military's use of torture during the war. This "case" is not as neatly defined as the others, though some scholars detect a through-line over this time period.[9] I focus on four areas of development and implementation. First, I examine the formation and growth of a U.S. intelligence service. The CIA followed several other iterations (and accompanying acronyms) of peacetime intelligence services, and all were the children of the Office of Strategic Services, or OSS, the U.S. intelligence agency during World War II. I argue that part of the OSS's philosophy was that war gave those willing to push limits an advantage. Thus, the OSS specialized in spying, a taboo activity thought at the time to be an underhanded and less than honorable practice of war. It also set about developing other tricks to gain the upper hand over the enemy. The CIA was founded in part on this approach. Both the CIA skeptics (e.g., Harry Truman) and its defenders (e.g., Gen. John Magruder) expected that the CIA would spend much of its time, money, and energy tiptoeing along the limits of normative and legal acceptability. They were not wrong. The CIA had shadiness baked into its foundations, suggesting an organizational culture partially defined by a willingness to do things other liberal-democratic organizations would not.

Second, I examine the origins and growth of the CIA's MKULTRA program and its cousins and predecessors (e.g., Project ARTICHOKE).[10] These programs attempted to copy and improve upon what the CIA believed to be Communist methods of mind and behavioral control through the use of drugs, hypnosis, and other techniques amounting to abuse.[11] One of the reasons for the growth of the programs stems from President Dwight Eisenhower's approach to the CIA. Eisenhower encouraged the shadowy, proactive, secretly funded side of the CIA, in contrast to Truman's preference for an above-board operation. Eisenhower's reasons stemmed from his belief that to fight the unscrupulous Communists, while at the same time not throwing out the American moral compass, the United States was going to have to bend some rules on the sly. As with the Philippine-American War case, the connection between the political leadership and detainee abuse here is loose but still meaningful: a brainwashing program was one symptom of Eisenhower's belief that the United States needed to fight a surreptitious, limits-pushing war against the Communists.

Chapter 5 also investigates the CIA's KUBARK interrogation manual of 1963 and its implementation in the Vietnam War. Techniques included sensory deprivation, hypnosis, and pain such as forced standing that makes the detainee believe that their suffering is somewhat self-inflicted. The KUBARK manual, partly a product of the mind-control research, contains evidence for the Lack of Specificity argument, specifically in the favorable comparisons between the CIA's preferred psychological methods and more blatantly physical tactics that it shuns. CIA interrogators in Vietnam drew similar contrasts to justify their methods.

The fourth area discussed in chapter 5 centers on the U.S. military. While some soldiers' behavior falls in line with my thesis's expectations, other testimony regarding torture challenges my argument. Torture in Vietnam was as much about anger, revenge, and racism as intelligence gathering. Moreover, soldiers returned from the war in a confessional mood, and they did not pretend that their actions were anything less than torture. My account would be incomplete without these explanations.

Chapter 6 covers torture during the post-2001 U.S. war on terror. This case is different from the others in that the Bush administration's embrace of abusive methods, though initially secret, was explicit. While the openness with which the administration defended torture has negative implications for the endurance of the antitorture norm, it does benefit the researcher, because administration officials have talked at length about their stances, and some of the memos and other materials documenting the early internal debate over interrogation tactics have come to light. I focus on the key decisions along three partially overlapping paths to abuse: the mix of vague instructions and detailed allowances that led to torture by the U.S. military, the selection of certain countries to which detainees were sent for abusive interrogation, and the development and approval of "enhanced interrogation techniques" used by the CIA.

I find strong evidence for my central claims in the war-on-terror case. Within a few days of the September 11 attacks, key Bush administration officials, including the president and vice president, were adamant about removing restrictions from those charged with carrying out the U.S. response. In the lead-up to the crucial 2002 decision to forgo the Geneva Conventions, backers of the torture program within the administration argued that Geneva would put too many constraints on interrogators. The CIA's internal program as well as its use of extraordinary rendition (in which it sent detainees to countries like Syria and Egypt to be tortured) exposes the same convictions about the efficacy of interrogations un-bound by norms and laws. Indeed, concerns about circumventing standards—rather than, say, experience or a proven track record—drove the administration's decision to have the CIA take the lead on interroga-tion of detainees. Throughout, the Bush administration equated effective intelligence-gathering with tactics that bent and broke the laws and norms prohibiting torture.

The Bush torture programs might have proven impossible if the adminis-tration hadn't been able to exploit the lack of specificity inherent in the tor-ture norm. The torture memos, the series of legal documents sanctioning abusive interrogation, (re)defined torture in the narrowest terms, freeing interrogators in the CIA and the military to use a wide range of methods, alone and in combination. The administration consistently denied that the euphemistically named enhanced interrogation techniques amounted to torture. If torture were more well-defined, the redefinitions, denials, and euphemisms might not have been possible.

Americans were desperate to prevent another major terrorist attack on the homeland in the early part of the war on terror, and this desperation played a part in their search for extraordinary means. The architects of the torture policy did not resemble fully rational actors, however, at least with reference to the goal of getting the most accurate intelligence. They did not sift care-fully through interrogation techniques looking for the most effective ones according to the best evidence, nor did they empower the most experienced interrogators to lead the teams. Early advocates of torture were more con-cerned with legality than effectiveness. And while the Bush administration did sell sketches of its muscular foreign policy approach to the public, the torture program was not in place simply to satisfy public demand. Much of the program was kept secret, and the administration revealed details only reluctantly.

Chapter 7 discusses the scope of generalizability for my central explana-tion. For instance, I investigate whether the recent rise of authoritarianism might be attributable to the impression among democratic leaders that autocrats possess the advantages of the unrestrained, combined with the no-tion that it is possible to chip away at liberal-democratic norms. I unpack the limits of the book's argument as well. My argument does not explain why tor-ture in the war on terror ended, for example. I also list the primary takeaways of the book, summarized as follows: (a) the antitorture norm's robustness problem is of long standing; (b) to lessen the chances of abuse, legislation must attack the gray zones at the edge of torture, especially in the United States; (c) implicit links between norm-breaking harshness and effectiveness are influential and need reexamination; and (d) norms can even define the preferences of violators, suggesting broad influence. The book ends with a look at the future of the antitorture norm in the United States.

2

Liberal-Democratic Torture

Answered and Unanswered Questions

The end of the Cold War was supposed to be the "end of history," marked by the conclusive victory of liberalism over competing political ideologies (Fukuyama 1989). Democratic peace theorists seemed to grow in numbers just as fast as the democracies they studied in the 1990s, and these scholars gave readers reason to believe that peace and improved human rights would follow political freedom (Fukuyama 1989).[1] Constructivism became a major player in international political theory at this time, too, founded on the idea that the anarchic world of international relations is not inherently or inevitably conflictual. Greater levels of cooperation could define new "cultures" of anarchy, and these arrangements could endure even if the benefits of defection from peaceful cohabitation temporarily outweighed the costs.[2] The past twenty-five years have borne out many of these optimistic expectations. War is still unthinkable in Western Europe, despite warnings from realists.[3] The recent spate of scholarship on the decline of war also shows that war and other forms of violence have been on the wane since the end of the Cold War.[4]

Yet torture persists, even in liberal democracies. Europeans turned to torture less than Americans did after 2001, producing real variation worth exploring and exploiting, but the recent European record has its blemishes, too. And while the U.S. Congress mandated that interrogations stick to the rapport-building methods of the *Army Field Manual*, future reversion to abuse is certainly conceivable (Jacobson 2017), especially in the aftermath of another 9/11-size attack.

Theoretically, explanations for the recurrence of torture fall partly in the blind spots of the two most prominent theoretical frameworks in international relations scholarship: rationalism and constructivism.[5] Rationalists insist that states make choices based on self-interested cost-benefit analysis. Sometimes these choices fall in line with international norms (which can impose costs for noncompliance), and sometimes they do not. As a result, rationalism can account for the norm-breaking side of the puzzle but cannot

American Torture from the Philippines to Iraq. William L. d'Ambruoso, Oxford University Press. © Oxford University Press 2022. DOI: 10.1093/oso/9780197570326.003.0002

easily explain why states often do not act in their self-interest or do not up-date when the returns from torture are poor. Social constructivists argue that shared understandings, norms, and rules constitute states' interests and identities, and so their choices are influenced, if not determined, by a sense of propriety, however thin. Hence constructivists are well-positioned to ac-count for why states might not maximize their utility, but they would have more trouble explaining why states operate outside of a norm that is widely held. This puzzle takes rationalist and constructivist orientations out of their comfort zones.

Still, the international relations approaches are useful lenses for un-derstanding the persistence of torture. While I draw primarily on con-structivism, rationalism plays a part as well in both complementary and competing explanations. In some instances (e.g., the war on terror), torture was a foreign policy choice at the highest levels of government. In others (e.g., the Philippine-American War), torture resulted in part from closely related foreign policy choices by the higher-ups. Theoretical approaches to international relations can tell us whether these choices were the result of careful calculations (rationalism), a (perverse) sense of what is appropriate for a given context (constructivism), or some combination of these.

Some of the key actors and decision-makers are foot soldiers, both liter-ally and figuratively. While they may not be elites, these actors are thinking about what war and anarchy require. They are grappling with the laws and norms of foreign war. As such, they confront classic questions and problems of international affairs, even if they do not hold high rank. International relations theorists are sometimes taken to task for spending too much time focusing on towering figures of government and ignoring how lower-level actors navigate international space. My study offers a partial corrective to this tendency.

This chapter sets out a definition for torture and also addresses the problem—one that I believe is serious enough to be part of my explanation for why torture occurs—of the gray area between torture and slightly less brutal deeds. With a working definition in hand, I then give a brief overview of liberal-democratic torture. Because I defend a relatively broad definition of torture, the history of torture by old, well-established democracies such as Britain, France, and the United States is more extensive than might be antici-pated. I then offer some explanations of torture by democracies based on the existing literature and conclude with a discussion of some of the questions—why people believe torture works, why the norm against it hasn't always obtained, etc.—that current scholarship leaves inadequately answered. I develop theoretical answers to those questions in the next chapter.

Defining Torture, Including the "Lite" Stuff

One of my principal arguments is that torture occurs because people redefine torture to exclude things that they want to do. So it may seem strange that I will now state a definition of something that I am claiming is inherently vague, with arbitrary boundaries. Yet norms typically have some agreed-upon terminology to which collective expectations can adhere, even if actors debate the terms' meanings. I adopt the widely used definition from the Convention against Torture (CAT) (United Nations 1984), which defines torture as

> any act by which severe pain or suffering, whether physical or mental, is intentionally inflicted on a person for such purposes as obtaining from him or a third person information or a confession, punishing him for an act he or a third person has committed or is suspected of having committed, or intimidating or coercing him or a third person, or for any reason based on discrimination of any kind, when such pain or suffering is inflicted by or at the instigation of or with the consent or acquiescence of a public official or other person acting in an official capacity. It does not include pain or suffering arising only from, inherent in or incidental to lawful sanctions.

The CAT, with 158 state parties, is the most salient, relevant example of antitorture norm codification.

Many of the psychologically abusive techniques favored by the CIA count as torture under the CAT definition. This includes the "regression" methods from the Cold War and "learned helplessness" from the war on terror. Methods sufficiently coercive to bring about a breakdown in personality and dignity qualify as acts causing "severe mental suffering."

The definition is also compatible with many of the "stealth techniques"—torture that leaves no trace—which democratic actors (and, increasingly, nondemocratic ones) apparently prefer (Rejali 2007). The CAT's definition does not stipulate that the pain and suffering must be long-lasting, as other definitions do. It does not require "organ failure . . . or even death," as Bush administration lawyers did (Bybee 2002a, 1). (If interrogators are really torturing for intelligence, the death of the subject would presumably be a failed outcome.)

Yet, holding the CAT definition aside for a moment, do stealth techniques, "torture lite," "enhanced interrogation techniques," or other methods with euphemistic monikers deserve the name "torture" as it is commonly understood? I argue that they usually do, for at least three reasons. First, many of the stealth techniques are worse than they sound, perhaps by design as a backup plan in case stealth fails. A volunteer in the French Foreign Legion described a technique in which detainees were forced to stand with one foot fixed to the ground: "Now, that doesn't sound very terrible, does it? Yet, after half-an-hour of it, I have heard men screaming and raving" (quoted in Rejali 2007, 316). The waterboard was rhetorically reduced to a "dunk in the water" to "save lives," which Vice President Dick Cheney agreed was so obviously the morally correct choice as to be a "no-brainer" (quoted in Eggen 2006). Yet after Erich "Mancow" Muller, a conservative radio host, submitted himself to the waterboard to prove that it was not a big deal, he admitted, "It was instantaneous . . . and I don't want to say this: absolutely torture" (Pollyea 2009).[6]

Second, the psychological damage can be long-lasting or permanent even if the visible, physical injuries are not. Christopher Hitchens, a journalist who submitted himself to the waterboard to give a firsthand account, reported nightmares of being smothered in the weeks that followed (Nizza 2008). Hitchens's (2008) experience is in some respects a best-case scenario, given that he was in control of his fate, he had plenty of professional and personal support, and he was "released into happy daylight rather than returned to a darkened cell."

We now know that the CIA's war-on-terror interrogation program did lasting damage to detainees. Even under the Bush administration Justice Department's narrow definition of psychological torture as techniques that would cause "significant psychological harm of significant duration, e.g., lasting for months or even years" (Bybee 2002a, 1), the "enhanced interrogation techniques" fail to elude the torture label. The *New York Times* ran a series of investigative reports in which it conducted over one hundred interviews with former detainees. It found no lack of stories like the following:

Today in Slovakia, Hussein al-Marfadi describes permanent headaches and disturbed sleep, plagued by memories of dogs inside a blackened jail.

In Kazakhstan, Lutfi bin Ali is haunted by nightmares of suffocating at the bottom of a well. In Libya, the radio from a passing car spurs rage in Majid Mokhtar Sasy al-Maghrebi, reminding him of the C.I.A. prison where earsplitting music was just one assault to his senses. (Apuzzo, Fink, and Risen 2016)

The *Times* series uncovered a lot of mental and physical health challenges, leading the authors to conclude that those who believed the mild nature of the program would bring only short-lived discomfort were simply wrong.

Third, psychological damage can be greater with stealth techniques than physical methods in certain instances. James Ron's (1997, 294–95) interview with a UN mental health officer dealing with cases of stealth torture shows why:

When prisoners had clear markings indicating they had been tortured, she explained, "the community understood why they broke down and implicated friends in real or imagined crimes." When released prisoners had no signs proving what they had experienced, however, they could not explain why they broke down and supplied interrogators with names. "The associated feelings of shame, remorse, and guilt can cause severe mental trauma that would not have been experienced had the subjects been physically scarred," she said.

The "severe mental trauma" mentioned by the UN worker sounds very similar to the CAT torture definition.

Mock executions, part of the stealth torturer's repertoire, can be scarier than beatings because of their long-lasting psychological effects. John McCain (2005), a U.S. senator who was tortured as a POW in the Vietnam War, explains:

[I]f you gave people who have suffered abuse as prisoners a choice between a beating and a mock execution, many, including me, would choose a beating. The effects of most beatings heal. The memory of an execution will haunt someone for a very long time and damage his or her psyche in ways that may never heal. In my view, to make someone believe that you are killing him by drowning is no different than holding a pistol to his head and firing a blank. I believe that it is torture, very exquisite torture.

In sum, most of the stealthy coercive interrogation techniques favored by liberal democracies deserve the name torture. They satisfy the basic condition of the widely accepted CAT definition by causing severe mental and/or physical suffering. They also do consistently more damage than the torture apologists claim.

Liberal-Democratic Torture in Britain, France, and the United States

Liberal democracies have committed their share of torture, lite or otherwise. Britain, France, and the United States have some of the oldest democratic features, such as free elections and laws enshrining human rights. Their histories are also marked by episodes and patterns of prisoner abuse. It's true that these countries can boast of some stories of restraint, and they have never reached the horrific heights of Stalinist Russia or Nazi Germany. Still, torture stuck around in Britain, France, and the United States much longer than their rhetorical and ratified commitments to human rights would indicate.

The decline of judicial torture in continental Europe was one of the watersheds separating pre- and post-Enlightenment. Because medieval European law relied so heavily on confessions for convictions, prosecutors leaned on torture to produce them. Near the end of the eighteenth century, reliance on judicial torture declined precipitously. France banned torture for confessions in 1780 as part of a general trend on the continent. To explain this broad decline, some scholars emphasize the importance of the changes in laws toward wider acceptance of circumstantial evidence— thereby reducing the need for confessions—in trials (Langbein 2004). Others stress the impact of strong critiques of torture by Enlightenment thinkers like Beccaria and Voltaire (Pinker 2011). Enlightenment writings had a strong effect on America's founders as well, and the prohibition against punitive torture was codified in the Eighth Amendment of the U.S. Constitution.

Medieval and early modern England had little in the way of judicial torture, save a brief period in the late sixteenth and early seventeenth centuries to generate confessions for crimes against the state. Typical English trials were based more on hearsay and the reputation of the accused than evidence of any quality, which sharply limited the prosecution's need for (coerced) confessions. The English were better known for instruments of punishment—whipping, keelhauling,[7] and so forth—that convicted criminals and errant military members were sentenced to suffer. Still, by the mid-nineteenth century, both punitive and juridical torture had been abolished everywhere in Europe (Einolf 2007).

Torture by liberal democracies survived the Enlightenment, of course, especially against those deemed to be undeserving of societal protections. During the nineteenth century, British and French colonial police used torture in the colonies to project the power of the state and generate confessions, though documentation of these events is limited. More well-known is the abuse of enslaved people in the southern United States, usually as punishment. At the same time, full citizens enjoyed a significant drop in torture at the hands of the state in comparison to years past (Einolf 2007).

The colonial wars of the twentieth century brought liberal democratic torture back into the spotlight.[8] The French engaged in widespread torture in Southeast Asia (in both policing and wartime contexts) and in the French-Algerian War. The British used torture for intelligence and punishment in the war against the Mau Mau in Kenya, against insurgents in Aden, and against rebellious factions in Northern Ireland. The United States, which fought fewer wars of decolonization, tortured detainees in the Philippine-American War and in Vietnam. American service members returning home from war would sometimes bring their methods with them. Consequently, the same techniques witnessed in the Philippines and Vietnam would appear in police interrogation rooms in New York and Chicago.

One significant difference between twentieth- and twenty-first-century torture and abuse of past centuries is how much "cleaner" the techniques have become. No longer does the state try to brand its victims so as to publicize its reach. Surveillance has displaced ostentatious suffering as the state's preferred way to exercise control (Foucault 1977; Ron 1997). Moreover, stealth techniques allow torturers to evade detection by human rights monitors, whose numbers and capabilities grew substantially in the second half of the twentieth century. I will also argue in the next chapter that stealth techniques allowed practitioners to navigate an increasingly robust norm against torture by permitting them to justify their behavior to others, and even themselves.

With the war on terror, the United States brought liberal democratic torture into the postcolonial twenty-first century. While most of the torture stayed stealthy in this war, two points of variation on other dimensions stand out. First, as I discuss further in chapter 6, the Bush administration was much more involved in the approval of torture techniques at the highest level than in years past. I argue that a slightly stronger antitorture norm led to a more explicit, top-down circumvention of that norm, because most torturers on the ground demanded legal and normative cover for their deeds. Second, the European record of abuses, though not spotless, has improved in postcolonial times. In the book's conclusion, I claim that Europeans have done a more thorough job than the United States of prohibiting the "torture lite" programs that American lawyers, bureaucrats, and politicians have used to smuggle abusive practices into interrogators' toolkits.

In sum, liberal democratic torture has persisted but has not gone unchanged. It is probably rarer today than it was before the Enlightenment or at the height of decolonization. It became stealthier in the twentieth century. And some liberal democracies have become more consistently compliant with human rights norms than others. Explanations of the recurrence and persistence of torture, which I explore in the next section, will gain persuasiveness if they square with these additional observations.

Leading Explanations

Torture, like war, has "so many causes." The difficulty in giving a comprehensive account of war is well known (Jervis 1988, 675). Surely the same can be said of torture, a practice permitted or prohibited at multiple levels, in different kinds of wars, with varying degrees of severity. Rejali (2007, 60) cautions that a full explanation of torture is impossible, both because of the complexity of the subject and the fragmented nature of the evidence, and I will not attempt one here. We might still profit from partial answers, however. Jervis (1988, 675) reduces his goal of linking misperception and war to "not[ing] several patterns," with the important payoff of learning how "misperception might lead to World War III." Concerning torture, Rejali (2007, 61, emphasis in original) focuses primarily on why a particular method is chosen, remarking that "[h]ow torture happens is an important check on misleading and overly general accounts of *why* torture happens." Likewise, I will be focusing on certain aspects of the "why torture" puzzle, specifically on its recurrence and the persistent coexistence of torture and the norm against it in liberal democracies.

How Democracy Matters

Since I am interested in how liberal democracies arrive at the decision to use torture, studies that show democracies torture less than autocracies do not directly pertain. However, research describing those elements that stand between democracies and torture may be relevant if torture occurs when the standard checks on abuse falter. R. J. Rummel (1994), who made a career of demonstrating that government without limits is abusive and deadly, argues that during war, democracies often kill civilians. The problem, he contends, is that the democratic leaders delegate too much authority to hierarchical, secretive agencies such as the military in the face of security threats, reducing oversight and restraint. His insights may apply to torture as well. In Rejali's National Security model explaining wartime torture, bureaucrats gain power during political emergencies because they are perceived to be the experts, while democratic politicians are mere amateurs. Because bureaucracies are closed institutions, bureaucrats may not be as responsive as politicians or the public to international human rights norms. Torture can occur because "bureaucrats overwhelm democrats." Rejali points to the French Army in Algeria as the most famous instance of the National Security model in action. After Gen. Jacques Massu authorized the use of "water and electricity," democratic institutions—including the judicial system and legislature—were "unwilling or unable to stop the turn to torture" (Rejali 2007, 46–47).[9]

The importance of democratic constraints receives support from Geoffrey P. R. Wallace's work on wartime prisoner abuse, interpreted broadly to include torture, neglect, or killing. Drawing on other wartime violence literature that privileges a rationalist framework (Downes 2008; Valentino, Huth, and Croco 2006), Wallace (2015) argues that democracies often have institutional incentives to avoid prisoner abuse. Democratic elites are accountable to those who bear the costs of war, leading them to fear revenge as a result of publicized prisoner abuse. Treating enemy prisoners well is essentially an "insurance policy," carrying the implied promise that good treatment of one's own prisoners will be reciprocated and encouraging even nasty regimes (e.g., Nazis on the Western Front) to outperform expectations in the realm of human rights (Wallace 2015, 9). For similar reasons of accountability, democratic leaders can also keep the human costs of war low by encouraging the enemy to surrender. Since democratic leaders have a stronger chance than autocrats of credibly promising to treat prisoners well, they can convince enemies that surrendering beats fighting on (9).

Wallace argues that where these institutional constraints are lacking, democracies are more likely to engage in abusive practices. In particular, "if concerns over retaliation weaken or disappear either because abuses by the adversary spiral out of control or because the adversary no longer possesses adequate numbers of prisoners to serve as a deterrent," then democratic actors may become more abusive (Wallace 2015, 65).[10] Under such conditions, Wallace finds that normative constraints are usually not up to the task of holding leaders back from committing human rights violations.

Although Wallace is mostly interested in regular interstate wars, he suggests that his findings may hold for colonial wars and counterterrorism as well. He argues that weaker adversaries that democratic states face in asymmetric wars will often lack the resources to capture large numbers of enemy prisoners, and expectations that terrorist or insurgent groups will follow human rights norms are low. This minimizes the costs of prisoner abuse for democracies, making the occurrence of such abuse more likely (Wallace 2015, 181–88).

While Wallace pays a lot of attention to the conditions under which democracies fight wars, other scholars focus on the details of formal liberal-democratic institutions themselves. Conrad and Moore (2010) break down liberal institutions into three groups: Voice (usually measured as competitive elections), Freedom of Expression (usually measured as freedom of the press), and Veto (diffusion of power or separation of powers).[11] The first two match roughly with an extension of Rejali's monitoring theory. Rejali argues that torture has become stealthier in recent times, because the number and capacity of human rights monitors has increased dramatically. If some monitoring causes torturers to use untraceable methods, perhaps more invasive, educated monitoring would stop torture altogether. In other words, if lack of monitoring is the problem, a vigilant, unencumbered press and ballot box accountability might be the solution.

Election timing may also be consequential for the occurrence of torture. If soldiers or their political superiors are worried about electoral accountability for human rights violations, they might wait until after an election to use repressive means, especially if waiting will not prove fatal to the mission. If they believe that the public wants to see that those in charge of waging war are "doing all they can," the lead-up to an election might be a more brutal time for detainees. In sum, if electoral accountability matters, perception of what the electorate (including key constituencies) wants will matter, too.

It is possible to imagine the Veto factor, like electoral accountability, leading toward or away from a torture policy. Some scholars argue that the diffusion of executive power, especially in the form of an independent judiciary, lowers the chances of human rights violations (Keith 2002; Powell and Staton 2009). Others disagree. Vetoes of executive authority slow down or halt changes in policy. Because they approach torture policy as the status quo and ask why torture policies sometimes end, Conrad and Moore (2010) argue that more veto points increase the likelihood that torture policies will continue.[12] The first argument is more applicable to my cases, because I argue that while torture policy has been persistent, it has not been constant. Rather, it keeps recurring. Therefore, Conrad and Moore's hypothesis is less likely to hold, and, according to my reading of the dependent variable, more veto points will potentially lessen the executive's ability to reintroduce torture as a viable alternative.

These dimensions of democracy may not be static during wars. Executives often have incentives to centralize power during war, and the rally-around-the-flag effect can pave the way for the suppression of criticism (Mueller 1970). While well-established liberal institutions can weather the war and rebound admirably when the dust settles, they can suffer setbacks in the midst of war (Starr 2010). Lincoln's suspension of habeas corpus during the American Civil War and the internment of Japanese Americans during World War II come to mind. And while, in a strict sense, Americans still enjoyed a free press during the war on terror, the Bush administration successfully bullied much of the media into compliant coverage after September 2001.[13]

Because I am interested in the recurrence of torture, I will be paying particular attention to the change that wars and other security emergencies bring in my cases. Do executives take advantage of the security concerns to consolidate power? Or do the legislature and the courts give over power freely? If it's the latter, then a counterfactual whereby the other branches do not relinquish control may not yield a different result. Likewise, if the press is stocked with cheerleaders for harsh treatment of the enemy, limiting or intimidating certain elements of the press would not change much. Finally, does the civilian leadership have a choice in the bureaucracy that will head up interrogations? If not, then they might have to rely on the "experts," as Rejali's argument suggests, and these bureaucrats may not have internalized liberal norms (see also the organizational culture argument presented later in the chapter). Delegation within organizations might bring interrogation choices even further from corrective liberal monitors and provide evidence that democratic bureaucracies are functionally autocratic.

These arguments focusing on liberal institutions have much to recommend them. They capture the messy way in which politics becomes policy in democracies, with multiple centers of power. Soldiers, bureaucrats, politicians, the media, international human rights organizations, and the public all have potentially distinct interests in, opinions about, and information regarding the necessary and proper treatment of detainees, and policies and political behavior will reflect some combination of these interests. Arguments focusing on democratic institutions highlight this complexity and distill it into testable, comprehensible hypotheses.

Several of these arguments are also based on solid social science, with a fair amount of evidence to corroborate their claims. Rejali finds no lack of examples of torturers discussing among themselves the necessity of staying stealthy and avoiding detection. I also find instances of torturers using, or trying to use, methods that leave no marks in each of my cases. Wallace uses both qualitative and quantitative data to show that prisoner abuse increases when institutional constraints wane. An argument about the occurrence of torture that uses these studies as points of departure is likely to be heading in fruitful directions.

One general limitation of these accounts, however, is that even strong evidence that some form of institutional breakdown was behind a torture policy would leave much unanswered. If human rights norms are not guiding behavior, what is? How does torture get a foothold in bureaucracies in the first place? If torture has multiple drawbacks, as I am claiming that it does, or is at the very least a risky proposition, then there ought to be positive reasons for such a policy.

Desperation

This discussion of democratic institutions focuses on the costs of a torture policy; when the costs are low, torture is more likely. But what about the benefits? What promise does torture hold?

Perhaps for the sake of simplicity, many scholars assume that torture is a rational response to certain conditions. That is, actors are choosing to torture because they believe it to be the best means to a given end (Mercer 2005,

79). Davenport, Armstrong, and Moore (2007), following Wantchekon and Healy (1999), assume that when faced with violence, executives have strong incentives to torture detainees. Merom (2003, 46) agrees: "The hasty acquisition of intelligence, often from sources unwilling to supply it, necessarily involves a great deal of personal violence." Merom (2003, 42–43) sees torture as a way to generate intelligence at a reasonable military cost, arguing that states resort to brutal interrogation methods during wars because they are both effective and efficient. Merom does not provide much in the way of careful, comparative evidence that torture is effective at gathering intelligence, and torture may be "working" in his cases by simply terrorizing and intimidating the opposition.[14] Still, the assumption that torture can be rational is productive for these scholars, and it allows them to theorize about the conditions under which it will occur and the consequences that wars of attrition will have.

In fact, actual effectiveness and rationality of torture are only loosely connected, and torture may be rational even if actors are wrong about its effectiveness. As Wallace (2015, 43) explains, what matters is whether military and civilian leaders *think* torture is effective. If they do, then torture will be rational if those leaders find themselves in an environment (such as a war of attrition) in which torture provides the best hope for realizing given ends according to given beliefs.

Moreover, leaders and soldiers need not be convinced that torture is always effective in order to use it, especially if they are desperate for intelligence. The word "desperate" is derived from the Latin *desparatus*, meaning "deprived of hope" (*Oxford English Dictionary*). Desperate actors do not necessarily have high confidence that their choices will yield success, but their situation may force them to try methods that they believe have slim prospects of being productive. Alexander Downes (2008) argues that leaders target civilians in war when they are desperate. He stresses that leaders are essentially cornered by circumstances into choosing civilian victimization as a strategy of war that allows them to either win at an affordable price, stave off defeat, save lots of their own soldiers' or civilian lives, or annex territory. Leaders need only believe that targeting civilians *might* work to achieve these ends. Thus, civilian victimization is "a calculated risk, not an irrational gamble" (Downes 2008, 39). Similarly, uncertainty about torture's effectiveness may not be enough to prevent desperate actors from using torture. The more desperate the actor, the less confident he needs to be in torture's effectiveness.

Rejali suggests that there are even times when it may not matter what actors believe. In fact, in some (rare) cases, the actors can believe that torture is ineffective and still end up condoning it, as the following example illustrates:

> In the late 1950's, Paul Teitgin, the prefect of Algiers, caught Fernand Yveton, a Communist placing a bomb in the gasworks. Teitgin knew Yveton had a second bomb, and if Yveton had planted and exploded it, it would set off gasometers, killing thousands. Teitgin could not persuade Yveton to tell him where the other bomb was. Nevertheless, said Teitgin, "I refused to have him tortured. I trembled the whole afternoon. Finally the bomb did not go off. Thank God I was right." . . . One can imagine what would have happened to Teitgin's career if the bomb had gone off. . . . It would have done Teitgin no good to explain that torture produces false leads and wasted resources, that it damages police professionalism and integrity, or that Yveton might say nothing despite the torture. . . . In such a circumstance, Teitgin could have been much more reassuring if he had tortured Yveton even if he knew torture did not work (Rejali 2007, 533–34).

Such unusual situations suggest that torture becomes more likely when actors become desperate. Torture may give comfort to those who can then say, "We are doing everything we can."

Desperate for *what*, exactly? Downes argues that leaders approve civilian victimization when they become desperate to win or desperate to save lives. Accordingly, he expects leaders to turn to civilian victimization as an "act of later resort," after other attempts have failed. Mapping these expectations to torture for intelligence during small wars is an imperfect exercise. Wallace (2015, 9) brings us most of the way by examining the nature of conflict as a cause of prisoner abuse. He claims that severe fighting, especially in long and costly wars of attrition, causes "embattled captors" facing "dire circumstances" to "make war more costly and painful for their adversary." Part of Wallace's argument reflects the fact that he includes both torture and killing of prisoners in his response variable. Killing prisoners may coerce opponents into ending the war sooner or remove a possible source of future resistance. But Wallace also maintains that desperate actors will be more tempted to torture for intelligence. When the going gets tough, civilian and military leaders will be more likely to value the potential benefits of torture more than they fear the risks (10). In his conclusion, Wallace extends his claims to counterinsurgency as well: "Given the greater challenges to gathering intelligence on insurgent adversaries, captors may be much more willing to turn to harsh interrogation techniques against detainees in an attempt to gain important information" (173–74).

The Teitgin example also suggests a feeling of desperation from events not unlike ticking time-bomb scenarios mostly specific to counterterrorism operations. Although these highly dramatic instances are exceedingly rare (Mayerfeld 2008), torturers might believe they have to act quickly to save lives even if their side is not (yet) concurrently suffering large numbers of casualties in a drawn-out war of attrition. For instance, both coercive and noncoercive interrogators of Abu Zubaydah and Khalid Sheik Mohammed, detainees in the war on terror, were looking for next-9/11-type threat information (U.S. Senate, Select Committee on Intelligence 2014, 28, 30, 81).

Finding evidence for the desperation hypothesis is a balancing act. Desperate actors should be in a hurry, especially if they think that timely intelligence will save lives, but rational actors should choose carefully among their options. When actors have more time under the desperation model, they will probably try noncoercive methods first, because the only risk of noncoercive methods is that they might not work. Torture carries greater risks, especially in states where it is illegal, and a rational actor should be at least interested in noncoercive methods so as to avoid those risks. Then the actor would evaluate results, find the intelligence to be lacking, become desperate, and try coercive methods.

The desperation hypothesis is compatible with realist theories of international politics. Torture follows need. The antitorture norm might have some regulative effects, but when the going gets tough, normative concerns are put aside. Like war, torture occurs under anarchy because there is nothing to stop it (Waltz 1959). Since realists believe that norms are only as meaningful and powerful as the states that enforce them, great powers are at an advantage in their ability to flout constraints when such a path is deemed necessary. Reflecting on torture during the war on terror, Stephen Walt (2009) summarizes:

> [F]or those of you who think that power is of declining relevance in world politics and that normative and legal standards are becoming increasingly important, I'd just point out that the various officials who sanctioned these abuses would be in a lot more trouble if they came from a weak and vulnerable state, as opposed to a global power like the United States. Not only does

power corrupt, but it allows people who sanction torture to get away with it, albeit at some considerable cost to America's image and reputation.

Realists argue that when leaders in powerful states are sufficiently desperate, they can enjoy the privilege of ignoring international law in a way that leaders of weaker states cannot. Since realists believe that force is the final arbiter in international politics, they would be likely to agree with rationalists like Wallace that the ability to retaliate in kind is an important check on torture.

The rational desperation explanation makes a crucial connection that is mostly consistent with the evidence I have found: wartime torture does indeed follow the need for intelligence, at least loosely. With a few exceptions, it does not occur randomly or out of pure sadism. In many of those wars in which torture becomes widespread, such as the French-Algerian War, intelligence is the key to locating the enemy or anticipating attacks, and both sides believe that much is at stake. Within these wars, torture is often aimed at those detainees who are likely to have the most valuable intelligence. This does not establish that torturers are logically ordering preferences or maximizing perceived utility, but it does suggest that the rationalists may be on to something when they say that torture follows a certain logic, however strained.

Explanations based on desperation have important limitations, however. By itself, desperation is indeterminate; it is unclear what desperation will actually produce. For instance, we can imagine a desperate leader in an intelligence crisis calling around to different agencies looking for the government's most experienced interrogators rather than the most brutal. In order to find out why certain leaders search for and empower the harshest intelligence officers and soldiers available, we need to theorize further.

Perhaps much of the problem lies in the fact that rationalist arguments do not tell us why some actors think that torture works, or think that it might work. Wantchekon and Healy (1999), for instance, assume that government actors believe torture to be a valuable interrogation method, and then show why they will probably use it when they develop a strong desire for intelligence. Yet the path by which governments come to believe that torture works is likely to be the most interesting and consequential part of the story. Once the state is convinced that torture is the right tool for the job, much of the process of deciding to use torture is already complete. Moreover, not all state actors agree on torture's utility; why are some convinced of it?

Intuition

Most rationalist explanations start with the belief that torture might work, and connect this belief to the outcome via cost-benefit analysis. But where does the belief originate? The simplest answer is that some interrogators find torture's appeal to be intuitive. Like the age-old trick of banging on an uncooperative television (back when televisions were thicker than a novel), it may be nothing more than intuition whispering to torturers that turning to force can loosen the tongues of otherwise taciturn detainees. Torturers defending their deeds often make assertions to the effect of "Anyone would do what I did." Statements such as these can be one indicator that torturers find the utility of their methods intuitive.[15]

One of the benefits of the intuition argument is that it tries to tackle the tough and crucial question of why people believe torture works. By implication, this explanation does not simply give over to the idea that greater need for intelligence connects unproblematically with torture. The connection needs a more complete theoretical storyline. The intuition argument represents an early attempt at filling in the blanks between need and outcome.

Unfortunately, intuitive arguments share some of the problems of the desperation argument; it is unclear where intuition will lead. It was intuitive to medieval and early modern Europeans that, in the interest of justice, reliance on confessions in trials would require torture to produce them. But it was also intuitive to Enlightenment critics like Beccaria that judicial torture would lead to a perverse result: "strong" criminals would successfully resist, and "weak," innocent victims would confess. Like desperation, intuition about interrogational torture suffers from indeterminacy. Maybe it is intuitive to torture, but it might also be intuitive to believe that torture victims will just say whatever they think will make the torture stop rather than the truth. At the least, more theorizing is needed to explain the content of what is supposedly intuitive.

Scholars have begun to do some of this additional theorizing. Rejali (2007, 449) helps the intuition argument along with what he calls "folklore about pain": the belief that "all people avoid pain and seek pleasure, more injury produces more pain, and so it is simply a matter of calibrating the quantity of pain for each individual" in order to extract information. Ruth Blakeley (2007, 376) also makes some progress on this problem when she argues that the "horribleness" of torture is behind its intuitive appeal. These are only early attempts, though, and I pick up where Rejali and Blakeley leave off in the next chapter.

Organizational Culture

States may use torture if coercive interrogation is ingrained in an organization's culture. Closed organizations such as intelligence agencies and military organizations develop their own set of ideas, beliefs, and norms which frame their approach to certain tasks (Kier 1997). Their singularity of focus gives them the image of possessing expertise in their fields, but it also limits their ability to see their actions in a larger context (Sagan 1994). Over time, the norms of closed institutions may contradict those on the outside. The secretive nature of these organizations hampers international norm penetration, insulates the organizations from the benefits of the marketplace of ideas, and makes state coordination difficult. The result is "decisions" (or rather, output) that do not reflect international sensibilities or work in the state's overall best interest. Torture may be a part of that output. Despite damning evidence, agencies may press on with torture as a matter of tradition and a lack of organizational learning.

The persistence of torture in agencies might be a matter of lack of knowledge. In his chapter titled "Why Governments Don't Learn," Rejali (2007) argues that militaries in particular do not learn from failures in torture as much as they learn from failure in war, because war takes place in the open, but torture is secretive. Knowledge of success and failure, and the roots of success and failure, cannot accumulate. Counterinsurgencies, often operating with more fragmented groups of soldiers, lead to less pooling of knowledge and centralized assessment. The result is a dearth of data and analysis. This, Rejali argues, is one reason that some torture sympathizers like Alan Dershowitz (2002) support "torture warrants": so observers can gauge torture's effectiveness in the light of day. Rejali then dismisses this idea as fanciful because torture is so difficult to regulate and often harms the perpetrator along with the victim.

Perhaps certain organizations lack more than just knowledge. Officials both inside and outside of an organization might understand the mission of the organization (Wilson 1989, 95) to include the government's "dirty work." The organization's job, then, is to be prepared to look past societal and human rights norms when duty calls. The "dirty work" mission affects recruitment, training, promotions, and informal socialization. Such a culture might lead to a race to the bottom in which organization members compete for the title of cruelest.

The organizational culture argument gets at a key empirical regularity. It explains why torture can take up residence in certain agencies and gives us tools for tracing the persistence of torture through organizational inertia or relapse. It can also tell us why certain organizations are more susceptible to abusive practices than others. The recurring flirtation with and indulgence in torturous practices by the CIA becomes more sensible when considering the culture—or perhaps subculture—that has endured since the agency's founding.

Yet organizational culture arguments can bring us only so far, because they cannot tell us why one particular culture rather than another takes root. Like the desperation and intuition arguments, organizational culture is something of a blank page on which any number of stories might be written. In cases in which political overseers can choose which organization should take the lead on interrogations, organizational culture's power as an explanation is further blunted. This does not mean that it is unimportant; it means only that it will be more convincing and more complete if it works together with other arguments to explain the outcome in question.

Racism

Perhaps torture recurs because wars across racial lines recur. Racism is a form of dehumanization, a process by which the denigration of victims "weakens the victimizer's normal restraints on violent behavior" (Haslam and Loughnan 2014, 401). The "other" is robbed of identity and community, both of which are instrumental in evoking empathy. Though Kelman (1973, 48–49) is principally concerned with massacres in the following passage, we can extend the same argument to torture as well:

> To accord a person identity is to perceive him as an individual, independent and distinguishable from others, capable of making choices, and entitled to live his own life on the basis of his own goals and values. To accord a person community is to perceive him—along with one's self—as a part of an interconnected network of individuals who care for each other, who recognize each other's individuality, and who respect each other's rights. . . .

Sanctioned massacres become possible to the extent that we deprive fellow human beings of identity and community.

Jean-Paul Sartre (1963, 15), writing on France's colonial wars, describes how French soldiers needed to adjust their definition of who is human in order to carry out their violent deeds while preserving their values: "Our soldiers overseas, rejecting the universalism of the mother country, apply the 'numerus clausus' to the human race: since none may enslave, rob, or kill his fellow man without committing a crime, they lay down the principle that the native is not one of our fellow men."

Later social-psychological research on dehumanization defines humanness in terms of uniqueness and nature. Human uniqueness refers to attributes that separate us from other animals. Human nature covers attributes that distinguish us from inanimate objects. Each provides a path for dehumanization. Individuals denied human uniqueness will be viewed as lacking intelligence or self-control. Those believed to be without human nature are seen to lack emotion (especially secondary emotion) and individuality (Haslam 2006; Haslam and Loughnon 2014). This rendering allows for more subtle forms of dehumanization (sometimes called "infrahumanization"), and does not require instances of blatant racial bigotry (though cases of torture have those, too) in order to demonstrate racism at work.

The causal arrow may go the other way as well: individuals may be motivated to devalue the enemy because doing so reduces the cognitive dissonance created by one's self-image and one's violent behavior. The more moral one thinks of oneself, the more likely one is to slander the other: "Consider the irony: It is precisely because I think I am such a nice person that, if I do something that causes you pain, I must convince myself that you are a rat. In other words, because nice guys like me don't go around hurting innocent people, you must have deserved every nasty thing that I did to you" (Aronson 2003, 240). Racism and violence may well beget one another.

It would be hard to deny that racism plays a part in the choice to torture, especially in colonial wars. Racism is often overlooked in international relations scholarship. Trying to explain U.S. torture in the Philippines or Vietnam without discussing race would be a glaring oversight. Racism may also structure interrogation settings in important ways that are difficult for social science to capture.

Whether racism is the *primary motivator* is a separate question. If it is, then we should see torture both inside and outside of interrogation settings.

(This is true of revenge as a primary explanation as well.) If torture is used only during interrogation, then there must be another factor that is absent when torturers and would-be torturers are showing forbearance in noninterrogation settings. My research generally finds the latter to be the case, necessitating an investigation of why torture and a sincere search for intelligence are so often paired in the empirical record.

Lingering Questions

Liberal democracies have engaged in their share of torture, by almost any definition. Previous scholars have done important work to explain torture as a symptom of the lack of institutional correctives, the dehumanizing forces of racism, the throes of desperation, and an enduring feature of certain organizational cultures. Yet each approach leaves unanswered several important questions. Arguments based on racism do not tell us what connects the need for intelligence and torture, and approaches that stress organizational-cultural origins do not tell us why a particular culture takes hold. Explanations emphasizing desperation for information help us understand why torture is so often chosen in pursuit of intelligence, but what explains the pervasive belief that torture works? Answers to this question based on intuition get us only so far, and scholars have just begun to unpack the content behind the intuitive explanation.

We also have more to learn about why the antitorture norm has frequently proven ineffective at preventing torture. Even if we dismiss international norms as having limited relevance in an anarchic world, we still need to address why many states that have codified these norms in their own domestic laws still violate them. Norms and laws may drive torturers to hide their deeds, but as I will show in later chapters, there are plenty of examples of actors playing down torture rather than hiding it. Why? The next chapter pursues these unanswered questions.

3

The Search for "Nasty" but "Safe" Interrogation Methods

The atmosphere was "excellent," John "Bruce" Jessen told a CIA investigator in January 2003, in reference to a "black site," one of the secret prison facilities that U.S. officials used to house what they believed to be high-level detainees in the war on terror (Central Intelligence Agency 2003, 13). Jessen, a CIA contractor hired to develop the agency's "enhanced interrogation" program, was singing the praises of a particularly notorious prison in Afghanistan, codenamed "Cobalt." Cobalt was dark, cold, and brutal. Most of the flooring was either dirt or concrete. The CIA's chief of interrogation called it a "dungeon." Another officer quipped that Cobalt was itself an "enhanced interrogation technique" (U.S. Senate, Select Committee on Intelligence 2014, 4). Prisoners simply called it "The Darkness" (Siems 2017). The architecture and thermostat were bad enough, but the techniques used within Cobalt were also ghastly: forced wearing of diapers, blaring music, marathon interrogation sessions, "rough take-downs," and the list goes on. What, then, was so "excellent" about Cobalt's atmosphere? In Jessen's words, it was "nasty, but safe" (Central Intelligence Agency 2003, 13).

Jessen's assessment is part of a pattern that explains why the United States has repeatedly turned to torture to fight insurgents and terrorists, despite norms and laws prohibiting its use. Coercive interrogators seek out methods that bend or break the rules—i.e., that are sufficiently "nasty"—to extract information from "nonstandard" detainees. They do not want to appear to be loose cannons, however, and often have an interest in arguing that their approach is mild, permissible, and not really torture—hence the "safe" qualifier.[1] The result is a kind of torturer's happy medium.

This argument helps to answer some of the lingering questions from the previous chapter. Why does the belief persist that torture works, despite evidence that is either too limited or too damning? I argue that torturers think their methods work because of a prior, general philosophy about the need to play dirty in a dangerous world. Why are antitorture norms so

American Torture from the Philippines to Iraq. William L. d'Ambruoso, Oxford University Press. © Oxford University Press 2022. DOI: 10.1093/oso/9780197570326.003.0003

often inadequate to the task of preventing torture? Not only is the norm against torture faced with the challenge of preventing behavior that coercive interrogators and their apologists believe can be redefined at will, but actors may also interpret norm-breaking as a sign that they are actually being sufficiently harsh. Why do torturers sometimes use stealth methods, and then freely admit to doing so? I argue that mark-less torture is not merely easier to hide; it also enhances the practitioner's ability to play down or deny the harshness of the deeds after revelation.

I lay out the logic of my argument in the next section, followed by a discussion of some of the most prevalent interactions between my explanations and other approaches. Then I detail the methodology I use in the empirical chapters to come, with special attention to a case selection that provides for a variety of test settings, and development of the kinds of questions that elucidate torturers' underlying beliefs and philosophy.

My Explanations for Torture's Recurrence

I will be explaining certain aspects of the "why torture" puzzle, specifically torture's recurrence and the persistent coexistence of torture and the norm against it in liberal democracies. Since both explanations feature norms in causal and constitutive roles, a short discussion about normative effects will help set up the argument.

Normative Effects

Norms are collective expectations of appropriate behavior for a given identity (Katzenstein 1996). Nina Tannenwald (1999, 2007) identifies three effects of norms in her work on the normative prohibition against the use of nuclear weapons. First, norms impose regulations on state actors, forcing them to consider the costs and benefits of compliance. Second, norms have constitutive effects, creating or defining forms of behavior, roles, and identities (Tannenwald 2007, 46). If X and Y are in a constitutive relationship, then "X is what it is in virtue of its relation to Y" (Wendt 1999, 25). For norms, that means forms of behavior, roles, and identities are what they are in virtue of their relation to collective expectations about appropriate behavior. Chemical weapons use might be categorized as outrageous and its users barbaric via their relation to a norm prohibiting weapons of mass destruction (WMD).

Third, norms can have "shadow" or permissive effects, in which a norm claims our attention, allowing other acts that are similar and equally (or nearly equally) deplorable, but categorically different, to escape condemnation. The fuel-air explosives that the United States used in the first Gulf War exemplify this latter effect. These weapons were as powerful as small nuclear devices, but because they were not actually in the nuclear category, they eluded harsh criticism.

Tannenwald (2007, 44) understands permissive effects to be a subcategory of constitutive effects; permissive effects "are defined in relation to the categories constituted by the norm or taboo and the larger normative context in which the taboo is nested." For instance, with regard to weapons of mass destruction, the anti-WMD norm defines the categorization of WMD; in doing so, it defines non-WMD weapons (like those fuel-air explosives). That said, permissive effects can arise in the shadow of regulative or constitutive effects. Regulative constraints on the use of WMD can make the use of non-WMD "cheaper" than might otherwise be the case. Likewise, the norm against WMD defines this categorization of weapons as unusable, part of the constitutive effect; by extension, it categorizes non-WMD as usable (47).

Other scholars have shown that norms can have unintended consequences. Charli Carpenter (2003) argues that civilian rescue norms privileging women and children for evacuation had the perverse effect of leaving the most frequently targeted group—military-age men—susceptible to mass killing. Ahead of the Srebrenica massacre in 1995, the norm-based definition of who was vulnerable in war mixed with self-interest to explain demographically informed evacuation choices: "[W]hen evacuations were negotiated, adult civilian men were excluded. This satisfied the Bosnian Serb fighters, who retained their 'legitimate targets'; the Bosnian Muslim authorities, who retained their pool of potential fighters; and the international community, who could satisfy itself at having 'at least' assisted the 'most vulnerable'" (Carpenter 2003, 682).

James Ron has shown that the norm against torture in particular has exhibited perverse effects. Drawing on Foucault's work chronicling the state-level shift from punishment to discipline, Ron (1997) explains how the horror over overt torture has forced governments to choose other forms of social control that are subtler but potentially more comprehensive. Instead of doing away with torture entirely, some states try to regulate and, by extension, legitimize the practice. As a result, Ron observes, there was a rise in the use of stealth interrogation techniques, including forced standing and restriction of air, by Israel in the early 1990s.[2] The Israeli government's shift in policy had multiple consequences. On the one hand, detainees suffered fewer broken bones and other lasting physical impairments from the techniques that were used. On the other hand, as noted in the previous chapter, the lack of physical scars added to the mental trauma by removing an obvious excuse for any confessions (real or fabricated) made under duress.

Ron's example shows how norms can have indirect effects. Domestic and international monitoring constrained the Israeli government (a regulative effect), but the government's response had the unforeseen consequence of increasing psychological damage among detainees in some cases. The norm against overt physical torture also paved the way for government efforts to legitimize alternative forms of "discipline."

The explanation that I present bears some similarities to Tannenwald's shadow effect, but without categorical boundaries on which everyone can agree. Because the torture norm is hard to specify, what constitutes torture is debated when the acts are not hidden. The boundaries of the shadow are contested. My first explanation is also an unintended consequence of a norm. The norm against torture constitutes torture as off-limits, attracting those who believe that international politics requires actors to either walk at the edge of, or venture beyond, normative constraints.

The "Cheaters Win" Argument

My explanation suggests that norms can have precisely the opposite of the intended effect. The causal story proceeds as follows. An actor (policymaker, bureaucrat, or soldier) faces a security challenge, such as a terrorist threat or an insurgency, which puts a premium on intelligence. This actor feels pressure from the domestic population, his peers, or even from himself, to produce results, but not necessarily explicit pressure to torture. He is looking for any advantage he can find, and he feels the need to get tough with the hardened opposition by thinking outside the box. Norms and laws define that box. The actor decides that he cannot afford to be hamstrung by the rules and that he needs either to push against them as far as he can without getting in trouble or to break the rules outright to obtain intelligence.

Two parts work together in this explanation. The first is a belief—or maybe just a suspicion—that in the nasty world of international politics, cheaters win. Second, norms and laws define what cheating is. As each part forms the whole of this explanation, each deserves elaboration.

We have plenty of reasons to suspect that the belief that cheaters have special advantages in the international realm, and sometimes in politics generally, is not unusual. Observers of international politics have appreciated cheaters' successes since Odysseus packed a wooden "gift" horse with soldiers. Machiavelli ([1513] 1882) celebrated wicked duplicity for the sake of the republic. After all, he reasoned, "One's country must be defended; whether with glory or shame; it must be defended anyhow" (quoted in Waltz 1975, 34). Some of history's most famous backstabbers, such as Bismarck and Hitler, saw considerable success, at least for a while, as a direct result of their backstabbing. The Prisoner's Dilemma rewards the defector in a world of defectors. The belief that cheaters win in international politics is sometimes a reasonable cognitive shortcut even if it is not always true.[3]

Feminist political thinkers have long noted traditional international relations theory's celebration of politics with no normative bounds. J. Ann Tickner (1988, 432) recalls Hans Morganthau's (1978) discussion of "political man, a beast completely lacking in moral restraints." She continues:

> Because states do not live up to the universal moral laws that govern the universe, those who behave morally in international politics are doomed to failure because of the immoral actions of others. To solve this tension, Morganthau postulates a realm of international politics in which the amoral behavior of political man is not only permissible but prudent. It is a Hobbesian world, separate and distinct from the world of domestic order, in which states may act like beasts, for survival depends on a maximisation of power and a willingness to fight. (432)

If and when some states behave morally in international politics, Morganthau contends, they become easy prey for their amoral peers.

Tickner is most interested in arguing that, just as one cannot divide public and private political realms, one also cannot neatly separate an autonomous, international, amoral political sphere from a domestic, moral one. When Morganthau attempts to do so, he constructs a world that privileges masculine ideals, presenting only a partial view of human nature and the consequences of political conditions. My argument is less concerned with demonstrating that assumptions about the advantages of amorality reflect masculine values, though that may well be the case. I aim to show that such assumptions are pervasive and can explain the recurring turn to torture as a method of interrogation. Those assumptions may have gendered origins, among other deep foundations.

Tickner's feminist critique also pertains to my argument in that it parallels my understanding of political behavior. If perfect rationality were attainable, then actors could always and constantly survey all the options and choose the best one in pursuit of their interests. I assume that perfect rationality is unattainable. This is not so controversial: rational choice theorists admit that the point of rational assumptions is to build theory and make predictions, not to portray individual decision-making with perfect accuracy.[4] Because rational calculations and constant updating are themselves costly and challenging endeavors, and because information is incomplete (especially when dealing with a phenomenon like torture, of which knowledge resists accumulation), actors must devise shortcuts to make choices. Just as (even) political man's view is more clouded and partial than Morganthau realizes, real people must cope with a lack of knowledge as well as a dearth of resources to organize what little they do know.

The second part of this explanation is the flip side of the usual constitutive effect of the norm. Proscriptive norms define what rule-following is. By extension, they also delineate what cheating is. By themselves, constitutive arguments are distinct from causal arguments, because they answer what and how-possible questions instead of why questions. Constitutive claims can play key roles in causal arguments, however (Wendt 1999, 83), and that is what I am claiming here. The off-limits nature of certain behaviors, defined by norms, can define "what it means to be a 'civilized' member of the international community" (Tannenwald 2007, 46), but it can also draw the gaze of those who believe that cheaters win in international politics.

The result is a kind of "upside-down world," where good is bad and bad is good. For instance, in the early 1930s, Japanese political leaders began to develop biological weapons, "in part because Japanese officials were impressed that germ warfare had been banned by the Geneva Convention of 1925. If it was so awful that it had to be banned under international law, the officers reasoned, it must make a great weapon" (Kristof 1995).[5] For these officials looking for an advantage in future wars, "awful" was "great."

The French-Algerian War in the late 1950s provides another example. The French, who suffered through World War II at the hands of the Germans, had been instrumental in developing and codifying norms pertaining to the treatment of prisoners during war, but the French Army was soon chafing under those restrictions in Algeria. Under pressure to produce intelligence, the resident minister urged the military to (continue to) use extreme measures: "The rebels' terrible threats and appalling crimes are forcing us to adopt certain behavior. . . . [I]n some cases strict compliance with the law may become a crime" (quoted in Branche 2007, 550). To stick with the law, the resident minister argued, would put the French at an inexcusable disadvantage. This attitude explains in part why French use of torture for intelligence in that war was systematic, widespread, and eventually habitual.

Given some of the work in political psychology on actors' interests in avoiding painful trade-offs, the Cheaters Win account may seem unlikely. People prefer to avoid decisions in which values conflict; stalling and buck-passing are some of the usual responses (Lebow 1983; Fiske and Tetlock 1997). I am suggesting a separate dynamic: people can *overestimate* the extent to which the world is comprised of trade-offs. Economists such as John Maynard Keynes have noted this tendency among their ranks. To explain why classical economics had more appeal than he thought it deserved, Keynes (1936, ch. 3) speculated that, among other ironies, the pain it prescribed gave it a noble air: "That its teaching, translated into practice, was austere and often unpalatable, lent it virtue." Paul Krugman (2010), citing Keynes, noted a similar development during the Great Recession: "Calling for austerity and tight money feels courageous, tough-minded, and virtuous; it allows the economist making such calls to take the pose of a Serious Person standing firm against the easy-money guys."[6] I am theorizing that political actors focused on security would be just as susceptible to a "no pain, no gain" mindset.

The theory of psychological reactance, associated most closely with the work of Jack Brehm, bears some similarities to my argument. Reactance is "the motivation to regain a freedom after it has been lost or threatened" (Steindl et al. 2015, 205) and explains why a movie that is forbidden can appear more attractive, or why people who are told that they must hold certain beliefs are more likely to adopt an opposing view.[7] People want to retain as much freedom of choice as they can and will sometimes reclaim their power by demonstration. Perhaps the norm against torture can inspire a "Don't tell me what I can't do" response from interrogators and leaders. While discrepancies exist between reactance theory and the Cheaters Win argument—most importantly, I am not assuming that actors are primarily concerned with maximizing behavioral freedom—the case chapters illustrate some overlap, too. The clearest instance of reactance is the Bush administration's sometimes aggressive refusal to allow international law to encroach on its interrogation options.

The Cheaters Win explanation does not always announce itself as plainly as some of this chapter's examples suggest. The historical record is not exactly replete with torturers spotting the norm, declaring "Ah-ha!," and deciding only then that torture must be effective. The reality is likely to be messier and subtler. People are generally brought up to believe that harming others is usually wrong. As some of them become international political actors of one form or another, they might notice these sentiments in international norms, both codified and informal. The norm against torture is one of these standards. Yet observations of some of the cruelties of international political life may convince the actor that there exists a kind of persistent race to the bottom in the world, and the wickedest players usually prevail. Those still restricted by norms risk rendering themselves defenseless in the face of danger. Actors such as these will then use words like "nasty" approvingly, as Bruce Jessen did in this chapter's opening vignette. Or they might use positive language to describe harsh things. We should search for these subtler clues to see the Cheaters Win explanation at work.

This explanation becomes more convincing when the lead-up to torture includes evidence of the following: (a) communication suggesting those without limitations have an advantage; (b) praise or promotion of unscrupulous agents for their unscrupulousness; (c) language suggesting a kind of "nascent moral inversion" (Adams, Balfour, and Reed 2006, 688)[8] in which "bad" becomes "good"; (d) suggestions that only a new or separate set of rules will do; and (e) approval of a package of norm-challenging items that may include torture. The last indicator confirms that it is not just torture that interests the approver, but generally pushing and exceeding limits, suggesting a mindset or a philosophy and not just the intention to perform a particular act (Jervis 2006, 649).

The Torture Norm's Robustness Problem

Typically, the more robust a norm is, the more compliance it engenders. As discussed earlier, there are both normative and rational reasons for this. A norm can inspire compliance because actors genuinely want to do what is appropriate, but even absent this, norms can impose costs on violators. Consistent lack of compliance may indicate that a certain norm is insufficiently robust, though for the sake of sound social science, it is important to measure robustness apart from behavior in order to avoid circular reasoning.

At a glance, the international antitorture norm may seem at least as robust as any other. Henry Shue (1978, 124) writes, "No other practice except slavery is so universally and unanimously condemned in law and human convention." Yet while most everyone condemns torture by name, not everyone can agree on what torture is. Some actors believe they can justify harsh interrogations because they see vagueness and malleability in torture's definition.

Jeffrey Legro (1997, 34–35) presents three dimensions for measuring a norm's robustness: specificity, referring to how clear the rules are; durability, which means how long standing the norm is and to what degree it can survive violations; and concordance, or how widely accepted the norm is. The torture norm has fairly strong durability and concordance, at least in liberal democracies. In addition to the earlier quote from Shue and some of the content from the previous chapters, I will add this: almost no U.S. politicians from the Philippine-American War to the present defend torture by name. Dick Cheney, one of the enhanced interrogation program's staunchest defenders, said that America didn't torture: "[I]t's against our laws and against our values" (Stout and Shane 2008). Time and again, actors deny that they are torturing, even when watchdogs reveal the details of the techniques and the suffering caused, and otherwise insist that their actions are not as severe as the critics claim.

The fact that actors believe these acts *could* be played down and argued as something less than torture suggests that the norm against torture lacks specificity. Much of the lack of specificity is inherent in torture itself: it is not neatly and clearly separated from its milder cousins. The authors of the UN Convention against Torture understood this when they included "cruel, inhuman, or degrading treatment" in their ban. Yet it is not clear how long a prisoner may be kept awake until the depravation of sleep becomes cruel treatment and then torture. Because some users of stealth torture want their techniques to sound more benign than they are, their methods are often based on extreme versions of normal acts. Asking a detainee to stand at attention for one minute would not be alarming; asking him to continue to stand for two days would be torture. It's unclear where the crossover points are. Since problems of definitional agreement are inherent in torture, the robustness of the torture norm has occupied a middle ground for some time; the norm has had durability and concordance, but not specificity.

Semi-robustness due to lack of specificity has opened up routes to violation. Potential violators can more easily justify (to themselves and others) acts that draw close to torture, because they can compare them favorably with even harsher (or harsher-sounding) methods, some of which may be used by the enemy.[9] They can use euphemisms and modifiers to soften the image of their techniques. They can also simply deny that a committed act is torture.

The use of favorable comparisons bears some resemblance to Tannenwald's "shadow effects," but with a little more emphasis on agency.[10] Nuclear weapons, Tannenwald's primary subject matter, are separated from conventional ones by what Schelling (2006) calls a "clear, bright line" or a "firebreak." The "shadow" falls on nonnuclear weapons, and disapproval of their use rarely, if ever, comes up. By contrast, torture and less coercive interrogation methods are not separated by a firebreak. Through favorable comparison, torturers try to push their own behavior into the shadow of their opponents' supposedly worse deeds.

Torturers may or may not believe their own justifications, which implies that the theory covers a range of actor-types. At one end of the spectrum, the actor is self-delusional (assuming the act really qualifies as torture). He believes his own justifications, thus preserving a moral image for himself, and perhaps even a sense of moral superiority if the justifications were comparative. The Machiavellian character at the other end of the spectrum knows that the behavior amounts to torture, and still thinks that either others will buy the justifications or, at least, the violations are unpunishable. Actors might fall somewhere in between these extremes, too. Telling one actor-type from another is challenging, because the justifications often sound the same. It is worthwhile to give an estimate of the actor-type in question, but the norm-specificity argument performs essentially the same causal function and does not require that we peer into the torturer's soul to find evidence for it.

Are justifications just cheap talk, post hoc add-ons that screen the real reasons for torture? Perhaps sometimes, but the fact that torture might be amenable to such justifications suggests a causal role. To see how justifications can amount to causation, imagine two friends, Joe and Bob, are out late having drinks. Joe announces that he has to go home. Bob says, "Come on, stay for one more." Joe responds, "What would I tell my wife?" Bob says, "Just tell her that ———." There are immediate causes for Joe's possible interest in staying that are worth noting: the promise of more camaraderie, a tasty beer, etc. But whether Joe stays or leaves may also depend on the justification that Bob offers (or one that Joe himself thinks up). Crucial here is how salable the justification is, and whether the behavior is amenable to salable justifications. The lack of specificity of the torture norm plays a causal role by making torture especially amenable to justifications that actors believe they can sell.

One example of the lack of specificity argument comes from Rachel Wahl's study of the use of torture among law enforcers in India, where the torture norm is weaker than in the United States, but human rights norms generally have some traction. Officers consistently downplayed their own culpability in undermining detainees' human rights by speaking of degrees of torture. One officer said that he used only "humane" torture: "A lot will depend on [an officer's] mind, his training, his upbringing. Maybe I will only use 50 percent of force but a younger person will use more. I have compassion. I have a different mindset. The degree of torture will depend on the mindset" (Wahl 2013, 231). Another officer maintained that torturers should try to uphold the dignity of the detainee as much as possible. Torture "should not go beyond a certain point" and should not "cause lasting damage" (232).

Wahl's example includes many routes to torture that the lack of specificity creates and shows the kinds of evidence that I will be presenting in later chapters. It has (a) direct appeal to the slippery slope: the "50 percent" and "beyond a certain point" comments; (b) modifiers, describing some kinds of torture as "humane"; (c) favorable comparison to "younger" officers. Imagine an officer trying out these justifications if the taboo had been cannibalism instead of torture; it would probably not occur to him to excuse himself by saying he just ate a toe, or that other officers were more likely to eat whole families rather than just a select few—such defenses would probably not convince anyone or enable anything. Some acts are more amenable to justifications than others.

Another example of the specificity problem comes from the French-Algerian War. When allegations of French torture in Algeria surfaced in Paris in 1955, the French government asked a colonial official named Roger Wuillaume to compile a report on the subject:

In March 1955, Wuillaume delivered his report for limited government consumption. The report not only acknowledged the use of torture in Algeria, but actually recommended sanctioning it because, on the one hand, Wuillaume decided it was effective and indispensable, and on the other, concluded that it could not be concealed. In fact, Wuillaume's only reservation was that torture must be exercised under "controlled conditions"—that is, its practice should be left only in the hands of professionals so as to prevent "abuse." (Merom 2003, 112)

Wuillaume's belief in the sliding scale of severity is clear and consequential. Because his recommendations for the French government leave room for forbearance at the end of the severity spectrum (no "abuse"), he can satisfy himself that he is not throwing out ethical concerns altogether.

Wuillaume envisions a carefully contained program run by "professionals," and the connection to my argument here needs further explanation. As Ron (1997) depicts in his study of Israel, and as we shall see in the later chapters, invocation of a process with internal monitoring, especially by physicians, can enable torture. The lack of specificity creates this possibility. Protests that an interrogation is carefully supervised may reassure concerned observers if they perceive that the methods are in some gray area between acceptably mild and illegitimately brutal. In contrast, when behavior is on the other side of a firebreak, professional monitoring is less likely to save it from condemnation. The legitimizing patina afforded by professionals projects the sense that an interrogation program will not slide into an abyss of amateurish sadism.

The lack of specificity clears the way for another enabling justification found in all three of my cases: the claim that a given technique was, in some sense, self-applied with no long-term adverse effects. The CIA's distribution of LSD among its own agents is one example. I am also including the "enhanced interrogation techniques" that were initially part of some advanced U.S. military training programs as another instance of self-application. As I demonstrate in chapters 5 and 6, torturers used both variations to protest their innocence along the lines of "We did it to ourselves and emerged unharmed."

Torture's blurry lines allow practitioners to try a mild version on themselves and their allies, and more potent variants, or more repetitions of the same treatment, on the enemy. Self-application specialists take advantage of the fact that methods can be bent subtly in more or less abusive directions, with infinite variety. We should not be fooled into thinking that these "tests" actually demonstrate something meaningful. Elements of torture like pain, fear, and mental suffering are subjective and can change drastically based on context, and the detainee's world is not comparable to that of the interrogator or a soldier in training.[11] Still, self-application offers a way of selling the idea that certain methods couldn't possibly be torture. In some instances, it also suggests that specificity justifications really have an enabling, causal effect, since these instances of self-application almost always predate use on detainees.

Ideally, we would find evidence for this explanation by eavesdropping on a conversation similar to the one between Bob and Joe. The actor conceives of the justification before the action, and the realization of this justification clearly tips the balance in favor of one policy over another. The world is not usually so compliant, unfortunately. Coping often requires reporting after-the-fact justifications—looking for the favorable comparisons, euphemisms, softening modifiers, and denials—and estimating how likely these justifications had a prior, enabling effect. The presence of after-the-fact justifications increases the likelihood that the possibility of making them occurred to actors ahead of time and had an enabling effect, but it's not conclusive. Where possible, evidence that actors used justifications "in the moment" or just prior is preferable. If the (scarcer) prior justifications match the (more prevalent) later ones in tenor, the later ones are more likely to have been conceived ahead of time.

Combining the Explanations: Finding the "Middle Ground"

Torture, then, becomes alluring for two reasons: its status as an off-limits practice suggests that it will be tough enough for even the most hardened detainees, and the torture norm's lack of specificity enables prospective torturers to anticipate that their behavior will be defensible. With help from a little motivated reasoning, torture—especially stealth torture—can transform from a despicable act to a method that seems to solve multiple problems. Torture's recurrence, despite a persistent norm against it, becomes much less mysterious.

If the torture norm lacks precise definition, how can it *clearly* define what cheating is, and therefore what "works"? The answer is that it doesn't. Instead, actors perceive severity of interrogations as a sliding scale. According to such perceptions, the most severe interrogation techniques may be effective, but are so condemned as to be off-limits even in the most desperate times. Conversely, interrogation methods that minimize severity would be widely accepted, but not harsh enough to extract information from

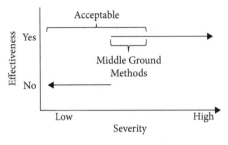

Figure 3.1 Perceptions of interrogation methods: the Middle Ground model.

hardened detainees. The trick is to find a magical middle ground in which interrogations are severe enough to be effective, but not so heinous that they invite condemnation and prosecution. Figure 3.1 shows a basic illustration of this idea.

As in the specificity argument, perception plays a major role. The actor perceives the severity, effectiveness, and acceptability of the interrogation methods in question. For acceptability in particular, torturers are interested in how others will interpret their behavior. Because of this, the middle ground is often occupied by the stealth methods discussed earlier. Torturers intentionally fence in the techniques—any suffering is brief, the methods leave no marks, there is no permanent damage—to differentiate them from the worst abuses, but they usually stop short of saying that the methods pose no difficulties for the detainees.

I treat perceived effectiveness as a binary variable in Figure 3.1. If we allow for continuous variation, more models emerge. Though many others are imaginable, I explore two in particular. First, the actor may believe that stealth methods are the best a civilized country can do, but a less scrupulous state would have even more effective methods at its disposal. The actor thus forfeits more effective but more brutal methods for the sake of propriety. The left panel of Figure 3.2 captures this relationship.

A second model with continuous perceived effectiveness adds separate theoretical elements, but it compares so closely to the other models in this section that I will present it here. Actors may come to believe that their middle ground methods are more effective than those that are less *or* more severe. The preference for one's own methods reveals in-group bias: one's own supposedly clever or scientific means of extracting information are in all ways preferable to the simple, barbaric ways of one's enemies or bureaucratic rivals. The right panel of Figure 3.2 gives an illustration.

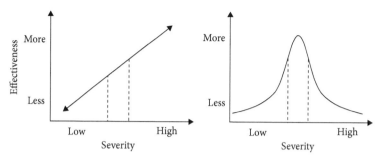

Figure 3.2 Two models capturing perceived degree of effectiveness based on perception of severity.

Moving away from the binary y-axis of Figure 3.1 has benefits and drawbacks. Most obviously, the richer models in Figure 3.2 can teach us more, and I use them where possible in the following chapters. They make more demands of the evidence, however, and sometimes it is hard to do better than speculate what actors might believe about the efficacy of interrogation measures outside the realm of their own practice. Furthermore, the sparser model can cover more cases and show that they are of a type, even if a higher-powered microscope—again, not always an option in the world of beliefs about torture—would reveal more variation.

In each of the graphed models, torturers are looking for a middle ground, methods that are tough but limited, and as we shall see, actors will frequently state plainly—sometimes in one carefully balanced sentence, sometimes in separate statements over time—that this is their goal. Bruce Jessen's "nasty, but safe" comment at the beginning of this chapter is one example. Such statements are key evidence for the Middle Ground argument.

The search for the middle ground can also account for the increased use of torture that leaves no marks. Recall that Rejali (2007) explains democracies' use of stealth methods as a reaction to "monitors": disapproving superiors, courts, human rights advocates, and journalists that report on prisoner abuse. Torture without marks, Rejali contends, allows torturers to "evade monitoring and preserve a thin [veneer] of legitimacy" (411). Rejali does not stipulate whether actors retain legitimacy *because* they evade monitoring, but we can surmise from the rest of his book that that is his emphasis. My explanation is complementary but distinct: actors can also try to preserve legitimacy by arguing that their methods are legitimate *even if monitors catch them*, and stealth methods make such claims more persuasive. Torturers can and do try to do both at once: hide *and* justify themselves if hiding fails. Stealth methods can serve both ends. While providing an alternative account of different specific torture methods is not my primary goal, stealth torture is an observable implication of the thesis. I argue that actors search for interrogation techniques that are nasty enough to work, but sufficiently mild-sounding to be sold as legitimate, and stealth torture usually fits the bill.

A More Complete Account

My explanations respond to a number of unanswered questions from the literature on the causes of torture. This does not mean that my argument is in a zero-sum competition with the others. By filling in blanks left by other explanations, the theory presented in this chapter, together with those presented in the previous chapter, create a more complete account of the recurrence of torture.

This chapter's explanations pick up where the previous ones leave off. In this section, I highlight points of closest connection by depicting hypothetical scenarios in which one explanation shades into another. While I leave the examples here unspecified, the cases include real instances of all of these variations.

Cheaters Win and . . .

. . . Desperation: Following a terrorist attack, the political leadership becomes authentically desperate to prevent another one. Drawing on assumptions about what effective counterterrorism demands, leaders pledge to themselves and each other not to tie their own hands with normative expectations. They then search their allies and their own bureaucracies for the seediest characters to carry out interrogations.

. . . Intuition: Ruthless enemy insurgents are waging a tough campaign. They obey no laws of war; they can pick whatever methods are most expedient without regard to norms. It just makes sense to the counterinsurgents that they too must look beyond normative bounds, including those related to interrogation, in order to compete.

. . . Organizational Culture: A group within a military or intelligence organization tasked with gathering intelligence from detainees develops certain separate norms not shared by wider communities.[12] The group is aware of national and international standards of conduct but believes that the jobs it must do require behavior at the edge of, or outside of, these norms. Because the secrecy of the work does not allow much knowledge to accumulate, group members use norm-bending or -breaking as an indicator that they are doing everything they can to produce intelligence. Dirty deeds, including torture, come to define the group's culture and the value-added that it promises political superiors.

Lack of Specificity and . . .

. . . Monitoring: An interrogation team deliberates over whether to begin a coercive program and decides to go forward with a set of stealth methods. Crucial to their decision is the belief that they run a low risk of getting caught, and failing that, they can argue that these methods are not really torture.

. . . Racism: Soldiers learn to dehumanize enemy insurgents through the shared use of negative stereotypes and racial slurs. Among the more common remarks is the complaint that the opponent is bound to fight "dirty." This comparison creates the possibility for coercive interrogation by these soldiers, which they argue is justified given the worse treatment they can expect from the other side (and perhaps necessary for fighting a barbaric, lawless enemy; see the Cheaters Win argument).

Empirical Strategy

I test these explanations with three case studies from U.S. history: the Philippine-American War (1899–1902), the early Cold War years up to the Vietnam War, and the post-9/11 war on terror. These cases capture the persistence of a revivable torture policy for over a century. Studying the persistence of something presents methodological challenges, particularly the inherent lack of variation in continuity, and I cannot pretend to solve all of those problems here. The cases hold some variation worth exploiting. Within the cases, support for torture varies, and I try to connect these differences to deeper philosophies. In the book's concluding chapter, I also draw comparisons between the United States and Europe, where the use of torture has leveled off or declined somewhat in recent times (Mayerfeld 2016). Still, the main value of my case studies is to demonstrate a repeated pattern in small wars set in different time periods and macro-strategic contexts.

Where possible, I focus most acutely on key moments when the decision to use interrogational torture is made. The fact that the choice to torture usually does not boil down to a single instance offers methodological advantages. The multiple points along the decision-making process, together with the numerous actors or groups involved, can serve to increase observations within each case and limit degrees-of-freedom problems (Bennett 2004, 41–42). The war-on-terror case offers the clearest view of the choices actors made just prior to torture. Bush administration officials set out their beliefs about how to fight the war on terror right after the 9/11 attacks, debated whether to forgo the Geneva Conventions, and justified their choices extensively, concurrently with torture in legal documents and later to the press. Most, but not all, of the evidence from the Philippine-American War comes from after-the-fact court-martial transcripts. In those instances, consistencies among testimonies and across time increase the chances that later evidence is more than just an after-the-fact justification. The early CIA case is the most secretive; I spend a considerable part of the chapter on the conditions that made a torture policy likely. In each case, I respond to a series of questions to determine the persuasiveness of each explanation, summarized in Table 3.1.

My main arguments emphasize the causal role of beliefs and justifications. Their impact becomes demonstrably more meaningful to the extent that I can show that they are (a) distinct from, and held prior to, the resulting behavior; (b) autonomous, or not directly following some competing factor; (c) powerful, or capable of actually producing behavior.[13] The focus, where possible, on decision-making and justification before torture helps with the first challenge. Generation of separate expectations for each theory addresses the autonomy problem. I also have shown how some explanations, such as the desperation hypothesis, are incomplete and require more theorizing about beliefs that connect desperation or panic and torture. Evidence that the same event (such as 9/11) produced disparate solutions from similarly desperate actors helps build the case that we cannot draw a straight and inevitable line from extreme need to torture.

We must avoid breezy assumptions about how powerful a belief is and whether a certain belief can be realized; domestic and international constraints and other factors can sever the connection between convictions and policy choices (George and Bennett 2005). Yet connecting beliefs to

Table 3.1 Questions to guide the search for evidence.

Questions for the Lack of Specificity Argument

Did torturers justify their actions?

If so, did their justifications take advantage of torture's blurry definition (through favorable comparisons, euphemisms, self-application, etc.)?

Did they try to (re)define torture to exclude their behavior?

Did their justifications occur before or concurrently with torture? If mostly after, did later justifications match earlier ones?

Questions for the Cheaters Win Argument

Did torturers believe that norm-breaking deeds yield advantages?

If so, did they cite this belief in the lead-up to torture?

Did they complain about being fenced in by laws and norms?

Did they violate a slate of norms, suggesting a consistent, deeper philosophy?

Questions for the Democratic Restraints Argument

Were torturers conscious of election timing? If so, did torture of detainees increase after elections?

Did torturers privately cite the election as a reason for a change in strategy?

Did torture increase the farther an interrogator was removed from central authorities?

Were higher-level commanders more likely to discourage and punish torture?

Did torturers try to hide from monitors?

Questions for the Desperation Argument

Did torturers seem greatly concerned about attacks and potential casualties?

Did they emphasize the need for timely intelligence to stop attacks before they occur?

Did torturers believe they had very little time to get intelligence?

Questions for the Racism Argument

Did torturers dehumanize their victims on the basis of race?

Did torture occur both inside and outside of interrogation settings?

Questions for the Organizational Culture Argument

Did authorities have only one option for interrogations?

Did norms within the organization come to contradict those outside over time?

Did members understand their own organization to be one that specializes in unsavory tasks? Was this understanding present at the founding of the organization?

Affirmative answers to the table's questions make the explanations more persuasive, contingent on the quality of the evidence they prompt.

action is probably easier in studies on subjects like torture. Because little knowledge has accumulated about the practice, prior hunches are likely to play an outsized role in determining torture's effectiveness. Furthermore, interrogations often occur at times of national emergency and/or war, when deference is the rule—from the media to politicians, legislators to executives, civilians to the military, and so forth. As a result, chances grow that a soldier's or bureaucrat's or president's beliefs about how to defeat terrorists or insurgents will influence and even determine outcomes.

Sometimes it is challenging to determine the power of a particular belief because of the issue of "belief overkill," the tendency of people to generate more arguments than they need to justify a given behavior. One way to overcome this problem is to find evidence that an allegedly important belief is consistent and held over a relatively long period of time and fits with other behaviors from the same actor (Jervis 2006). War-on-terror Vice President Cheney is a clear example of this. Although he held many beliefs that were probably compatible with coercive interrogation, his long-standing contention that oversight of the executive authority should be limited and intelligence agencies especially need to operate without their hands tied stands out. He gave this issue the highest priority *before* September 11, 2001, about which more will be said in chapters 5 and 6.

While it is not shocking to find prior beliefs in harsh measures continuing over centuries, the persistence of the antitorture norm is more surprising. The norm was at least somewhat robust at the societal level, if not within the military, even as far back as 1899. Following Legro's (1997) measure of robustness, the antitorture norm had durability, dating at least to the Constitution's prohibition of cruel and unusual punishment. It also had concordance: almost no one defended torture by name. Using Tannenwald's (2007) alternate measurement of robustness, the "burden of proof" lay with torture's advocates. During the Philippine-American War, pro-imperialists in Congress took pains to show that torture was unusual and the work of a few bad apples in the U.S. Army. Though they often suggested that such occurrences were unsurprising under the circumstances, they never played up torture as a necessary method in a nasty war. The antitorture norm received further codification, most importantly through the Convention against Torture, in intervening years, and part of this codification included attempts to solve the specificity problem. Still, the norm is semi-robust (because it lacks the specificity dimension in Legro's conceptualization) in all three of my cases.[14]

The cases do not quite qualify as "most different" cases in which three cases with almost nothing in common still contain similar causal mechanisms leading to similar outcomes. A set from a single country could hardly do so. Still, the cases depict torture and the semi-robust norm against it through fundamentally different historical times. The United States was an emerging power during the Philippine-American War, not yet a hegemon with global reach. The war was typical of colonial times, with commensurate levels of racism. Race plays a part in all the cases, but racism is most blatant, pervasive, and widely accepted in the Philippine-American War. The Vietnam War shares some similarities with the Philippine-American War, but the interrogation techniques that the CIA used in Vietnam have their roots in the early Cold War, when the main concern of the United States was the Soviet Union. Given the threat of Great Power war, the stakes were higher during the Cold War than in the other two cases. The post-2001 war on terror was another thing entirely, as the Bush administration claimed—except for the pattern of abusive interrogation that the administration (perhaps unknowingly)[15] resurrected. A theory that can explain a colonial soldier's turn to torture in the early twentieth century, the development of a secret behavioral control program at midcentury, and the Bush administration's approval of torture in the early twenty-first century would be showing good range.

My selection does not include all imaginable cases. The most conspicuous omission may be the American Civil War, which had guerrilla/counterguerrilla phases. Detainee treatment norms were unsettled at the time. Much of the abuse that occurred on both sides had as much or more to do with neglect and poor planning as with coercion, and it is difficult to parse out premeditated abuse, interrogational or otherwise, from plain sloppiness (Einolf 2018; Brundage 2018). The three included cases are more directly comparable (Einolf 2018).

Since I am interested in the recurrence of torture, the war-on-terror case is especially crucial. The war on terror represents the latest iteration of liberal-democratic torture and makes for an important update that might have lasting consequences for the norm itself (McKeown 2009). It is also notable because hegemonic countries are supposed to be somewhat less susceptible to normative effects (Sikkink 2013). If norms influence actors (one way or another) even in a noncompliant hegemon, then we can conclude that their importance is considerable.

4

Justifying Torture in the Philippine-American War

Cars heading northeast out of Anchorage, Alaska, would be hard-pressed to avoid Glenn Highway, one of the state's busiest roads, named after Edwin F. Glenn. The son of a surgeon in the Civil War, Glenn led a tough but successful expedition through the Alaskan wilderness in 1898 to establish gold rush routes.[1] Glenn's varied career included much more: he was a graduate of West Point Military Academy and in command of Buffalo Soldiers stationed in the American West in the 1870s; he earned a law degree and practiced in Minnesota for two years in the 1890s before returning to the army; he led a division in World War I in France in 1918; and he finished his career as a two-star general in command of Camp Sherman in Ohio a year later. Along the way, Glenn wrote two books on the laws of war, including the U.S. Army's 1914 *Rules of Land War*. The army's choice of author is either ironic or telling, depending on one's views, for Glenn was also the most notorious torturer of the Philippine-American War.

No doubt if Glenn were alive today, he would quarrel with my use of the label "torturer." Of all the folders in the National Archives containing court-martial transcripts and related documents for soldiers on trial for detainee abuse in the Philippines, Glenn's is the thickest, and he uses much of his airtime arguing that his methods did not constitute torture. In fact, in his effort to exonerate himself via the torture norm's lack of specificity, Glenn puts on a clinic: he asserts that the act does no injury or permanent damage, compares it favorably to prisoner treatment by Filipinos and U.S. police forces, claims to have endured the procedure himself to no ill effect, and argues over the minute details of the procedures, always to convince observers that his application was too mild to warrant condemnation.

At the same time, Glenn argued, detainee treatment needed to be severe enough to generate intelligence. Some sort of "pressure" or "fright" would be necessary. Glenn was convinced that soldiers would have to push as far as the laws of war would allow. Usual norms of decency would not do. Interrogators

American Torture from the Philippines to Iraq. William L. d'Ambruoso, Oxford University Press. © Oxford University Press 2022. DOI: 10.1093/oso/9780197570326.003.0004

needed a technique that was harsh, but not too harsh-sounding. This was the promise of the "water cure," a mixture of stomach pumping and choking with water, Glenn's method of choice, and an increasingly popular technique among U.S. soldiers as the counterinsurgency campaign in the Philippines wore on.

Glenn was also racist, at least by today's standards, and his views on people with "oriental characteristics" must have played a part in his decision to be as coercive as he was. Still, when he tortured, he was after intelligence, though his unit may not really have been as desperate for it as he claimed. His timing also follows political developments, at least loosely: torture by Glenn and others picked up around the election of 1900, either in anticipation of or in response to orders for tougher measures that were to follow Republican victories. I detail these alternatives later in the chapter. Yet Glenn's initial attraction to torture stems from his belief that it was tough enough to produce results from "treacherous" foes, but not so obviously egregious that it would lead to condemnation or punishment.

If Glenn were the only torturer to hold such views, then my explanation of torture in the Philippines would be limited. But he was not. A belief in the need to push the envelope was widely held, and playing down the severity of the acts became *the way* of pleading one's innocence. Much of this is now contained in court-martial transcripts at the National Archives.[2] Within these files, the written statements are especially valuable for my study, because they allow accused torturers the space and time to connect their deeds to deeper philosophies and reflections. Supplementing these are testimony by soldiers to a congressional committee and other investigations by the military. While most of the testimony comes a short time after the occurrences of torture, it is consistent with the more limited, concurrent evidence, some of it from letters and diaries held at the archives attached to the U.S. Army War College in Carlisle, Pennsylvania. I turn to this evidence in detail after a summary of the war and the torture therein.

Background

Overview of the War

For both sides, the Philippine-American War (also known as the War of Philippine Independence and the Philippine Insurrection, among other appellations) continued earlier fights with a mutual foe.[3] Filipinos had been fighting the Spanish for independence since at least 1896. When the United States emerged victorious from the Spanish-American War in 1898, a debate emerged among American foreign policy thinkers about whether the Philippines should be granted independence. The imperialists prevailed in their argument with the anti-imperialists, and with the signing and ratification of the Treaty of Paris in 1898–99, the United States bought the Philippines, Guam, Puerto Rico, and a few other territories from the Spanish for the light (but, for the Spanish, face-saving) sum of $20 million.

Filipinos agitating for independence had thought at first that an American victory over the Spanish would mean independence for the Philippines. Emilio Aguinaldo y Fami, the Filipino leader, certainly thought this, which is why he led his troops to fight alongside the Americans against the Spanish. The Treaty of Paris disillusioned him. Aguinaldo and his fellow Filipinos then turned their sights on the Americans, first in conventional battles, and then using guerrilla tactics, the latter of which proved more effective, but not ultimately successful, against the better-armed Americans.

Though President William McKinley was an imperialist, he was a less enthusiastic one than some of his peers, especially his second vice president and successor, Theodore Roosevelt. In language typical of the times, McKinley came around to the idea that it was the duty of the United States "to educate the Filipinos, and uplift and Christianize them" (quoted in Miller 1982, 24). McKinley's desire for "benevolent assimilation" of Filipinos through a "policy of attraction" set the tone early on, and contrasted with Roosevelt's repeated desire to "smash" the enemy en route to similar, imperial ends.

From the beginning of the war until the end of 1899, the Philippine Army of Liberation held together and put up a conventional fight. During this time, the Americans mostly confined their interest to the island of Luzon, the largest in the Philippine archipelago. Manila, on the west side of Luzon, was the political and economic center of the islands and the U.S. Army's headquarters in the Philippines. U.S. soldiers would depart Manila, a few hundred at a time, and pursue the Philippine Army. Because the Americans were almost always better armed and usually better trained, they invited pitched battles and typically prevailed. By November 1899, the Army of Liberation was no longer a coherent organization. Aguinaldo called for guerrilla tactics to continue the resistance.

McKinley's highest military commander in the Philippines for most of the early war period (1899–1900) was Gen. Elwell Otis. Otis, eager to please those back home who wanted a quick and decisive victory, consistently downplayed any and all bad news on the war front. He carefully censored correspondence from those in the Philippines who suggested the war was going anything but swimmingly, and when word of difficulties did slip past his heavy editing he accused the naysayers of exaggerating and overreacting (Jones 2012, 140–45; Miller 1982, ch. 5). Finally, Otis resigned and returned home to a hero's welcome (Shilling 2003), a production that had a lot to do with Republican interest in putting the best possible face on the war in the run-up to the November 1900 elections (Miller 1982).

Roosevelt, riding a wave of popularity from his own participation in the Spanish-American War, steadily gained more influence until he joined the McKinley ticket for the 1900 election. A staunch imperialist, Roosevelt was enthusiastic about the U.S. acquisition of the Philippines, and, together with some of his military friends and contacts, he petitioned McKinley early in the war for tougher measures implemented by tougher commanders (Jones 2012). Roosevelt would have to wait until six months after the election of 1900 to see one of his ilk appointed supreme commander in the Philippines, but the U.S. shift toward harsher measures came earlier.

In May 1900, McKinley picked Gen. Arthur MacArthur to succeed Otis as supreme commander. Initially, McKinley was intent on continuing the policy of attraction under MacArthur, but such a policy was becoming more challenging. The guerrilla war, which began in earnest in early 1900 and intensified as the election neared, convinced both soldiers and civilians that a change of tactics was necessary. MacArthur and his fellow officers drew up sterner plans, but most of these measures were postponed until after the elections. The decision to wait to enact harsher war methods was twofold. First, "MacArthur and other senior officers had expected the resistance to collapse in the wake of the Republican victory" (Jones 2012, 205), and while morale did take a hit among Filipino soldiers when McKinley won, the resistance wasn't finished. Second, and perhaps more important, the Republicans, including the McKinley administration, had been selling the line that the war was over, or all but over (Miller 1982, ch. 6). While some tough measures certainly predated the elections (Jones 2012, 207–10), the change was noticeable.

General MacArthur made impressive strides until July 1901, when he relinquished his post. With aggressive sweeps, crop and property destruction, and the segregation of civilians from guerrillas through the establishment of "protected zones," the army "ended armed resistance in twenty-one of the thirty-eight unpacified provinces" (Linn 2000, 214). Aguinaldo was captured in March 2001, a significant victory that would have been even more important had resistance not already been on the wane since the beginning of that year. Due in part to his strained relations with his civilian counterparts and superiors, MacArthur ceded civilian control of the Philippines to William H. Taft, and military control to one of Roosevelt's favored men, Adna Chaffee.

Though the war was very much in hand for most of his tenure as military commander in the Philippines, Chaffee presided over the most well-known campaign of the war, the pacification of the island of Samar. Summary executions and orders to turn the island into a "howling wilderness" led to charges against Maj. Gen. Littleton Waller and Brig. Gen. Jacob Smith. Historians often write about these two trials alongside a third, that of Maj. Edwin F. Glenn, who tortured detainees in Samar and Panay. Glenn was found guilty of the practice and given a light sentence.

With the conclusion of the Samar campaign in 1902, President Roosevelt declared the war over and offered a general amnesty to participants in the Philippine insurrection. Limited uprisings would continue for the next several years, finally abating in 1913. The Philippines remained an American colony until 1946.

Torture in the Philippine-American War

Atrocities in general were rare during the conventional part of the war (1899), but there were a few exceptions. The most well-known was Maj. Gen. Lloyd Wheaton's proclivity for burning villages. Wheaton, who served under William Tecumseh Sherman during the American Civil War, was partial to Sherman's scorched-earth approach. After one battle in March 1899, a brigade under Wheaton burned house after house near Laguna de Bay, southeast of Manila (Linn 2000, 94). But the army generally followed the laws of war for most of 1899 with regard to detainee treatment. The first reports of torture by the United States came in December 1899, immediately after Aguinaldo's turn to guerrilla tactics, but torture would not be widely used for a while still (Einolf 2014, 42). Eventually, harsh measures would consist of free-fire zones, burning of homes and crops, summary executions, and torture, including beatings, hanging by the neck with rope in a manner that did not lead to death, and restricted diet.

The most famous family of torture techniques was known collectively as the "water cure." The water cure overlaps in part with the waterboard, but Rejali's (2007) account gives them distinct origins. The water cure as pumping involves "forcibly filling the stomach with water," inflicting "some of the most intense pain that visceral tissues can experience." The pumping version was "one of the most fearful tortures of the Inquisition" and almost certainly came to the Philippines first by way of Spanish colonization (279–80). By contrast, the waterboard, which resembles a "Dutch cloth" method used by mariners from the Netherlands in the seventeenth century, is a slow drowning induced by pouring water over a cloth covering a person's face. In practice, the choking and pumping effects can blend, especially given the informal and improvisatory way in which torture is so often applied (279–80). According to one soldier, "Now, this is the way we give them the water cure. Lay them on their backs, a man standing on each hand and each foot, then put a round stick in the mouth and pour a pail of water in the mouth and nose, and if they don't give up pour in another pail. They swell up like toads. I'll tell you it is a terrible torture" (quoted in Kramer 2008). Water in the nose would choke the victim, but the swelling could come only from swallowing water. A Filipino mayor given the water cure testified to both swallowing water and breathing some in through his nose.[4] Other variants involved several soldiers lifting a detainee, inverting him, and submerging his head in water for several seconds, otherwise known as "ducking."[5]

As is so often the case with torture, it is impossible to estimate with precision the extent of the abuse in the Philippine-American War. For politicians of the time as well as historians of today, estimates of atrocity levels at the hands of American soldiers seem to vary with sympathy for the overall endeavor. Sharp critics like Gregg Jones (2012) and Paul Kramer (2006) describe a "war without limits." Brian McAllister Linn, whose collected works on the war are probably the most thorough, takes a more cautious tone. In the preface to one of his books, Linn (2000, ix) complains:

Nowadays textbooks and popular histories summarize the Philippine war in a few clichés—the water cure, civilize 'em with a Krag [rifle], kill everyone over ten, reconcentration camps—all of which convey an overall impression of a conflict characterized by brutality and atrocities. Any reader who questions the proposition that in barely three years an expeditionary force of 25,000 combat troops terrorized over 7 million people into submission—an argument grossly insulting to Americans and Filipinos alike—is currently at a loss.

Linn promises to "apply some much needed correction to the popular view" (ix). Yet even Linn (1989, 145) acknowledges that use of torture like the water cure was a "distressingly common manner of interrogation among officers assigned to intelligence work." Stuart Creighton Miller (1982, 213) calls the use of the water cure "widespread," and Christopher Einolf (2014, 4) argues that "soldiers used torture extensively during the final campaigns of 1901 and 1902." John Gates (1973, viii, 175) describes the reports of atrocities as "exaggerated," though he acknowledges that both American soldiers and the Filipinos under their command "resorted to the water cure and other forms of terror" by the middle of 1900. On the whole, most historians of this subject characterize torture as an increasingly common form of interrogation, especially in the second half of the war.

Mid- to high-level officials, both civilian and military, fall into three camps on the subject of directing, approving, condoning, or tolerating torture. The first consists of the "benevolent assimilation" folks, the most prominent being President McKinley. These leaders did not want to follow the ways of other imperialists' ugly campaigns. The British scorched-earth approach in South Africa was the most commonly cited example of the kind of behavior that members of this camp wished to avoid. Torture, among other atrocities, was antithetical to the hearts-and-minds campaign they envisioned.

A second contingent criticized the benevolent assimilators for going too easy on the enemy, but they did not openly endorse torture. They usually held that the laws of war at the time, called General Orders 100, when taken as far as could be permitted, would be harsh enough to put down the insurrection. I call them the "General Orders" group. These include Theodore Roosevelt, first in his capacity as an outside critic of McKinley's policies, then as vice president, and finally as president following McKinley's assassination. Supreme commanders MacArthur and Chaffee also belong to this camp, as do influential officers like Maj. John Parker and Brig. Gen. J. Franklin Bell.

During the Civil War, under Abraham Lincoln's direction, jurist Franz Lieber (1863) developed General Orders 100, also known as the Lieber Code. This forerunner to modern laws of war laid out prescriptions for soldier behavior while hostilities endure. Parts of the code allow for harsh measures. Article 20, for instance, allows that surprise may be essential even if it means killing many noncombatants instead of warning them of an imminent attack. However, Article 16 bans torture: "Military necessity does not admit of cruelty—that is, the infliction of suffering for the sake of suffering or for revenge, nor of maiming or wounding except in fight, nor of torture to extort confessions." While many in the General Orders camp played down techniques like the water cure as a serious offense, they did not pretend that a court-martial judge would or should find this technique permissible.

Drawing on examples from the General Orders camp, Linn (1989, quoted in Wallach 2007, 496) argues that detainee abuse received no official blessing: "Physical mistreatment and torture were never sanctioned by either Division headquarters in Manila or district headquarters, and there were constant warnings against it; but it clearly occurred." Torture never became official policy. Generals MacArthur and Chaffee, despite orders for an increasingly aggressive counterinsurgency, called for more guilty verdicts than the court-martial proceedings yielded in torture cases, and, in the cases of guilty verdicts, stiffer penalties than judges typically assigned. The White House often concurred with these generals.

Andrew Birtle (1998, 132), another historian of the war, claims that there was tacit approval among officers, including high-level ones presiding over courts-martial:

Officially, the Army condemned the water cure, which fell under [General Orders] 100's proscription of torture. Unofficially, many officers winked at the practice, and military courts proved exceedingly reluctant to punish officers charged with applying coercive methods. As the war progressed the number of incidences of abuse grew as officers, disenchanted by the failure of benevolent policies, came to believe that the "cure" was the only effective way to uproot the guerrilla infrastructure.

Because the semi-approval that Birtle alleges is unofficial, there is not much direct evidence for it. So if officers really did "wink" at torture, what does this mean in practice? General Bell, one of the most respected officers in the Philippines, makes a clear case in point. In court papers, he was against the use of the water cure:

Nobody in the Philippine Islands has ever been more opposed than I to the use of the water cure. I have always forbidden it. . . . I felt certain we could achieve success by the simple enforcement of the laws of war, without the assistance of unwise and unauthorized expedients. G.O. 100 [has] never been fully or strictly enforced in these islands because [it was] deemed inconsistent with the policy of benevolent assimilation—of conciliation and attraction—announced by President McKinley. In conscientious and commendable efforts to adhere to what appeared to be the policy of the American Nation, troops in the field have been so restrained and corrected for attempting to enforce some of the well-known provisions of the laws of war, that, in some places, they had become discouraged and inefficient, and failed to do their duty through fear of getting in trouble.[6]

At first blush, Bell and other General Orders folks appear to stick to the law and prohibit cruelty, claiming it unnecessary for achieving the end of victory in the Philippines. The real story is more complicated than this. Bell relates the following tale in a letter to a fellow officer:

[A] young officer of the 13th Infantry told him that he once went to a man's house to get some rifles which he was absolutely certain he had hid there. That he demanded the rifles and indicated clearly to the mans [sic] mind that he knew he had them, but notwithstanding this the native persisted in lying and denied having any arms. That he then strung him up by the neck, whereupon the rope broke. That he then threatened to shoot him and did actually fire his pistol very near to him as if he were trying to hit him, but still the native persisted that he had no guns. That he then raked up some leaves against his home and lit a match preparatory to setting the leaves on fire whereupon the native weakened and disclosed the hiding place of 13 guns.

Bell continues, "In my opinion, the end justified the means, but I fear my superiors would not agree with me." Earlier in the same letter, Bell guessed that his superiors (Otis and MacArthur) "both have no personal objection to using a little judicious force" to extract information; rather, they feared backlash, and Bell could not overrule them: "[A]lthough I fully believe that such methods are *necessary and justifiable* under the circumstances, I have no authority in the matter and therefore would not be able to protect any officer whose employment of such methods became a matter of complaint or scandal."[7] Linn (2000, 224) argues that this amounts to a "don't ask, don't tell" policy, but he could go further. By calling the use of such interrogation methods "necessary," Bell implies that interrogators *must* occasionally use coercive methods if the army is to prevail. Perhaps "Don't ask, don't tell, but do what you have to do without making a fuss" is a more accurate summary of Bell's position, as well as his estimate of others'. This, I am arguing, is the content of the "wink" that Birtle describes.

A third group, including most of the employers of torture, claimed that techniques like the water cure were permissible under General Orders 100. They pointed to the tough measures that the code allowed for soldiers to impress enemy guides into their service. They also emphasized the importance that the laws of war placed on saving the country. At the same time, they frequently emphasized how "mild" the techniques were. In this camp are several mid- and low-level officers and enlisted soldiers, including Edwin F. Glenn and James Ryan. It is this camp that approves and justifies American torture in the Philippines, and its members are my focus in explaining why some U.S. soldiers believed it was a good idea to choke and pump enemy detainees with water in search of information.

Explaining Torture in the Philippine-American War

"Inspiring the Same Fear": Evidence for the Cheaters Win Argument

While some officers and veterans believed that the laws of war did not include the water cure and need not do so in order to be effectively applied, others saw a high degree of malleability in the laws' stipulations. In fact, some understood General Orders 100 to be so lenient as to undo itself in certain circumstances. Ryan, who favored a submersion variant of the water cure, quoted General Orders 100 in the written defense accompanying his court-martial: "To save the country is paramount to all other considerations."[8] Ryan's interpretation seems to be that when the safety of the country is at stake, the law is that there is no law. Even the judge advocate general George B. Davis admitted that soldiers could exceed the limits of General Orders 100 in certain emergencies in a letter to Secretary of War Elihu Root regarding Glenn's case. Davis simply thought that Glenn's company did not face sufficiently dire circumstances.[9]

Glenn argued at trial that his actions were well within orders. He understood MacArthur's orders to be a call for a "relentless" campaign of martial law, granting wide latitude to commanders in the field.[10] He quoted orders from Chaffee to the commanding general of southern Luzon as follows: "The

Division Commander directs, no matter what measures be adopted, information as to whereabouts of this force must be obtained." He also brought the court's attention to a similar relayed note: "In compliance with instructions from Division Commander, Department Commander directs that information of the whereabouts of the Caballes [a Filipino officer] be obtained, no matter what measures be taken."[11] Though orders such as these almost always came with caveats, Glenn may have interpreted them to mean that he should push as far as he could against the laws of war. He believed that only "pressure" and "punishment" would work for gathering intelligence in the Philippines. Through questioning of his own witnesses, Glenn (who, as a lawyer with knowledge of the laws of war, represented himself) attempted to show that Filipinos never gave information voluntarily, only when they were "punished."[12]

Ryan echoed the idea that, in terms of coercion, American soldiers were necessarily in a kind of race to the bottom with the enemy. Because American soldiers' hands were so often tied, Ryan argued, they could not "inspire . . . the same fear" in the Filipino population that the enemy could. "The result is simple; they [the population] took their chances with the less rigorous of the two parties, and events have proven their reasoning was correct. [A]s long as these [less severe] methods are pursued, [t]he Filipino will delight in an outward show of Americanism, and gloat inwardly over his real loyalty to insurrection."[13] This, Ryan claimed, is why the U.S. Army could not play nice: "Having arrested them and knowing that the truth can be gotten from the average native only under pressure or fright, especially this being true during active insurrection; must I lay aside my sword and take up the functions of a missionary?"[14]

Effective intelligence-gathering during war, Ryan is asserting, requires a different set of standards from what most people find wholesome. This is a recurring theme among U.S. soldiers in the Philippines and constitutes the clearest evidence that soldiers equated boundary-pushing with effectiveness. Glenn's written statement opens with the idea that the nature of war requires that soldiers follow separate laws, which is intuitive enough given that war, but not civilian life, necessarily involves trying to kill or incapacitate an enemy. Later in the same document, he argues that interrogations meant to reveal hidden weapons or press enemy soldiers into service as scouts should not be too mild: "I have never been taught by any of the books I have studied, nor by any of those able soldiers whose rules of war or practice it has been my good fortune to study that a campaign or scout had to be conducted upon the lines of a woman's afternoon tea or a Sunday school picnic."[15] For Glenn, confining oneself to norms of decency would compromise effectiveness.

Other cases suggest that the belief that U.S. soldiers must act in unseemly ways to be effective became an increasingly pervasive philosophy over the duration of the war. For example, when Lt. Edward Hickman was tried for ducking detainees, Capt. Daniel Boughton, writing on Hickman's behalf, sounded the same notes as Glenn and Ryan. The U.S. Army, Boughton argues, has done "work that may or may not have been distasteful. It was sent to the Philippines by the American people. What for? To hold receptions, dress parades, and pink teas?"[16] Things that may appear distasteful to others are often a necessary part of the soldier's charge, Boughton contends.

These defenses of interrogational torture match broadly held assumptions about what constitutes effective war-fighting. General Wheaton, for example, viewed effective counterinsurgency as an activity set apart from the "gentler" activities of peacetime: "You can't put down a rebellion by throwing confetti and sprinkling perfumery" (quoted in Birtle 1998, 135). Birtle estimates that "by the end of the Philippine War there were few American soldiers who would have argued with him" (135).[17]

One repeated theme in these quotes is how soldiers illustrated the norms of peacetime with caricatures of feminine imagery: "pink teas," "perfumery," and the like. This conforms with the feminist theoretical expectation that soldiers' philosophies of war-fighting will be defined not just in normative terms but in ways that reflect gender hierarchy. That these are probably the most overt examples of machismo in this book should come as no surprise given that the war comes before many women's rights milestones like suffrage in the United States. That's not to say that method selection is not still gendered after the Philippine War, just that these instances are more blatant.

While feminism complements my argument, other interpretations of the evidence present potential problems. First, the example of General Wheaton indicates that many soldiers, civilian policymakers, and observers believed that war-fighting would require tough and sometimes disturbing measures, but not all became torturers or endorsed the water cure. Those in the General Orders camp fit this description well. Why, we might wonder, did some become torture advocates while others—perhaps most strikingly, Roosevelt—did not?

It's an important question, and I address it later, in the section on domestic political pressures. I also return to the issue of "law-and-order warriors," which includes figures like Roosevelt and (years later) John McCain in the book's conclusion, when I discuss the limitations of my argument. For now, however, rather than parse this variation on a soldier-by-soldier basis, I show how the General Orders camp advocated pushing the law to the limit, which opened up various interpretations along the law's frontier.

MacArthur was probably not picked for his reputation for enacting tough measures, but he did preside over increasingly coercive policies. Civilians and soldiers were both on board with the policy. In the fall of 1900, Taft said that after the election, "the time will have come to change our lenient policy" (quoted in Jones 2012, 204). Taft did not have much direct influence on the military given his frosty relationship with many of the officers, especially MacArthur (Miller 1982). Taft may have been indirectly influential, however; officers would have been encouraged by the fact that even the man who described the Filipino as "our little brown brother" was comfortable with harsher methods and became an advocate for them. MacArthur instructed his commanders to "completely destroy" the rebels' infrastructure in cities and towns. To do this, they would need to apply martial law and those provisions of General Orders 100 that allow for crackdowns, "*the more drastic the application the better.*" MacArthur also stipulated "that unnecessary hardships should not be imposed upon persons arrested and that the laws of war are not violated in any respect touching the treatment of prisoners" (quoted in Jones 2012, 206), though, as noted earlier, some interrogators may have dismissed this as an obligatory disclaimer.

MacArthur's announcement may have been more of a summary of what officers had already agreed to than brand-new guidelines. Roosevelt had continued to hear from his military friends in the Philippines that a change was necessary. One such friend was Maj. John Parker. Parker wrote in October 1900 that "the fundamental obstruction to complete pacification" was "the attempt to meet a half-civilized foe . . . with the same methods devised for civilized warfare against people of our own race, country and blood" (quoted in Gates 1973, 190–91). The U.S. military was too hamstrung by rules based on the policy of benevolence; they had "applied the methods of the kindergarten where other nations habitually, and successfully, use the most stringent measures." Officers needed to be allowed to "make a few punitive examples" (quoted in Jones 2012, 204). Roosevelt forwarded Parker's note to Secretary of War Root, and soon some of the changes that Parker requested became official policy (Jones 2012). Violence instigated by U.S. forces (which included Major Glenn and those under him on "water detail") escalated around this time, especially on the island of Panay, suggesting that Parker was not alone.

In the fall of 1901, just two weeks after Roosevelt took the oath of office following McKinley's assassination, a company of seventy-six American soldiers lost over half of their men in a surprise attack. The event became known as the Balangiga massacre after the town in which it occurred. Chaffee immediately blamed the massacre on the "soft mollycoddling of treacherous natives." Roosevelt was right with him. He ordered Chaffee "in no unmistakable terms" to use "the most stern measures to pacify Samar" (quoted in Miller 1982, 205–6). Chaffee used the shift of mood following the massacre to apply tough measures elsewhere as well.

Chaffee assigned Bell to pacify another problematic region, the Batangas Province in southwestern Luzon. In early December 1901, Bell counted off a number of transgressions of civilized war that Filipino insurgents had committed. He wrote that he intended to "severely punish, in the same or lesser degree, the commission of acts denounced in the aforementioned articles" (quoted in Miller 1982, 207). It is highly likely that much of the military shared Bell's sentiments. For one, Chaffee approved the document. More telling was the wide respect accorded to Bell throughout the war. In a moment of rare agreement, both Chaffee and Taft thought he would be the best person for the Batangas post, and part of the reason for this was his "ruthlessness." Linn (2000, 300) suggests that Bell probably would have been the choice of "the vast majority of soldiers if consulted."[18] In Batangas, Bell proceeded to herd people from the rural areas into camps, outside of which scorched-earth tactics— including free-fire zones and the burning of crops—were used. Ironically, McKinley had once condemned Spain for such tactics, claiming, "It was not civilized warfare. It was extermination" (quoted in Kramer 2006, 153).

The point of the preceding paragraphs is not to argue that every instance of tough talk led directly to torture. Rather, the idea is to expose how the military's and Roosevelt's beliefs about what the counterguerrilla war required created conditions ripe for torture. The occurrence of other atrocities, endorsements for harsher methods by key leaders like Bell and Parker, and broad encouragement of "stern measures" by Roosevelt suggest an overarching philosophy that steadily gained the upper hand over the Benevolent Assimilation camp throughout the war. Roosevelt and the U.S. Army thought that General Orders 100 should be pushed to the limit. Some soldiers believed that this included use of harsh interrogation methods like the water cure, which, as I show in the next section, practitioners tried to play down as not so terrible.

In sum, while Roosevelt and the supreme commanders (Otis, MacArthur, and Chaffee) in the Philippines never condoned torture, the general push to take the laws of war as far as they would go created a context in which torture occurred. Evidence for the Cheaters Win hypothesis is stronger among midlevel officers and other soldiers. Interrogators did not want to be confined by rules. As one veteran of the Philippine-American War put it, when it comes to gathering intelligence, "[S]cruples often mean flat failure or belated action" (quoted in Einolf 2014, 179).

Endless Quibbling: Evidence for the Lack of Specificity Argument

Most soldiers justified their use of torture such as the water cure not by denying that it had happened but by playing down its severity. Even though many of the justifications came after torture had occurred, they make the existence of earlier justifications more likely, because they are widespread and mostly uniform, they come from the practitioners and witnesses themselves, and they match what earlier evidence does exist. One example comes in a letter from Gen. Fred Funston, who commanded soldiers who used and witnessed the water cure. Funston shows that the military also used the tactic of favorable comparison: Filipinos working with the Americans (he claimed that the Americans themselves never used the water cure) who used the water cure "were merely repaying the insurgents for worse treatment received by them in the past."[19]

Funston also played down the importance of the use of the water cure by suggesting that the method was not as bad as his subordinate officer had implied:

> The so-called "water cure," as it has been described to me by Macabebe soldiers [Filipino soldiers from a company friendly to American soldiers], was by no means so severe an ordeal as would be indicated in the extract mentioned. The method was merely to throw a native on his back, hold his nose with one hand, and pour water down his throat from a canteen or other vessel. It occasioned nothing more than a few moments of strangling, and never resulted fatally.[20]

How long are "moments" to General Funston? How much is "a few"? Torture's lack of specificity allows for these vague descriptions and the justifications they support.

The court-martial transcripts are full of quibbling on various dimensions over what constitutes torture. Glenn never denied using the water cure. His primary defense was that the technique was not really torture. The plaintiff in the trial, Joveniano Ealdama, claimed that the water cure sessions lasted about fifteen minutes; Glenn said they were not longer than five minutes, and "probably not more than three."[21] Ealdama accused Glenn and his subordinates of putting salt in the water; Glenn did not recall using salt. Even if salt were added, Glenn claimed, it would have amounted only to "a trifle more sensation, not amounting to pain, in the nose."[22] Ealdama said he was first put under a faucet eighteen inches high; Glenn estimated it to be lower than a foot, implying less force from the water on the detainee's face.[23] Glenn argued his detainee's "mouth was opened," but it "was not held open, since he could and did close it from time to time." The discomfort, Glenn claimed, "is nothing more than may be experienced in swallowing, gargling, or taking a nasal douche."[24]

Other defendants tried the same approach: confess to the alleged methods and argue that they did not amount to torture. Lt. Bissell Thomas, accused of beating prisoners for information, based much of his defense on details meant to persuade the court that he was showing "extreme aversion and re-luctance."[25] Most of the strikes, he protested, were dealt with an open hand, not a fist; the prisoners fell from shoves, not blows to the face; the strikes were from the side, not straight out from the shoulder.[26] A soldier testified in the trial of Capt. George Brandle that the rope used to hang detainees for sev-eral seconds in order to produce information was wrapped on their jaws, not their necks, causing no wounds or suffocation but only slight marks.[27] Glenn went so far as to suggest that the water cure carried the health benefits of cleaning out the stomach and even curing fevers, as if the "cure" were merely an uncomfortable medical procedure or spa treatment.[28]

In fact, Glenn brought medical professionals into his trial to testify that the water cure would not have long-term deleterious effects on detainees. He summarizes their findings in writing:

Medical experts testify that but a small portion of the water used enters the stomach, and that only by the act of swallowing; that the [detainee] could not have swallowed anything like three or four bottlefuls in the time stated . . . that excessive distention of the stomach was impossible under the circumstances, as the water would be rejected by vomiting before excessive distention occurred, and this without pain of any kind; and that the subject could limit, if he wished, the amount which entered the stomach.[29]

Ryan's trial also included testimony from doctors stating that the water cure did not endanger victims.[30] The inclusion of medical professionals' opinions, a move that is replayed in the war on terror (chapter 6), is a clear effort to build the legitimacy of the chosen methods. This is in keeping with James Ron's (1997) argument that modern torturers try to legitimize, rationalize, and professionalize their work. It is telling *how* Glenn tries to use the patina of legitimacy that the doctors provide: to fuss over the details of the technique in order to demonstrate that it did not cause serious injury.

Capt. Cornelius Brownell, who was tried for ordering the torture of Father Augustin de la Peña in late 1900 in pursuit of insurgent funding sources, also played down the severity of the water cure in part by claiming that he carefully selected the administrators. Even though Father Augustin died as a result, Brownell stuck to his implausible defense: "The water cure was administered by my order several times to different natives. . . . I do not and never have believed it cruel or barbarous in any manner, and whenever it became necessary, in my judgment, to administer it, the men chosen for that duty were chosen with a view to having only intelligent, careful, humane men perform the operation" (quoted in Vestal 2017, 51–52). Only if a norm lacks specificity can the act it proscribes be thought of as lacking cruelty when "humane men" perform it.

Interrogators also claimed to have endured self-application of their favorite interrogation methods without much lasting damage. Hickman compared his interrogation techniques to part of his upbringing: "I took [the detainee] to a nearby stream and had two of my men duck him as I have been ducked as a youth in a swimming hole with my own companions slightly my superiors in strength."[31] The detainee "was simply ducked and in no way hurt."[32] Glenn claimed to have given himself and a soldier with him the water cure before they took their show on the road:

I knew from previous experiment upon myself and upon Lieut. Conger that the so-called "water cure" . . . is a "bugaboo" for those only who have never seen or tried it. . . . [T]he evidence of every man who has tried this so-called "water cure" both involuntarily and voluntarily, including myself who took it several months before the alleged injured man in this case was appointed a guide, stated distinctly, positively, and without exception that there was no pain and nothing more than a temporary discomfort attending it.[33]

The point of discussing self-application, as these examples make clear, is to convince others—and perhaps themselves—that their deeds were legitimate and that they caused no pain or lasting damage.

If interrogators were not causing severe pain and suffering, what were they doing? Ryan claimed that his intent was to "frighten" the enemy into divulging information.[34] Likewise, Glenn says that the water cure "did frighten [his] guide. It did not injure him in any way."[35] Another officer testified to a board of inquiry that he was merely trying to "frighten" captured guerrillas, not "injure" them (quoted in Einolf 2014, 184). Hickman uses nearly the same language (quoted in Einolf 2014, 86–87). Thomas softened the verb even further, pleading that he merely wished to "*surprise* these prisoners into an unwilling confession" (quoted in Einolf 2014, 45, emphasis added).

Frequently, defendants matched these arguments with favorable comparisons to what the enemy did. At Glenn's trial, another American soldier discussed other tortures by the Filipino insurgents, including burning noses to a crisp and beating U.S. soldiers to death with clubs.[36] Other witnesses talked of insurgents burying people alive.[37] Some courts took the bait. Hickman was accused and acquitted of administering the water cure, and favorable comparisons were an integral part of the legal defense's strategy:

> [A] considerable amount of evidence was put before the court by the defense to show the illegal methods used by the insurgents in the conduct of their own operations and their complete disregard for the laws of war. . . . In *Hickman* in particular, the court "invite[d] attention to the abnormal and disgraceful methods of armed resistance to the authority of the United States [and] the treachery of the natives generally." (Mettraux 2003, 144)[38]

Citing, among other reasons, difficult circumstances, the court also showed "leniency" toward Glenn, fining him fifty dollars and giving him a month off without pay.[39]

Glenn made other comparisons as well. He described his methods as "far gentler" than the interrogation tactics that the New York and San Francisco police departments used. He lamented the use of the term "water cure," because it brought to mind "old-fashioned" uses of water that he claimed were "intensely painful" and much more severe: pelting the subject with "a thin stream of water . . . from a great height . . . forcing water down the throat of the victim in such a way as to burst his stomach," or using water pressure to force "a rag tied to a string" into a detainee's stomach. Glenn protested that he did not engage in such barbarity. By contrast, "the so-called water cure as it is administered here causes neither pain nor permanent injury."[40] Moreover, the water cure was mild compared to what Glenn was able to do according to General Orders 100, so he argued. He claimed that he had the legal authority to kill his guide but refrained from doing so.[41]

Following Glenn's light sentence, Army Judge Advocate General Davis protested to Secretary Root in a memorandum. Davis names the danger posed by the Specificity problem: that the difference between levels of coercion is one of degree rather than kind:

> No modern state, which is a party to international law, can sanction, either expressly or by a silence which imports consent, a resort to torture with a view of obtaining confessions. If it does, where is the line to be drawn? If the "water cure" is ineffective, what shall be the next step? Shall the victim be suspended, head down, over the smoke of a smouldering fire; shall he be tightly bound and dropped from a distance of several feet; shall he be beaten with rods; shall his shins be rubbed with a broomstick until they bleed? [The United States] cannot afford to sanction the addition of torture to the several forms of force which may be legitimately employed in war. (quoted in Jones 2012, 384)

Davis wonders where the line should be drawn because torture is not inherently delineated.

Soldiers separated words like "abuse" and "torture" from what they were doing. Witnesses for Glenn said that no "force" was used when Ealdama was suffering the water cure. "I never saw any cruelty," reported one soldier. "He was not abused in any way," claimed another.[42] None were denying the use of the water cure; they only viewed the technique as being in a realm separate from cruelty and abuse. Some of the evidence, while gathered after the fact, strongly suggests the prior importance of a spectrum of severity for creating justifications. Sgt. Januarius Manning testified that his commanding officer told him to oversee the application of the water cure to Filipino prisoners "and to see that the men did not abuse the prisoners . . . to see that they did not get too much" (U.S. Senate 1902, 2252). That the officer thought his soldiers could administer the water cure to the prisoners without abusing them is a paradox resolved only by the torture norm's lack of specificity (and some wishful thinking).

The diary of cavalryman Frederic Presher also suggests that officers divided the water cure from other forms of abuse at the time the abuses occurred. Presher describes one incident in which detainees held and interrogated by his company

> were kicked and cuffed and beaten but no information was forthcoming. One was knocked senseless by a blow from the butt of a scout's carbine and the other one tied up by his thumbs but the officers would not allow that so he was cut down in a few seconds. Other means of persuasion were used to be sure, but still "No habla." Then the "Water Cure" was tried, a cure which is said to be sure.[43]

The officers were willing to countenance the water cure, but tying a man up by his thumbs went too far.

Experimentation: Searching for the Middle Ground

Einolf calls American torture in the Philippines before the second half of 1900 "early experimentation."[44] The term is apt. But what was the goal of the experimentation? Einolf implies that the soldiers were searching for techniques that worked and would not result in their prosecution. My interpretation runs along these lines. Soldiers were trying to find an interrogational middle ground—not too overtly harsh, not too mild. Eventually, many interrogators came to believe that the water cure fits the bill.

Early attempts to find this middle ground were not sufficiently convincing. Bissell Thomas, who slapped and punched prisoners for information, testified, "I adopted this method . . . because I believed it to be the least brutal and painful which would be efficacious."[45] In other words, the entire set of possible effective methods lay on the "more severe" end of the spectrum, but Thomas was choosing the lower end of the range. Other court-martial transcripts reveal a similar approach. Glenn brought several witnesses to the stand to discuss the "classes" of punishment that the Spanish had used in the Philippines in order to show that the water cure was the mildest among them.[46] In fact, Glenn appears to have chosen the water cure specifically because it could be made more or less severe:

> There is a further distinction between punishments which are <u>manifestly</u> cruel and unusual, and those which are cruel and unusual when taken to excess. The former class invariably results in some physical injury, and the instances cited are burning at the stake, crucifixion, and breaking on the wheel. The present treatment cannot be included with punishments of this character. It is equally difficult to include it in the second class, since punishment can hardly have been carried to excess when it has scarcely begun.[47]

Yet he claimed that "if information is to [be] obtained, pressure of some sort is necessary with these people."[48]

Some soldiers expressed satisfaction with the extent to which the water cure functioned as a middle-ground method. Samuel Lyon, in a letter to his wife, wrote about his plans for getting information from a Filipino soldier whose cooperation Lyon found lacking: "I fear I will have to give the insurgent officer a touch of high life by means of a little water properly applied—he may do better next time. The beauty of the 'water cure' is—that if you know how to apply it—there is no lasting bad effect—but it certainly is discouraging at the time."[49] For Lyon, the water cure struck a perfect balance: it was sufficiently "discouraging" to produce information, but did not produce such a "lasting bad effect" as to be beyond the pale. Figure 4.1 illustrates this balance.

The focus on the water cure by war contemporaries and later historians alike has thrown other techniques into a normative shadow, but soldiers

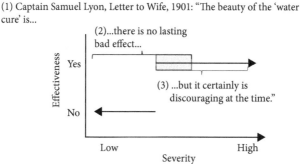

(1) Captain Samuel Lyon, Letter to Wife, 1901: "The beauty of the 'water cure' is...

(2)...there is no lasting bad effect...

(3) ...but it certainly is discouraging at the time."

Effectiveness

Yes

No

Low

High

Severity

Figure 4.1 The "beauty" of a middle-ground method.

used other methods that they claimed to be a reasonable compromise between humanity and necessity. In June 1900, Lt. Ernst Hagedorn was investigating recent attacks on U.S. soldiers in a city north of Manila. When he concluded that the townspeople themselves were probably involved, he "seized three suspicious-looking characters" and questioned them. When they refused to answer, he "ordered them confined to the stocks, with a diet of salt fish without water" for forty-eight hours. Hagedorn claimed that he would have been justified in executing the soldiers if he had wished to do so, as the circumstances called for "the most severe measures." Still, he insisted, "the health of none of these men were [sic] ever injured by this [dehydration/restricted diet] treatment" (U.S. Senate 1902, 967).[50]

Alternative Explanations

Racism

Can racism explain torture in the Philippine-American War? Racialized motives certainly inspired America's imperial impulses in the late nineteenth and early twentieth centuries. Kramer (2006, 4) argues that "race as a mode of power and knowledge was a core element in the making of formal colonialism in the Philippines." Albert Beveridge, the most outspoken pro-imperialist senator of the era, frequently invoked racially infused language on behalf of his cause. According to Kramer (2006, 2), Beveridge believed that

[t]he American cause was nothing less than that of the "English-speaking and Teutonic peoples" whom God had prepared for "a thousand years" to become "the master organizers of the world," possessors of what he had called, in the 1898 address, "the blood of government." The enemy had also become more focused in Beveridge's imagination as Filipino guerrillas disappeared into villages and forests. He urged his colleagues to "remember that we are not dealing with Americans or Europeans but with "Malays" corrupted by "hundreds of years of savagery, other hundreds of years of Orientalism, and still other hundreds of years of Spanish character and custom." What "alchemy," he asked, "will change the oriental quality of their blood and set the self-governing currents of the American pouring through their Malay veins?"

Even McKinley's phrase "benevolent assimilation" suggests hierarchy and paternalism resembling a "White Man's Burden" tone typical of the times, in which a "superior race," in its condescending magnanimity, offers a helping hand to the "lower races."

Racism played a role specifically in motivations for the use of more hard-nosed war-fighting tactics. Certainly Major Parker's letter to Roosevelt, with its comments about the need to get tough with a "half-civilized foe," suggests the importance of race in characterizing the methods of the enemy. Soldiers and politicians frequently used racially charged words like "savage" to describe the insurgents' primary methods of war and justify a severe response. These apologists, Kramer (2006, 146) explains, "claimed that the Filipinos' guerrilla war, as 'savage' war, was entirely outside the moral and legal standards and strictures of 'civilized' war. Those who adopted guerrilla war, it was argued, surrendered all claims to bounded violence and mercy from their opponent."

Kramer (2006, 140–41) finds evidence specifically connecting torturers with racist sentiments:

> In 1902, Albert Gardner, in Troop B of the First U.S. Cavalry, composed comic works that made light of torture in a way that suggested familiarity and ease. The first, playing with the torture's name, was a mock-testimonial patent-medicine advertisement addressed to "My Dear Doctor Uncle Sam," by a certain "Mariano Gugu." The author complained of a recent bout of "loss of memory, loss of speech [*sic*] and other symptoms" of a disease called "insurectos"; among other things, he "had forgotten where I placed my Bolo and my rifle." He had been miraculously cured with "only one treatment of your wonderful water cure." "No hombre's shack is complete without a barrel of it," he concluded in a postscript.

Gardner wrote an ode to the water cure that began, "Get the good old syringe boys and fill it to the brim / We've caught another nigger and we'll operate on him" (quoted in Kramer 2006, 141). Kramer notes the absence in the song of any need, pretended or real, for gathering intelligence, suggesting that racism and hatred are the primary motivators.

I agree that racism cannot be ignored. White American soldiers' letters and diaries were peppered with references to "gugus" and "niggers,"[51] and use of the latter term was sufficient in frequency to draw scorn from the African American soldiers in the islands (Brundage 2018, 182). Some white soldiers even tried their hand at amateur racialized anthropology. For instance, Glenn compared Filipinos to the Indian insurgents the British faced in 1857–58:

> The East Indian resembles the Malay in certain racial characteristics, but in point of civilization and education and in many of the manly virtues our English friends state that they are so far superior to our Filipinos that a comparison is useless. It is fair, however, to make a comparison of them as to their treachery, duplicity, the wonderful power of collective secrecy and some other distinctly oriental characteristics.[52]

Racism played a major role in Senator Henry Cabot Lodge's favorite explanation for abuses during the war:

> What is it which has led [American soldiers] to commit these atrocities which we all so much regret and over which we sorrow? I think I know why these things have happened. I think they have grown out of the conditions of warfare, of the war that was waged by the Filipinos themselves, a semi-civilized people, with all the tendencies and characteristics of Asiatics, with the Asiatic indifference to life, with the Asiatic treachery and the Asiatic cruelty, all tinctured and increased by three hundred years of subjection to Spain. (quoted in Kramer 2006, 148)

Though Lodge's sentiments may sound outrageous to modern ears, they were common at the time.

If racism (or revenge or hatred rooted in something else) were the primary motivator for torture, then we might expect to see a lot of examples of torture without interrogation that Kramer finds in Gardner's water-cure song. But there are not many. In the court-martial trials, all the defendants claimed to be seeking intelligence, and no one, including the prosecution, the victims, the prosecution's other witnesses, or the judge, challenged the defendants on that point. All the cases involved interrogation settings. Ryan maintained that the interrogation stopped as soon as the prisoners confessed.[53] First Lieut. Julien E. Gaujot, who tortured three priests on the island of Samar, claimed, "I did not coerce them for my own gratification, but for the purposes of obtaining information."[54] There is no evidence that these claims are not true. The regularity with which torture matches interrogation suggests that arguments based strictly on racism, hatred, and revenge are incomplete.

Rational Choice and Desperation

Linn (2000, 222) argues that torture did not occur at random: "Unlike executions, which usually were retaliatory, torture had a very practical motive—it was used to secure information or extort confessions." A basic rational choice model that does not evaluate actors' beliefs for their soundness provides a very simple explanation for torture: certain actors believed torture to be the best means to a given end. This argument gets extra force from soldiers' beliefs that insurgents would kill any Filipinos who cooperated with Americans voluntarily, but they would forgive those who divulged information under torture. Taft reported to a Senate committee that "there were some amusing instances of Filipinos who came in and said they would not say anything unless tortured; that they must have an excuse for saying what they proposed to say" (quoted in Miller 1982, 213).[55]Strangely, Taft's testimony implies that American torture was rational because *Filipino insurgents* believed that it was effective—too effective to fault their brethren for breaking under its yoke.

Soldiers' use of torture increased as the war continued, suggesting that it may have been a "strategy of later resort," to use Alexander Downes's phrase. The argument that the United States turned to torture out of strategic desperation has timing problems, however. Torture was most prevalent toward the end of the war, when the writing was already on the wall for the insurgency. Torture under Chaffee's appointments, in addition to the harsh counterinsurgency tactics by Bell and others, occurred after the Americans had captured Aguinaldo and much of the insurrection had given up. Perhaps American soldiers and politicians were desperate for the war to be over, but they were not facing imminent defeat at any point, and certainly not in mid-1901 or later.

There is also little evidence that soldiers updated their beliefs and preferences according to torture's results, as a standard rational choice argument would suggest. Ryan testified that the *presidente* "admitted what [Ryan] already knew" under torture.[56] This makes Ryan's necessity defense strange, since he needed only to consult his own memory to replicate what the detainee produced. Glenn described his use of the water cure against Ealdama as only slightly successful, but even this appears to be an exaggeration. Ealdama was supposed to lead a group of American soldiers to an insurgent camp. Instead, the party only caught glimpses of insurgents, and nothing came of the semi-encounter.[57] It's not that torture, including the water cure, never worked or was never a tactic that soldiers turned to only after other methods failed. Overall, however, there is little evidence of soldiers carefully and systematically evaluating the water cure for effectiveness.

The search for the "middle ground" interrogation tactics that were sufficiently harsh but did not go too far has rational choice elements. Soldiers were looking for a method that fit the bill, according to their beliefs. Yet the rational choice argument by itself is at best a partial account because it skips over a crucial part: the origins of those beliefs. As I argued earlier, norms structure and shape the search for middle-ground methods, enough to make a rational choice explanation incomplete by itself.

Domestic Politics

The election of 1900 held implications for both sides during the war. The Philippine resistance leaders stepped up the guerrilla campaign in the months leading up to the election to try to turn the American people against the war. These leaders hoped that Americans would show their dissatisfaction by voting for William Jennings Bryan over McKinley. In August 1900, a Filipino general implored his soldiers, "Let us for a little while longer put forth heroic deeds of arms. . . . McKinley falls by the way side, the people abandon him and incline to the political party of Mr. Bryan whose fundamental teaching is the recognition of our independence" (quoted in Linn 2000, 187). The move was risky, and it ultimately backfired: "[B]y tying independence to the election, the revolutionaries increased their short-term appeal, but at the cost of widespread demoralization when McKinley was reelected" (Linn 2000, 187).[58]

The U.S. Army, unsurprisingly, experienced the opposite effect. In the lead-up to the election, the army tried to keep the war news quiet. Then, when the potential for electoral accountability was in the rearview mirror, MacArthur and his subordinates ramped up coercive measures. This was not purely in reaction to insurgent tactics; the guerrilla war had been ongoing for almost a year. It wasn't out of desperation, either; the defeat of Bryan put the wind at the U.S. Army's back. The election governed the timing. MacArthur's official announcement came in December 1900, but as Glenn recalled while on trial, MacArthur met with his top officers, and plans were leaked immediately after the election.[59]

The election may have mattered for torture as well. Torture became increasingly widespread after the election of 1900, but it is not clear why. Perhaps soldiers feared that any revelations of abuse would prompt campaign-pressured politicians to call for their heads. Maybe the army leadership wanted to avoid casualties before the election, which caused it to be more cautious, which in turn presented less need for prompt intelligence, reducing the urge to torture. The latter seems more likely. Officers under MacArthur believed that army policy was "much influenced by fear of what the newspapers may say and its possible effect upon the election" (quoted in Linn 2000, 213). It also may have been difficult to plan effective campaigns because a victory for Bryan could have resulted in a reversal of overall strategy. The force of these arguments is tempered in part by instances of torture in the late summer of 1900, before the election.

Whatever the case, American torture in the Philippines did not occur by popular demand. While the White House may have considered recalling MacArthur from duty close to the time of the election because of "his apparent passivity and his failure to communicate his plans" (quoted in Linn 2000, 222), there is no evidence that McKinley or Roosevelt felt the need to appoint someone who would bend or break rules because of electoral concerns. The lack of accountability, especially the substantial autonomy of local commanders, seems to be positively correlated with the frequency of torture. The further an actor was from electoral accountability, the more likely he would be to support torture. Hence, the elected officials and the commanding officers never condoned it, the officers below the commanding officers "winked" at it, and local commanders sometimes advocated and practiced it. This gives some credence to Wallace's (2015) speculation that the fragmentation of forces in counterinsurgencies can reduce accountability and lower barriers to detainee abuse.

Domestic political concerns seemed to constrain Roosevelt and others in the General Orders camp, which helps explain why they took a wide-ranging and not always internally consistent approach to revelations of torture. Roosevelt shows a willingness to play down the abuse *and* hold torturers accountable for their deeds in a letter to a German diplomat:

In the Philippines our men have done well, and on the whole have been exceedingly merciful, but there have been some blots. . . . The conditions were most exasperating. The enemy was very treacherous, and it was well-nigh impossible to find out who among all the pretended friends really had committed outrages; and in order to find out, not a few of the officers, especially those of the native scouts, and not a few of the enlisted men, began to use the old Filipino method of mild torture, the water cure. Nobody was seriously damaged, whereas the Filipinos had inflicted incredible tortures on our own people. Nevertheless, torture is not a thing that we can tolerate. . . . [I]t was necessary to call some of those who were guilty of shortcomings to sharp account.[60]

If the water cure was not such a big deal, why invest in pursuing the guilty? Perhaps the administration wanted to project competence and minimize domestic political fallout, claiming that they were on top of even this relatively minor problem. Secretary of War Root followed his boss's lead. At times, he claimed that the administration was ready for a thorough investigation: "The President desires to know in the fullest and most circumstantial manner all the facts, nothing concealed and no man being for any reason favored or shielded" (Root 1902). Yet Root also believed that these examples of atrocities would prove "few and occasional." These statements followed his earlier attempt to convince a Senate committee tasked with investigating charges of abuse by U.S. soldiers against Filipinos that such instances were expressly prohibited, rare, and inevitable. He spent most of his communicative efforts describing the "barbarous cruelty" of the Filipino forces (quoted in U.S. Senate 1902, 950).

Root's maneuvers smack of damage control. His communications followed public accusations, and his simultaneous downplaying and pledges to investigate are most easily explained by the perceived need to limit political fallout. This suggests that norms against torture and other human rights violations held by the wider public, if not the administration itself, were having a standard, regulative effect, and were partly responsible for some of the courts-martial that resulted.

Organizational Culture

Torture was not embedded in the U.S. Army's organizational culture at the beginning of the war. If it had been, the army would have been torturing detainees right away. Even in counterinsurgency mode after 1899, soldiers did not automatically start torturing people.

Yet torture grew on certain members of the army and became something the army did despite its own leadership. A letter from Henry T. Allen, an army major who became chief of the Philippine Constabulary, to another officer suggests as much:

> You, as well as I, know that in bringing to a successful issue war measures out here certain things will take place not intended by the higher authorities; that the "watercure" and other unauthorized methods will be resorted to in spite of the strictest instructions. I have heard that under me, although against my orders, the "watercure" and other measures just as bad, or worse, were adopted, and probably under you the same; moreover, it can be said that such things have taken place under all commanders out here. (quoted in Linn 2000, 223)

Allen could have been exaggerating about the extent of abuse to cover any shortcomings he might have had as a leader. Still, the inevitability of detainee abuse was part of the narrative both the army and its civilian oversight told themselves.[61]

While torture was not an explicit part of the army's organizational culture, at least initially, vigorous fighting was. Gen. Samuel Young spelled out the idea in a speech near the end of the war:

> To carry on a war, disguise it as we may, is to be cruel; it is to kill and burn, burn and kill, and <u>again kill</u> and <u>burn</u>. If such an adjective as humane can be applied to war, I would define a humane war as a short war, which is in fact furious and bloody from the very beginning, the more furious a war is in the beginning, the shorter it will be and the less will be the eventual loss of life and property.[62]

Young's philosophy lacks some internal consistency. He claims that the "American army is the most humane army that ever waged war,"[63] but he implies that this is because of the army's forbearance, not its ruthlessness. Young is confident that "our little Jap friends" and "the aggressive army of our German friends" would have ended the war much sooner.[64] The lack of internal consistency is beside the point, however; what matters is what the army told itself, true or not.

Much of the army shared Young's beliefs. General Bell, a barometer for wider sentiments because of his enormous popularity in the army, wrote in a generally circulated telegraph, "A short and severe war creates in the aggregate less loss and suffering than a benevolent war indefinitely prolonged." For this reason, Bell advocated a highly coercive policy that would make resisters "want peace and want it badly."[65]

One reason for this "severe war" culture was the army's admiration for William Tecumseh Sherman, who once said, "War is cruelty. There is no use trying to reform it. The crueler it is, the sooner it will be over" (quoted in Risjord 2002, 143). The connection to torturers in the Philippine-American War is clear: in his written defense, Glenn spent pages quoting Sherman on the classification of detainees as guerrillas and criminals rather than prisoners of war.[66] In a separate trial, Glenn also presented his superiors' orders, which sound very much like Bell's: "The policy to be pursued in this Brigade, from this time on, will be to wage war in the sharpest and most decisive manner possible. . . . [S]hort, severe wars are the most humane in the end."[67] Glenn tried to fit his use of the water cure into the army's vigorous fighting culture, arguing that he chose the morally superior and "humane" route since his action "directly resulted in the saving of many human lives and directly injured no one."[68]

The Organizational Culture argument is most convincing in this case when combined with the Cheaters Win argument, because the latter partly informs the content of the former. Soldiers encouraged each other to pursue a short and severe war from both a practical and an ethical standpoint. Some intelligence officers applied severity to interrogation, a small and unsurprising leap given the context that the culture created. The temporal arc of detainee abuse—increasing gradually throughout the war and continuing even after it was all but over—provides some evidence of the two explanations' complementarity. While a Cheaters Win explains the turn to torture, borne out by interrogators' reflections about the initial attraction, developing norms and habits[69]—the stuff of an emerging organizational subculture—can account for torture's expanded use over time, beyond what strategic desperation would expect.

Summary

Contrary to some authors' assessments, the United States did not wage a "war without limits" in the Philippines, even after the counterinsurgency heated up in late 1900 (Kramer 2006; Jones 2012). Limits mattered, though not always in a straightforward way. Lack of norm specificity allowed actors to argue that the water cure was merely mild punishment, to downplay its severity by comparing it favorably to what the enemy was doing, and to suggest that self-application did no lasting damage. Limits, especially domestic or insufficiently masculine ones, defined what would amount to ineffective interrogation, according to certain soldiers. They helped to convince these actors that the United States would have to do as the adversary does or risk being stifled by their own rules. Limits—that is, norms and laws—can still structure the decisions of those who appear to operate without them.

Given its modern relevance as a small war with human rights scandals, one might wonder why we do not hear more about the Philippine-American War today. Only a few authors have pointed out the parallels in the torture stories since the revelations of detainee abuse from the war on terror, and there was almost no chatter *before* the invasions of Afghanistan or Iraq about America's dealings in the Philippines. If the Korean War is the "forgotten" war in the elementary study of American history, we need a stronger adjective for the Philippine-American War.

Surely the eclipsing immensity of the two world wars played a part in throwing the Philippine War into history's shadow. But perhaps the U.S. public was eager to forget the war and its scandals soon after they happened. Near the end of war, the newspaper *The World* (1902) noticed that publication of the atrocities was not translating into the kind of political outcry that one might expect:

> The American Public eats its breakfast and reads in its newspaper of our doings in the Philippines.
>
> It sips its coffee and reads of its soldiers administering the "water cure" to rebels; of how water with handfuls of salt thrown in to make it more efficacious, is forced down the throats of the patients until their bodies become distended to the point of bursting; of how our soldiers then jump on the distended bodies to force the water out quickly so that the "treatment" can begin all over again. The American Public takes another sip of its coffee and remarks, "How very unpleasant!"
>
> It then butters its bread and reads of the ingenious Major Waller, who murdered his defenseless victim on the installment plan, tying him to a tree, shooting him in non-mortal places for two days, and forgoing till the third day the delights of killing him outright.

The American Public reaches out for another tab of butter and remarks, "How distressing!"

It cracks an egg and reads . . . of the orders of Gen. Smith to "kill and burn," to "take no prisoners," to kill "everything over ten," and to "make Samar a howling wilderness."

"Rather extreme," is the comment of the American Public as it eats its egg.

All this delectable reading fills the American Public, seated at its breakfast, with a feeling of mild disapproval, not unmingled, perhaps, with disgust.

But where is that vast national outburst of astounded horror which an old-fashioned American would have predicted at the reading of such news? Is it lost somewhere in the 8,000 miles which divide us from the scenes of these abominations? Is it led astray by the darker skins of the alien race among which these abominations are perpetrated? Or is it rotted away by that inevitable demoralization which the wrong-doing of a great nation must inflict on the consciences of the least of its citizens?

Public pressure to investigate crimes by the U.S. Army in the Philippines waned after 1902. Miller's (1982, ch. 13) chapter title on the subject is fitting: the collective decision to turn the page on the war amounted to a "triumph of American innocence." Furthermore, as imperialism fell out of fashion, so too did Americans' eagerness to think on their war of annexation in the Philippines. By the time the United States was embroiled in the Vietnam War and its attending atrocities—the subject of the next chapter—the Philippine-American War held memories and lessons that few could retrieve.

5

The Roots and Rationalizations of U.S. Torture in Vietnam

The story of the origins of American torture in Vietnam is really two separate tales. The shorter one involves the U.S. military's abusive practices against North Vietnamese soldiers, suspected Vietcong insurgents, alleged collaborators and sympathizers, and unlucky civilians. While much of the torture consisted of turning a blind eye to their South Vietnamese partners' interrogation methods, exasperated American soldiers on difficult missions were also guilty of violating the basic rights of some detainees and villagers. There is little evidence that civilian overseers or the military's top brass encouraged or even condoned torture by U.S. soldiers, and the techniques appear to have been improvised or learned in Vietnam rather than through centralized training. Some soldiers, in fits of rage, chose mutilating and sexual tortures, seemingly in an effort to be as brutal as possible. These soldiers had few illusions about the severity of their techniques. My argument explains neither their behavior nor their justifications particularly well. Other soldiers, however, chose their techniques—plenty of electric shocks by magneto and some water torture—to be rough enough to be effective but sufficiently mild as to be compared favorably with the Vietnamese's "bare-fisted" methods. In these cases, U.S. soldiers' behavior in Vietnam appears strikingly similar to that of their predecessors in the Philippines as well as Bush administration officials thirty-five years later.

The longer story ends with the CIA's interrogation of high-value detainees in Vietnam and begins around the time of the agency's founding in the late 1940s. Unlike soldiers in the Philippines or Vietnam, the CIA showed up in Vietnam having already developed a program of coercive interrogation going back to the beginning of the Cold War. This chapter is thus constructed to capture (a) the years before the Vietnam War, when the CIA developed a repertoire consisting of psychologically coercive interrogation methods; and (b) what turning to the CIA signified in terms of government interest. A broader temporal focus on the CIA helps to overcome the lack of extensive

American Torture from the Philippines to Iraq. William L. d'Ambruoso, Oxford University Press. © Oxford University Press 2022. DOI: 10.1093/oso/9780197570326.003.0005

documentation for any one particular time covered in this chapter. Finally, including the early Cold War allows me to flag the beginning of a new theme that recurs in the war on terror: an effort by the CIA to develop a kind of "science of torture."

Much of what the CIA did in the early Cold War now sounds like ridiculous conspiracy theorizing from overexcited critics of government. Yet we have evidence that the United States really did have a program in which prostitutes surreptitiously drugged their customers with LSD while CIA agents looked on. And the CIA really did develop other chemical agents for poisoning. And there really was an effort to learn how to "program" people. However, we should *not* believe that the drug experiments amounted to more than so much wasted time and energy, or that the CIA in any sense cracked the code to the human psyche. Many of these programs make the CIA look downright amateurish in hindsight, and the agency abandoned much of its drugs-for-interrogation research in the early 1960s. It did, however, hang on to isolation and sensory-deprivation methods, and used these against certain Vietnamese detainees.

The thread that connects these early years with later ones is the agency's abiding interest in psychological methods of interrogation. I argue that the CIA programs came about in part because U.S. foreign policy elites were convinced that their enemies' unscrupulousness put the United States at a disadvantage. Whether this clubby bunch from the political haut monde of the 1940s and 1950s actually knew all the details of the behavior-control programs is unclear. What is clear is that almost all of them shared a sense of urgency about geopolitical developments and the need for rule-bending and sometimes rule-breaking measures in order to keep up with the Soviets. Plus, a subset of these elites did, in fact, approve of and develop the program. Eventually, the result was a psychological approach that CIA interrogators believed to be less harsh than what they would see practiced by the Vietnamese, while still sufficiently coercive to be effective. Here again, we see interrogators searching for that magical middle ground in which interrogation methods are tough but not egregious. As a result of the supposedly scientific roots of the CIA's approach, agents believed their methods to be both more morally sound *and* more effective than a more physically brutal, scarring approach.

Next, I recount in more detail these twin origin stories of U.S. torture in Vietnam, followed by an exploration of the causes. My arguments explain quite a bit of American torture in this era, but not all of it, and I supplement my account with discussions of how desperation, racism, revenge, and organizational culture play important roles as well. I conclude by connecting this case with the next one, the war on terror.

Torture in the Vietnam War and the Cold War Road Thereto

The Central Intelligence Agency grew out of the Office of Strategic Services (OSS), an intelligence agency set up during, and exclusively for, World War II. The OSS engaged in intelligence reporting, spying, counterespionage, and special operations under the direction of Gen. William J. Donovan. The OSS conducted many daring missions, including parachuting teams behind enemy lines and delivering arms to fortify pockets of resistance. When it was dissolved at the end of World War II, many of its members and fervent supporters despaired. They had envisioned a permanent intelligence agency to counter the emerging primary threat: the Soviet Union.

After intense lobbying, the CIA was created by the National Security Act of 1947. The act included a crucial allowance: it authorized the CIA to perform "such other functions and duties related to intelligence affecting the national security as the National Security Council may from time-to-time direct." These "other functions and duties," mostly clandestine operations, would become the main focus of the CIA, involving the majority of the agency's employees and financial resources (Weiner 2007, 32).

Some of those functions and duties included experiments in mind control. The show trials under Stalin, as well as Joseph Cardinal Mindszenty's almost hypnotic, false confession of treason in Budapest in 1949, made an enormous impression on the CIA. Perceptions that other Communists, such as the North Koreans and the Chinese, were involved in mind control also played a role in the CIA's decision to begin its own research (*New York Times* 1977). The projects on mind control took on various, random names, including BLUEBIRD, ARTICHOKE, and the most well-known, MKULTRA. Much of what is known about these programs comes from an inspector general's report from 1963 and a request through the Freedom of Information Act by the author John Marks in the 1970s. Marks's request turned up seven previously overlooked boxes of material on MKULTRA and its predecessors. Although the documents were mostly accounting data of marginal value, they include some gems, like an overview of the program and other sprinkled hints of program content. Richard Helms, longtime overseer of behavioral control research and director of Central Intelligence in the early 1970s, ordered most of the material on MKULTRA destroyed in 1973. Senate hearings from the middle of same decade, one of which was inspired by what Marks unearthed, are also informative.

These projects consisted of various experiments, some of which now sound strange and almost comical. The most well-known tests involved giving LSD to unwitting subjects, with the hope of using the drug at some point in real interrogations. The CIA also used a number of other drugs, including a combination of stimulants and depressants, as well as the drug that became known as the "truth serum," sodium pentothal (Marks 1979). The connection to interrogation is direct: the drugs were meant to "cause mental confusion of such a type that the individual under its influence will find it difficult to maintain a fabrication under questioning" (quoted in Smith 2003, 170). Some of the first subjects—that is, drug recipients—in the series of mind-control programs were North Korean detainees in real interrogations (Marks 1979, 22). The military did some LSD testing in the 1950s as well, with similar intentions. Access to LSD in the early 1950s was mostly limited to the CIA, however. (*Kronisch v. United States* 1998).

By the early 1960s, the CIA's interest in LSD and other drugs had waned. Dr. Sidney Gottlieb, the chemist who oversaw MKULTRA, wrote in 1964, "It has become increasingly obvious over the last several years that the general area [of biological and chemical control of human behavior] had less and less relevance to current complex operations. On the scientific side these materials and techniques are too unpredictable in their effect on individual human beings to be operationally useful" (quoted in Melton and Wallace 2009, 22).

In parallel with the drug testing, another set of techniques emerged as a result of the CIA's obsession with Communist mind control. The CIA and the military hired Lawrence Hinkle and Harold Wolff, two doctors from Cornell University Medical College, to study the methods that produced the show trials and docile, compliant captives in Russia, China, and North Korea. Hinkle and Wolff first shared their results privately with CIA director Allen Dulles and others at the agency, and then published them in a medical journal. Hinkle and Wolff looked through agency files on the subject and also interviewed former Communist interrogators and prisoners. They did not find that the Communists used drugs, hypnosis, or any other "magical weapons" for drawing out confessions (Marks 1979, 112), as earlier observers had expected.[1] Rather, through systematic isolation, a deadening routine, and removal of mental and sensory stimuli (see Table 5.1), prisoners broke down until they welcomed the chance to deliver a false confession, even in some cases with the promise of a death sentence (Hinkle and Wolff 1957).[2] The authors describe the treatment as "torture," but only in a passing sentence on the ninth page of their study. Although the LSD testing got more attention when it was revealed, the isolation and sensory-deprivation techniques that Hinkle and Wolff describe would have a more lasting impact in both manuals and actual interrogations.

In the early 1960s, the CIA secretly issued the KUBARK interrogation manual. The manual eschews physical methods; instead, it emphasizes psychological coercion. Techniques include sensory deprivation and positional tortures such as forced standing to make the detainee believe that the pain is self-inflicted (Central Intelligence Agency 1963). The overall intended effect is "regression," in which layers of personality are peeled back in an attempt to undo those elements of the person that facilitate resistance. Several of the methods described made appearances in Vietnam, in the 1983 CIA manual used to train military and police forces in other countries, and in the war on terror after the September 11 attacks.

Table 5.1 "The Detention Regimen" Practiced by the Soviets

---

1. Total Isolation: No Communication of Any Sort with Any Person
2. Cell: 6 x 10—Barren—No View Outside—Light in Ceiling Burns Constantly
3. Rigid Regimen—Strict Time Table. For Example:
   a. Early Rising
   b. Short Time for Washing
   c. Eat—(No Utensils)
   d. Sit—(Fixed Position)
   e. Exercise—(Walk Alone)
   f. Sit—(Fixed Position)
   g. Eat—(No Utensils)
   h. Sit—(Fixed Position)
   i. Sleep—(On Back, Hands Out, Face to Light)
4. Immediate Punishment for Infractions
5. Food: Plain, Distasteful—Just Sufficient to Sustain Nutrition—Sometimes Excessively Salty
6. Elimination: Slop Jar in Cell—Removed for Infractions—Thereafter, Taken to Latrine Only at Pleasure of the Guard
7. Temperature: May Be Hot, or Cold and Damp
8. Pain May Result from Fixed Positions During Sleep and When Awake

---

Source: Hinkle and Wolff 1957, 605.

The most notorious early case of the CIA putting into practice its research on drugless psychological methods involved the KGB officer Yuri Nosenko. Nosenko defected to the United States in 1962, and although he had proved his worth by exposing a high-level mole in Western Europe, his handlers still believed that he might be a KGB plant. They subjected him to solitary confinement under constant lights and constant watch for more than three years. He was given nothing to read. He made calendars and chess sets out of lint on the floor of his cell, but these basic occupations were swept away when he was forced to clean his room. He suffered hallucinations from isolation, a result that echoed some Soviet prisoner responses to similar treatment (U.S. House of Representatives 1978).[3]

Some authors draw a straight line from the behavioral control experiments through Vietnam (and beyond), suggesting that these markers are all part of a single story about the CIA's obsession with the use and dissemination of torture and mind control. For example, Alfred McCoy (2006, 64) argues, "From its overall strategy to its specific interrogation techniques, [the] Phoenix [Program, a CIA and South Vietnamese collaboration featuring torture and targeted killings] was the culmination of the CIA's mind control project." Though the connections are lacking with respect to the use of drugs, McCoy is right that Wolff and Hinkle's findings receive attention in KUBARK and show up in CIA interrogation practices in Vietnam. For lower-level detainees, the CIA sometimes protested and sometimes looked the other way while the South Vietnamese used bare-fisted techniques. The CIA saved its more tightly controlled program of extended isolation and sensory deprivation for detainees it deemed of higher value (Duffett 1968, 437).

The U.S. military did its share of torturing in the Vietnam War, sometimes in connection with the CIA's Phoenix Program, and sometimes separately. Observers seem to agree that torture by both the North and South Vietnamese was widespread, and the United States often turned a blind eye to its ally's brutal methods. How much the U.S. military actively participated is hotly contested. Some, like Nick Turse (2013) and Douglas Valentine (2000), suggest lots of American torture, with at least an off-the-record blessing from higher-ups. Others, such as Guenter Lewy (1978) and Mark Moyar (1997), believe direct U.S. participation was more limited and rarely if ever encouraged by high-level officers or their civilian overseers.

Much of what is known about American torture in Vietnam comes from soldiers' testimony in various contexts. Lawyer and activist Mark Lane's (1970) book *Conversations with Americans* is made up mostly of interviews in which soldiers confess to torturing and killing Vietnamese soldiers and civilians.[4] Together with other journalists and scholars who were unsympathetic to the U.S. policy in Southeast Asia, Bertrand Russell headed an international tribunal on American war crimes in Vietnam.[5] Veterans also testified either directly before Congress or, in the case of the "Winter Soldier" gathering in Detroit, had their testimony read into the congressional record.

Darius Rejali (2007, 176) carefully and critically reviews the testimony, removes the likely fabrications, and presents the following helpful summary:

> American electrotorture in Vietnam began with some military interrogators adopting magneto torture in the Mekong region between 1963 and 1964. This technique, particularly the use of field telephones for interrogations, spread among American units, peaking around 1967 or 1968. . . . Interrogators also adopted other clean techniques, such as slapping and stress positions, and after My Lai and similar scandals that publicized magneto and water torture in Vietnam, some of these lesser-known techniques became more prominent. Torture techniques migrated stateside, appearing sometimes in military training exercises. They were also discussed informally after interrogation training or indirectly through courses training soldiers to resist torture.

Rejali argues that both the testimonies and the government record actually paint a somewhat similar picture: clean techniques using electricity and water, midlevel commander approval or intentional neglect, and no evidence of overall approval by Washington of military torture. Finally, as is usually the case, "just how widespread [torture] was among military interrogators will be impossible to determine" (177).

The military's torture techniques did not begin with the CIA's behavioral control research. Donald Duncan, a military interrogator in Vietnam, testified to the Russell Tribunal that he and his classmates received training in Russian secret police methods, including both "psychological" techniques (isolation, temperature control, etc.) and more physical methods. But he also says that soldiers "were not interested in using [psychological methods, Russian or otherwise], they weren't properly motivated to use them, they were tremendously unsuccessful using them, and . . . they reverted to the physical methods of interrogation" (quoted in Duffett 1968, 465). Instead, military interrogators probably adapted techniques from the South Vietnamese, especially given the prevalence of American use of the telephone magneto, a favorite of French colonists in Vietnam in previous decades. Other techniques, such as continuous slapping, can be traced to American prison practices, but not through any official, centralized channels. Rather, the methods spread through whispers, unofficial conversations, and apprenticeships (Rejali 2007, 177–78). Still other techniques, especially sexual abuse of villagers, suggest improvisation.

Since the military and CIA techniques and programs follow distinct tracks, their causes are best considered separately. I start with the desperation that U.S. policymakers felt during the early Cold War, which got the ball rolling toward a CIA behavioral control program.

Evidence

Desperation? (Or Frustration?)

Although there are theoretical reasons to doubt the Desperation argument's determinacy, it can help us begin to explain the development of a behavioral control program. CIA officials saw their situation in desperate terms that they claimed were difficult for others to understand after the fact. Long after his time heading up covert operations for the CIA, Michael Burke told Marks (1979, 26), "One was totally absorbed in something that has become misunderstood now, but the Cold War in those days was a very real thing with hundreds of thousands of Soviet troops, tanks, and planes poised on the East German border, capable of moving to the English Channel in forty-eight hours." Similarly, Dr. Gottlieb began his statement to a U.S. Senate subcommittee hearing about MKULTRA by referencing a "Soviet threat" that was "very real and tangible," and claiming that the CIA believed that the Communist advancement in behavioral control projects had "implications for national survival" (U.S. Senate 1977, 169–70). With regard to LSD and the suspicion that Russian scientists had developed an offensive capability with it, one officer testified:

> [It] is awfully hard in this day and age to reproduce how frightening all of this was to us at the time, particularly after the drug scene has become as widespread and as knowledgeable in this country as it did. But we were literally terrified, because this was the one material that we had ever been

able to locate that really had potential fantastic possibilities if used wrongly. (U.S. Senate 1976, 392–93)

Agency official Hugh Cunningham sums up the mood: "What you were made to feel was that the country was in desperate peril and we had to do whatever it took to save it" (quoted in Marks 1979, 26).

Cunningham's remark shows how the Desperation argument shades into the Cheaters Win explanation: "whatever it takes" always seems to mean extreme measures, never modest ones. The Cheaters Win evidence continues the story: actors were desperate, and acceptable practices were deemed insufficient for Cold War–size challenges. "We were in World War II mode," recalls one former CIA psychologist when asked to offer thoughts following Gottlieb's death in 1999. "And when fighting a war, you do things that you might not ordinarily do." "Intelligence services should not be confused with the Boy Scouts," mused another former officer (quoted in Kinzer 2019, ch. 15).

Because much of the "desperation" talk comes from former CIA agents defending themselves before a panel of U.S. senators, it is tempting to dismiss their comments as a retrospective cover-up of more sinister or sadistic motivations. Yet the agents' later rhetoric matches earlier statements. In 1953, Director Dulles gave a speech on what he termed "brain warfare," the Communist plot to indoctrinate and control the minds of "hundreds of millions of people." The Communists were making a strong effort to "standardize the mind," with techniques "so subtle and so abhorrent to our way of life that we have recoiled from facing up to them." The Communists were trying to indoctrinate the masses in part to justify "any type of aggressive action against the free world." Communists were also interested in "brain-conditioning" on an individual basis, Dulles warned, and he believed they were advancing "rapidly" and becoming more "refined" in their use of monotony, "minor tortures" like forced standing, and possibly drugs. The overall tone of Dulles's speech is dark and alarmist, and it matches the Desperation argument well. On the whole, desperation is the go-to justification for both the most important figures in the CIA's behavioral control program and close observers.

U.S. soldiers in Vietnam also became desperate at times. Peter Martinsen, an interrogator in the war, described how his fellow interrogators felt about their work: "They had been trying to rationalize and say: 'I'd rather torture one Viet Cong than have one of my friends die because we didn't get some vital information.' This was a very common rationalization."[6] Martinsen reported being under a lot of pressure from officers above him to produce results: "They kept telling me, 'You must get information now. *Now!'* "[7] Under this pressure, Martinsen and his fellow interrogators tortured prisoners, usually with beatings or electricity from field telephones, to try to get them to talk.

In explaining when he would take coercion to another level, Martinsen describes his own feelings in a way that is close to, but not quite captured by, desperation:

> My interpreter was beating this man with a wooden mallet . . . on the knee-caps and shoulder blades. . . . This didn't yield much information. We were being watched by my commanding officer and I got *very frustrated*. I decided to try out a new idea. I had the man dig his own grave with a gun at his head, and he dug his grave until I counted off the minutes that he had to live.[8]

Martinsen also uses the word "frustrated" to describe a fellow interrogator's decision to stick bamboo splinters beneath a detainee's fingernails.[9] Frustration is not reducible to desperation. Perhaps U.S. interrogators and their superiors started out as desperate, but soon exasperation and anger took over. In this way, the desperation argument takes a few steps toward a revenge-based explanation. Although Martinsen is not referring to specific retribution, both desperation and a desire for revenge share anger as a potential intermediate step on the way to torture.

The Cheaters Win Belief among Foreign Policy Elites in the Early Cold War

The tenets that birthed the CIA's experiments and interrogations connect the Desperation and Cheaters Win arguments and can be summarized as follows: (a) the United States was in a fight for its life in the middle of the twentieth century, especially in its face-off against Communism; (b) in order to prevail, the United States would have to start bending and breaking rules, in part because its opponents were not rule-bound; and (c) the CIA would function as an equalizer in the Cold War, giving the United States the ability to fight toe-to-toe with its Communist opponents. Much of the foreign policy elite held these beliefs, and the result was the CIA's psychological program, the adaptation of Soviet interrogation techniques, and the implementation of some of these methods in Vietnam. This section will focus on those beliefs and their translation into practice.

The CIA's belief that cheaters have the advantage was first the OSS's belief in World War II. Donovan, the director of the OSS, told the head of the organization's Research and Development branch, Stanley Lovell, "I need every subtle device and every underhanded trick to use against the Germans and Japanese—by our own people—but especially by the underground resistance programs in all the occupied countries. You'll have to invent them all, Lovell, because you're going to be my man" (quoted in Marks 1979, 12–13). For Donovan, deviousness had utility. This wasn't the only appeal of OSS work, however. Lovell seemed to get special pleasure from doing unscrupulous work, and he figured that others would, too. He writes that his strategy for recruitment was "to stimulate the Peck's Bad Boy beneath the surface of every American scientist and to say to him, 'Throw all your normal law-abiding concepts out the window. Here's a chance to raise merry hell' " (quoted in Marks 1979, 12–13). Raising merry hell is not the same as believing that cheaters have an advantage. Still, early advocates for a peacetime intelligence agency understood that it would likely be a vessel for out-of-bounds operations.

Harry Truman, who was president during the CIA's founding, feared what the agency might become but also condoned quite a bit of early covert action and experimentation. Following the war, he told an advisor, "[W]e have to guard against a Gestapo. . . . You must be careful to keep [national defense] under the control of officers who are elected by the people" (quoted in Jeffreys-Jones 1989, 30). Truman understood that because intelligence gathering is necessarily done in secret, any agency put in charge of intelligence could also be a clandestine arm of the U.S. government, beyond the corrective reach of a democratic populace. He finally relented and inaugurated the first director of Central Intelligence, Sidney Souers, in charge of the Central Intelligence Group, a chronological bridge between the OSS and the CIA. Truman invited Souers and Adm. William Leahy to a lunch and an "induction ceremony." Leahy recalls, "At lunch today in the White House, with only members of the Staff present, Rear Admiral Sidney Souers and I were presented [by President Truman] with black cloaks, black hats, and wooden daggers, and the President read an amusing directive to us outlining some of our duties in the Central Intelligence Agency [*sic*], 'Cloak and Dagger Group of Snoopers'" (Central Intelligence Agency 2008). Truman, through this strange satire, foresaw that the CIA would be the place to which politicians would turn to do distasteful deeds in the name of national security.

While Truman was sounding weak alarm bells, he was also signing over power to early proponents of an independent intelligence agency. These men viewed the extralegal character of clandestine operations as a necessary and integral component of quality intelligence-gathering right from the start. One was Gen. John Magruder, director of the Strategic Services Unit, another forerunner to the CIA. According to Magruder (undated):

> Clandestine intelligence operations involve a constant breaking of all the rules of correct procedure according to which the regular government departments must operate. To put it baldly, such operations are necessarily extra-legal and sometimes illegal. No regular government department, be it War, State or Navy, can afford to house such operations within itself or otherwise identify itself with them. Independence of association with them is therefore essential.

Magruder believed that part of an independent intelligence agency's raison d'être was its value as a vehicle for activities that flirted with lawlessness. James Angleton, a longtime counterintelligence officer with the CIA, would echo the sentiment years later in Senate hearings: "[I]t is inconceivable that a secret intelligence arm has to comply with all the overt orders of the government" (quoted in Holzman 2008, 202). While there is little in writing to suggest that Truman was enthusiastic about the CIA's more adventurous projects, Magruder maintained that even the Truman White House understood that the CIA was going to have to push the bounds of acceptability in order to be successful (Weiner 2007, 14).

Specific interest in human experimentation dates back at least to the waning days of World War II. American officials searched Germany and the rest of Europe for Nazi scientists and their findings. Chemical and biological weapons research were of particular interest, as was the science behind the V2 rockets, among the most advanced in the world at that time. One part of the Americans' concern was simply to make sure other countries did not get their hands on these things—and guarantee that Germany would not retain them. The other part was that intelligence officials and parts of the U.S. military wanted to use German research to improve offensive capabilities. This is why, under the names Operation Overcast and Operation Paperclip, the United States imported several German scientists (many of whom might otherwise have been convicted of war crimes) along with their written records (Cockburn and St. Clair 1998, ch. 6; Kinzer 2019, ch. 2).

The CIA and the U.S. military were especially interested in Nazi scientists because of their experiments on humans. Six medical doctors who experimented on prisoners at Dachau contracted with the United States after the war to develop behavioral control methods (Jacobsen 2014). American facilitators may have been convinced that a certain Nazi-like ruthlessness was just the ticket for the harsh environs of mid-twentieth-century international politics. Dwight Eisenhower would echo this sentiment with regard to Germany's wartime economy a few years later when he was president: "We could lick the whole world if we were willing to adopt the system of Adolph [sic] Hitler" (Gleason 1953). While Eisenhower worried about the implications of a permanent war economy for American democracy, he saw inherent instrumental value in a less encumbered, more aggressive national posture.

Both Truman and Eisenhower were worried about the dangers that the requirements of fighting the Cold War would have for democracy. The belief that following democratic norms would hinder America's ability to fight the Cold War suggests a trade-off between standards and effectiveness. At times during his tenure, Truman tried to weaken the CIA, and he criticized the agency for going too far a decade after his presidency was over. In an op-ed in the *Washington Post*, Truman (1963) called for the CIA to refocus on delivering intelligence briefs and distance itself from covert activities. Dulles visited Truman shortly after the piece was published, and then claimed that Truman had retracted his statements and had reaffirmed support for clandestine operations (Talbot 2015, 570). In fact, Truman refused to disavow his article, but Dulles was not completely wrong: Truman longed for a more docile CIA that never really existed, even on his own watch. Still, while both Dulles and Truman are guilty of legacy protection, there is no evidence that Truman was an enthusiastic supporter of the CIA's seedier deeds.

Eisenhower was much keener on use of the CIA. As his biographer Stephen Ambrose (1983, 111) puts it, Eisenhower believed that "nuclear war was unimaginable, limited conventional war unwinnable, and stalemate unacceptable. That left the CIA's covert action capability." Eisenhower would turn to the CIA time and again to pay off political allies abroad, undermine and overthrow unfriendly governments (including democratically elected ones), and plot assassinations. Under the leadership of Eisenhower's pick, Allen Dulles, the CIA also considerably expanded its mind-control research via the MKULTRA program.

It's not clear how much Eisenhower or other foreign policy elites besides Dulles knew about MKULTRA, so the evidence I will be presenting on their beliefs is not tightly linked with the outcome of human rights abuses. Still, we should pay attention to what these thinkers believed for at least two reasons. First, and most important, we are trying to determine the philosophies that gave rise to the program. The overall assessment of the security situation and the general beliefs about how to counter it, especially from highly influential sources, are therefore pertinent. The consistency of belief across elites, including those who promoted and developed the program and those who may not have known about it, suggests a political climate very much in keeping with the Cheaters Win argument.

Second, there's no evidence that Eisenhower and other elites did *not* know about the CIA's various programs. Prominent foreign policy thinkers were a kind of fraternity, and Dulles, who helped develop the behavioral control program and was briefed regularly on MKULTRA, ran in those circles. Moreover, Dulles briefed Eisenhower on a regular basis, in addition to their informal conversations.[10] The lack of a written record of knowledge is not particularly surprising, especially given Dulles's interest in "plausible deniability."[11]

Central figures of the early Cold War feared that in some aspects of the Great Power struggle, the Soviet Union had the upper hand because it was not bound by accepted norms of conduct or the corrective force of public opinion and the vote. The authors of National Security Council Paper #68 (or NSC-68), a key document laying out America's early Cold War strategy, claim that "[t]he free society is limited in its choice of means to achieve its ends," since it must use force only as a last resort. Meanwhile:

> The Kremlin is able to select whatever means are expedient in seeking to carry out its fundamental design. Thus it can make the best of several possible worlds, conducting the struggle on those levels where it considers it profitable and enjoying the benefits of a pseudo-peace on those levels where it is not ready for a contest. At the ideological or psychological level, in the struggle for men's minds, the conflict is worldwide. At the political and economic level, within states and in the relations between states, the struggle for power is being intensified. And at the military level, the Kremlin has

thus far been careful not to commit a technical breach of the peace, although using its vast forces to intimidate its neighbors, and to support an aggressive foreign policy, and not hesitating through its agents to resort to arms in favorable circumstances. (National Security Council 1950, pt. IV)[12]

The Soviet Union, unbound by any norm or corrective, would have the advantage of choosing the most expedient means and timing. Moscow-based diplomat George F. Kennan's (1947, 573) famous article on the challenges posed by the Soviet Union also hints at the advantages of foreign policy untethered by norms, including in the realm of ideas: "[T]he [Soviet] leadership is at liberty to put forward for tactical purposes any particular thesis which it finds useful to the cause at any particular moment and to require the faithful and unquestioning acceptance of that thesis by the members of the movement as a whole." For Kennan as well as the NSC-68 authors, the Soviets' flexibility and lack of restraints were assets.

To keep close tabs on his favorite outlet for fighting the Cold War, Eisenhower appointed a committee to investigate and summarize the work of the CIA. Gen. James Doolittle (1954), the committee's chairman and a friend and advisor to Eisenhower, included this in his report:

It is now clear that we are facing an implacable enemy whose avowed objective is world domination by whatever means and at whatever costs. There are no rules in such a game. Hitherto acceptable norms of human conduct do not apply. If the US is to survive, longstanding American concepts of "fair play" must be reconsidered. We must develop effective espionage and counterespionage services and must learn to subvert, sabotage and destroy our enemies by more clever, more sophisticated means than those used against us. It may become necessary that the American people be made acquainted with, understand and support this fundamentally repugnant philosophy.

Ambrose (1983, 227) calls this passage "a concise summary of Eisenhower's own views." It gets to the heart of the matter: "fair play" endangers survival.

This is the political context in which the CIA built its behavior control programs. The political elites believed that the situation was desperate, the Soviets had the advantage of being unfenced by norms, and the CIA was the right vehicle to push against the norms and laws of the time. As with the Philippine-American War, we cannot draw a simple line between leaders like

Eisenhower and programs like MKULTRA. The connection is stronger here, however, because Eisenhower likely knew something of and approved of the CIA programs, and of course Dulles knew about and approved the program by signature. A Cheaters Win philosophy set the stage and drove the approval of the CIA's interrogation strategies and experimentation in the early Cold War.

The CIA was engaged in more than just torture. It was involved in chemical and biological weapons research, both of which were considered taboo at the time. The agency would soon add assassination to its tally of norm-flouting deeds. And as Ward Thomas (2001) argues and the Doolittle quote implies, even espionage was considered unsavory business at the time. All of this suggests that the CIA and those politicians who were enthusiastic about empowering it possessed a general philosophy about the need to bend and occasionally break the rules in a dangerous world.

The CIA looked specifically for people of questionable moral fiber to carry out its riskier programs. When searching for an assassin to do its bidding in the Congo in 1960, the agency settled on a "forger and a former bank robber" who would "try anything once." According to one CIA officer:

> He [the assassin] is indeed aware of the precepts of right and wrong, but if he is given an assignment which may be morally wrong in the eyes of the world, but necessary because his case officer ordered him to carry it out, then it is right, and he will dutifully undertake appropriate action for its execution without pangs of conscience. In a word, he can rationalize all actions. (quoted in Macy and Kaplan 1980, 165)

Similarly, the CIA looked for deviants to carry out its behavioral control program, and those in charge of hiring and contracting out research would either pass over those who were too squeamish or hide from them the true reasons for the work. In one ARTICHOKE memo, an agent worried that a certain potential hire's "ethics might be such that he might not care to cooperate in certain more revolutionary phases of our project." In another memo, the author reports approvingly, "His ethics are such that he would be completely cooperative in any phase of our program, regardless of how revolutionary it may be" (quoted in Marks 1979, 28).[13] In other words, the less ethical, the better.

George White is the quintessential example of an ethically challenged CIA hire. White was a former OSS operative who worked for the Federal Narcotics Bureau in New York. According to Marks (1979, 80):

White lived with extreme personal contradictions. . . . He was a law-en-forcement official who regularly violated the law. Indeed, the CIA turned to him because of his willingness to use the power of his office to ride roughshod over the rights of others—in the name of "national secu-rity," when he tested LSD for the Agency, in the name of stamping out drug abuse, for the Narcotics Bureau. As [a] close associate summed up White's attitude toward his job, "He really believed the ends justified the means."

White was just the man to help the CIA implement its unwitting testing pro-gram on "marginal" subjects. Because White was surrounded by drugs and knew the cops, he could pay prostitutes in heroin or get them out of legal trouble in exchange for secretly slipping their customers drugs. White seemed too crazy for the CIA at times. According to another CIA official, "He was a pretty wild man. I know I was afraid of him. You couldn't control this guy. . . . I had a little trouble telling who was controlling who in those days" (quoted in Marks 1979, 80).

The CIA's core was cut from only slightly different cloth than was George White. They usually had a similar ends-means philosophy, plus more edu-cation and other markers of high society. Yale graduate Nelson Brickham, a longtime CIA officer who helped develop a forerunner to the Phoenix Program in Vietnam, summarized: "I have described the intelligence service as a socially acceptable way of expressing criminal tendencies. A guy who has strong criminal tendencies—but is too much of a coward to be one—would wind up in a place like the CIA if he had the education" (quoted in Valentine 2000, 114).

The Phoenix Program in Vietnam is another example of the implemen-tation of the belief that advantages can be gained by trespassing normative bounds. "CIA representatives recruited, organized, supplied, and directly paid CT [counterterror] teams, whose function was to use Viet Cong techniques of terror—assassination, abuses, kidnappings, and intimida-tion—against the Viet Cong leadership" (Marchetti 1974, 236–37). Or, as Chalmers Roberts of the *Washington Post* put it, these CIA-directed teams "work[ed] on the theory of giving back what the Viet Cong deals out—as-sassination and butchery" (quoted in Otterman 2007, 63). One could add torture to this grisly list. It was an effort to "beat the enemy at his own game," according to one SEAL veteran who worked with Phoenix's counterterror teams (quoted in Valentine 2000, 76).

The historical record lacks most of the details of CIA torture in Vietnam. I discuss more in the section covering how the philosophy that cheaters have an advantage mixed with the need to demonstrate restraint. For now, what is known about the CIA's in-house program is that its agents preferred coercive psychological methods that were born of the belief that the CIA would need to learn some unsavory things if the United States was to prevail in the Cold War. The CIA was founded to compete with the Soviets' supposed advantages of normative boundlessness. It conducted pseudo-scientific experiments on subjects, both witting and unwitting, in developing a behavioral control program, and it employed some ethically compromised characters for the purpose. While the storied drug trials faded, the CIA came to favor psychological methods that its interrogators in Vietnam like Frank Snepp (1977) were trained to use.[14]

The "Slippery Slope": Lack of Specificity Evidence

In the documents covering the programs BLUEBIRD and ARTICHOKE, the predecessors to MKULTRA, CIA agents at times play down the danger and emphasize that everything will be under control. Richard Helms, then the assistant deputy director for plans, wrote to Director Dulles the purpose of the program: "[W]e intend to investigate the development of a chemical material which causes a *reversible non-toxic* aberrant mental state, the specific nature of which can be reasonably well predicted for each individual. This material could potentially aid in discrediting individuals, eliciting information, and implanting suggestions and other forms of mental control" (Helms 1953, quoted in U.S. Senate 1977, 79, emphasis added). Calling chemicals like LSD "non-toxic" is selective and misleading, as is the emphasis on damage from the experiments being "reversible." CIA officials also reassured their superiors (and perhaps themselves as well) that a medical team would "backstop" the interrogation experiments to make sure things did not get out of hand.[15] In response, "Mr. Dulles agreed that these experiments should go ahead on a laboratory basis under medical and security controls which would insure that no damage was done to the individuals who volunteer for the experiments."[16]

The behavioral control program was really an array of programs, however, and some focused on unwitting experiments (i.e., those for which the term "volunteer" should not apply). The most famous case concerns Frank

Olson.[17] In November 1953, Olson, a member of the Army Chemical Corps' Special Operations Division, met members of the CIA division primarily responsible for LSD caretaking and experimentation, including Gottlieb, the head of the division. The meeting was part of a three-day retreat to discuss collaborations between the army and the CIA on the subject of chemical storage. At the retreat, Gottlieb surreptitiously spiked several drinks, including Olson's, with LSD. According to one observer, Olson became "psychotic. He couldn't understand what happened. He thought someone was playing tricks on him" (quoted in Marks 1979, 68). According to his family, Olson was never the same again. He became by turns agitated, paranoid, and deeply depressed. He committed suicide (if the CIA did not murder him in an effort to keep him quiet) before the end of the month.

Twenty-two years later, Gottlieb defended himself before a congressional hearing by downplaying the perceived dangers: "[G]iven the information we knew up to this time, and based on a lot of our own self-administration, we thought it was a fairly benign substance in terms of potential harm" (U.S. Senate 1977, app. A, n35). Such a comment on "self-administration" of LSD might produce snickers now, but this is a standard way of taking advantage of the blurriness of torture. Earlier memos show that Gottlieb's defense was not just an ex-post rationalization. CIA documents touted LSD as a limited measure at the time the drug was being tested: "The use of LSD-25 is relatively safe because of the wide margin of safety between an effective and lethal dose."[18]

The difference in context between applying techniques to oneself and experiencing them at the hands of others lurks as a potential problem in all instances of this type of defense, but may be the most pronounced in cases of unwitting LSD administration. A person unknowingly given LSD might believe that he or she is going insane or being attacked, and the drug mixed very poorly with certain personalities. Dr. Albert Hofmann, who accidentally discovered the drug, describes the feeling as "horrific": "I was afraid. I feared I was becoming crazy. I had the idea I was out of my body. I thought I had died. I did not know how it would finish. If you know you will come back from this very strange world, only then can you enjoy it" (quoted in Marks 1979, 6). Another victim of Gottlieb's unwitting testing recalls his LSD trip as "the most frightening experience I ever had or hope to have" (68).

The CIA set up brothels in New York and San Francisco so that they could pass LSD and other drugs to clients of these establishments. The CIA brothels were the stuff of legend, set up with cameras and two-way mirrors so that agents could observe. Because prostitutes already endured social marginalization, the CIA operated with little fear of wider exposure or legal reprisal. So agents pushed the envelope further. One explains, "If we were scared enough of a drug not to try it ourselves, we sent it to San Francisco" (quoted in Marks 1979, 98). Some officers were hesitant to go along with the unwitting tests. According to the inspector general's 1963 report on MKULTRA, "The concepts involved in manipulating human behavior are found by many people both within and outside the agency to be distasteful and unethical" (Earman 1963, 2). Other agents were less principled. One retired CIA officer told Marks (1979, 45), "I never gave a thought to legality or morality. Frankly, I did what worked."

In Vietnam, some American soldiers made distinctions between methods that the South Vietnamese and U.S. militaries used compared to "classic" images of torture. Richard Welcome, advisor to Provincial Reconnaissance Units, the local interrogation centers connected with the Phoenix Program, divides abuse from torture: "Prisoners were abused. Were they tortured? It depends on what you call torture. Electricity was used by the Vietnamese, water was used, occasionally some of the prisoners got beaten up. Were any of them put on the rack, eyes gouged out, bones broken? No, I never saw any evidence of that" (quoted in Moyar 1997, 91). Welcome's "could be worse" attitude tries to take advantage of what he sees as a blurry line between torture and acts that fall just short.

CIA agents in Vietnam also separated their "psychological" methods from the more physically coercive ones that the South Vietnamese used. Frank Snepp, the most outspoken of the CIA's interrogators from that era, apparently made such a distinction. He was put in charge of interrogating Nguyen Van Tai, a former North Vietnamese deputy minister of "public security" who became one of the architects of the 1968 attack on the U.S. embassy. After his arrest in 1970, Tai was held first by the South Vietnamese for several months: "They administered electric shock, beat him with clubs, poured water down his nose while his mouth was gagged, applied 'Chinese water torture' (dripping water slowly, drop by drop, on the bridge of his nose for days on end), and kept him tied to a stool for days at a time without food or water while questioning him around the clock" (Pribbenow 2007). After he was shown pictures of himself with Ho Chi Minh, Tai partially confessed to his identity. The CIA, convinced of his value, moved him to the National Interrogation Center in Saigon. There, Tai was kept in solitary confinement for three years in a completely white room with no windows and the lights on around the clock. Tai's CIA handlers kept the industrial air-conditioning on all the time, reasoning that, "like many Vietnamese, [Tai] believed his blood vessels contracted when exposed to frigid air" (Snepp 1977, 31).

Snepp's reaction to beatings of other prisoners suggests that he viewed South Vietnamese treatment as condemnable (on both moral and instrumental grounds) while simultaneously exempting the CIA's methods from reproof. Snepp (1977, 43–44) describes paying a visit to another detainee at the National Interrogation Center and noticing that he was covered in bruises from beatings by the South Vietnamese:

> I made a full report to the CIA officer responsible for coordinating the Station's dealings with the Interrogation Center. I had always been against strong-arm tactics and said so. Apart from the moral aspect, such techniques made it impossible to develop any rapport with the suspect, which is the key to effective interrogation. I suggested that we send one of our doctors over there to look at the man. That at least would discourage further beatings, since the Vietnamese never like to have their indiscretions exposed to the Americans. The officer, an old Asia hand who always sported a jaunty bow tie, listened to me in silence and then laughed. "Well, now, don't get so excited. The boys over there are just having a little fun. Anyway we can't rock the boat. The Viets would lock us out of the Interrogation Center if we did. We'll just have to overlook this one and go on."
>
> I remember yelling at him, something about his cowardice and the Station's moral responsibilities, and storming out of his office. I wrote a letter of resignation and sent it to the Station Chief. He called me in just before the end of the day and promised he would set things right.
>
> This morning I was taken off the case.

While Snepp was protesting physically brutal methods, he was also directing Tai's sensory deprivation and solitary confinement, which shows his willingness to give the CIA's methods a pass as compared to those of the South Vietnamese. The quote also shows that Snepp's colleague had ways of downplaying their Vietnamese counterparts' behavior, minimizing the acts as just "boys . . . having a little fun."

Years later, after journalists and leaked documents exposed prisoner abuse by the Bush administration, Snepp (2009) had a different take on the methods he used:

Tai asserts that his American interrogators never mistreated him. Indeed, I never laid a hand on him, never humiliated him, and when he asked for medical care, extra rations or clothing, I accommodated him. I even tried to establish rapport by discussing French poetry with him.

But I did become complicit in the psychological manipulation and torment of a prisoner. Never mind that the North Vietnamese inflicted far more brutal treatment on the American inmates of the "Hanoi Hilton." My "success" in promoting a "dialogue" with Tai was based on his lingering fear that, without dialogue, he would be tossed back to the brutal South Vietnamese—an impression I encouraged. The isolation, the chilled air, the disorienting new routine were all things I imposed.

My CIA colleagues and I used to rationalize our tactics, and some still insist that psychological intimidation, verbal threats and tight handcuffs are perfectly acceptable in terms of both morality and expediency. But I believe there is an organic connection between the tactics I applied against Tai and those approved by the Bush Justice Department. Controlled brutality is a slippery slope, and once you pass through the moral membrane that should contain our worst impulses, it becomes so very easy to rationalize another step, and yet another, in the wrong direction.

Snepp's warning about brutality's "slippery slope" suggests that the Lack of Specificity argument can help explain torture in both Vietnam and the Bush administration's war on terror, the next chapter's case.

There is some evidence that does not support the Lack of Specificity argument. With unwitting LSD testing, the CIA knew that it was crossing a line. The agency worked hard to keep the whole program a secret. The department in charge of MKULTRA was given considerable autonomy so as to minimize exposure both within and outside of the department (Helms 1953). The inspector general's report summarizes why:

The sensitive aspects of the program as it has evolved over the ensuing ten years are the following:

a. Research in the manipulation of human behavior is considered by many authorities in medicine and related fields to be professionally unethical, therefore the reputations of professional participants in the MKULTRA program are on occasion in jeopardy.

b. Some MKULTRA activities raise questions of legality implicit in the original charter.

  c. A final phase of the testing of MKULTRA products places the rights and interests of U.S. citizens in jeopardy.

  d. Public disclosure of some aspects of MKULTRA activity could induce serious adverse reaction in U.S. public opinion, as well as stimulate offensive and defensive action in this field on the part of foreign intelligence services. (Earman 1963, 1–2)

Though some CIA agents believed that the agency could play down the level of danger to which it exposed its subjects, others didn't agree that such an effort would be sufficient.

Then again, maybe a skilled lawyer with questionable principles can rationalize anything. When the CIA compiled a list of "potential violations of, or at least questionable activities in regard to, the CIA's charter" (called the "Family Jewels"), soon-to-be director of intelligence William Colby (1978, 341) was underwhelmed, as he summarized later:

> [P]erhaps I revealed my own long career in, and resulting bias in favor of, the clandestine profession, when I concluded that this list of CIA misdeeds over twenty-five years really was not so bad. Certainly there were activities on it that could not be justified under any rule or by any rationalization, were outside CIA's proper charter, and were just plain wrong whether technically forbidden or not. But I was familiar with the procedures of other intelligence and security services in the world; was aware of the kind of encouragement and exhortations CIA received from government leaders and public alike during the Cold War, to be "more effective, more unique and, if necessary, more ruthless than the enemy"; knew the difficulty of enforcing disciplined behavior in an atmosphere of secrecy and intrigue; and knew personally some of CIA's more bizarre characters, such as . . . Peter Lorre–like scientists fertile with ideas as to how drugs might help the "mission."
>
> So I found the most remarkable thing about the list is that it was not more serious, that it did not include more widespread dangers to the lives and liberties of our citizens.[19]

Mixing caveats and allowances with justifications, Colby attempted to play down the entirety of the CIA's history of violations. It could have been worse, he concludes.

Some soldiers coming home from Vietnam made little effort to soft-pedal the severity of their acts. When Sgt. D. J. Lewis was asked whether the use of field telephones to electrocute prisoners was painful, he answered, "Oh, hell yes, it's painful. I mean, you can hold the two wires and barely crank it and get a jolt. The more you crank the higher the voltage, and it's DC voltage, so that's more intense shock" (quoted in Conroy 2005). Lewis could have said that the shocks were not so bad, but he actually volunteered information (i.e., the DC voltage bit) about how the use of electricity was perhaps worse than we might imagine.

Much of the testimony from soldiers—in Lane's book, at the Winter Soldier gathering, and before Congress—does not include efforts to minimize culpability by taking advantage of torture's blurry definition. If anything, the violence is exaggerated. This may be because their incentives were the reverse of soldiers from the Philippine-American War. U.S. soldiers in the Philippines were defensive, trying to save themselves from prosecution and opprobrium. By contrast, many veterans of Vietnam who came to oppose the war were in a confessional mood, with the intention of showing that the wartime violence was beyond the pale and beneath the country's ideals. Lack of Specificity tactics served no function for them anymore. They came home not to defend their behavior but to try to hold their superiors and politicians accountable for creating the conditions under which such behavior was likely. Perhaps these soldiers rationalized at first, and confessed later, as Snepp did. Indeed, the next section includes some soldiers (as well as CIA agents) choosing methods they thought were mild enough to be defensible while still being harsh enough to work.

"Maximum Mental Discomfort" and Other Middle-Ground Efforts

The CIA wanted to make sure that the United States did not fall behind the Soviet Union in the use of behavioral control measures, but agents were also worried about keeping tight control over operations:

> There is ample evidence in the reports of innumerable interrogations that the Communists were utilizing drugs, physical duress, electric shock, and possibly hypnosis against their enemies. With such evidence it is difficult not to keep from becoming rabid about our apparent laxity. We are forced by this mounting evidence to assume a more aggressive role in the development of these techniques, but must be cautious to maintain strict inviolable

control because of the havoc that could be wrought by such techniques in unscrupulous hands. (from 1952, quoted in U.S. Senate 1976, 393)

The CIA was convinced that it could be "aggressive" as long as the program was "controlled." Agents aimed for a middle ground in which methods of behavioral control were vigorous enough to be effective but restrained enough to be moral.

The KUBARK manual sounds by turns limited and boundless, enough so that observers have drawn opposite conclusions from its pages. John Prados (2013, 116–17) emphasizes that KUBARK "discusses at length how friendly relations with a subject are best suited to eliciting information. It specifically finds strong-arm methods counterproductive." From this perspective, Prados argues, when CIA agents interrogated Soviet defector Yuri Nosenko, they "threw away the book." Michael Holzman, by contrast, highlights the darker parts of KUBARK: "[I]t was a way of forming the character of the interrogator, an instrument, not to put too fine a point on it, of moral corruption." He reminds readers that KUBARK does not prohibit illegal methods; it merely mandates that interrogators check with headquarters before proceeding (see Central Intelligence Agency 1963, 8). According to Holzman (2008, 201–2), "A person who has accepted and internalized KUBARK Counterintelligence Interrogation has become quite a different type of person than the one who has not. He is no longer a member of civil society, of a constitutional order."

These tensions are partly resolved with the recognition that KUBARK advocated few limits for psychological methods, but more restrictions for physical techniques.[20] From the time of the arrest of the subject, the manual advises achieving the "maximum amount of mental discomfort in order to catch the suspect off balance and to deprive him of the initiative" (Central Intelligence Agency 1963, 85, emphasis in original). And when it comes to sensory deprivation, more is more:

> The more completely the place of confinement eliminates sensory stimuli, the more rapidly and deeply will the interrogatee be affected. Results produced only after weeks or months of imprisonment in an ordinary cell can be duplicated in hours or days in a cell which has no light (or weak artificial light which never varies), which is sound-proofed, in which odors are eliminated, etc. An environment still more subject to control, such as watertank or iron lung, is even more effective. (90)

Yet KUBARK does warn against physical coercion, and this is a fairly consistent theme among CIA agents as well. As we have seen, Snepp's methods followed KUBARK's emphasis, privileging a psychological approach and condemning "strong-arm tactics" on both ethical and instrumental grounds. Figure 5.1 summarizes the perspective.

Snepp was not alone. He describes a conversation with another CIA interrogator who seemed to be fishing for just the right middle-ground method:

> The chief CIA officer in My Tho took time out over lunch to give me some pointers on an interrogation technique he insists will break a prisoner in less than forty-eight hours, without the need for violence. The "Arabic Method," he calls it. Simply undress the subject, bandage his eyes, tie him to an armless, straight-backed chair, then let him sit—and sit. Eventually, after three or four hours, he loses all sense of orientation ("returns to the womb"). Then you begin questioning him, softly and soothingly at half-hour intervals, a voice out of the gloom. Guaranteed: he'll be eating out of your hand by the following morning. (Snepp 1977, 44)

No violence is needed, the CIA officer contends; just forced sitting, loss of "orientation," and "gloom."

Some U.S. soldiers also opted for what they believed to be middle-ground methods, including use of water and electricity. Next to a *Washington Post* (1968) picture of 1st Cavalry soldiers temporarily suffocating a Vietnamese detainee with water, the caption reads, "The water technique is said to be in fairly common use among Allied soldiers in Vietnam. Those who practice it say it combines the advantages of being unpleasant enough to make

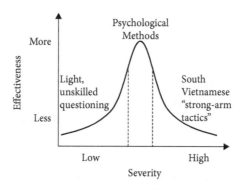

Figure 5.1 CIA perceptions from the early Cold War through the Vietnam War.

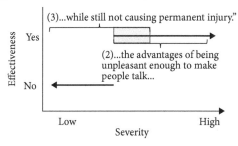

(1) *Washington Post*, 1968: "Those who practice [water torture] say it combines...

Figure 5.2   Perceptions of water torture in Vietnam.

people talk while still not causing permanent injury."[21] Figure 5.2 illustrates soldiers' efforts to find a technique that was simultaneously effective and acceptable.

Former Army Ranger Philip Wolever expresses a similar view of the use of electricity as a reasonable middle-ground method that avoids going too far:

> I heard one report—and again, this is just a report. If I had witnessed it I would have pressed charges—[that] a hammer was used to interrogate a female prisoner. It was placed right in the vagina. And something like that you just do not do. I mean a field telephone, if it wasn't overused—I'd have used it because, I mean, in the field, if you had contact, if somebody was just shooting at you, you'd want information. The field telephone is, you know, I think on the lower end of the list of things that probably was used. (quoted in Conroy 2005)

That is, something sufficiently harsh like a magneto may be necessary for getting information, but it is low enough on the severity spectrum that it can be considered acceptable.

Racism and Revenge

A PBS documentary on Charlie Company, the unit behind the My Lai massacre in 1968, captures how a group of soldiers can descend into a violent rage:

JOE GRIMES, Squad Leader: I believe that the month of February was our most devastating month for Charlie Company. It drove us to the ground. It's just like if you had a wound, and they would stick something in that wound and go a little bit deeper. Every time somebody else got killed, and it was like that wound, and it would go a little deeper. And the hurt never stopped.

FRED WIDMER, Radio Operator: Your mindset has to change and you've got to somehow figure out how to adapt. Your attitude towards the villagers, now—everybody's an enemy. You don't know who to trust. You don't know who is a friend, who is a foe. You don't have a scorecard to tell you, well, this village over here is friendly to you, it's okay to go there. Or, this village over here is sympathetic to the Communists . . . and you start to wonder who's who.

LAWRENCE LA CROIX, Squad Leader: They know where the mines and booby traps are, they have to or they can't work in the fields, they can't move between villages, you know. So they know where everything is. But they're not gonna tell you. They're gonna let you blow your leg off. You begin to hate and the hatred becomes very intense and very real.

FRED WIDMER, Radio Operator: Finally, you just throw the rulebook away. The rules of the game have changed. Instead of just going through villages, casually going through them, you went into villages, started ripping shit apart. That became the standard now—we're not nice guys anymore. (Goodman 2010)

Charlie Company's crimes include torture using mock execution with a gun, tiger cages (which induce stress positions), electricity, water, and various combinations of these (Calley 1971, 76–78, 95–96).[22] Widmer's statement about the "rulebook" sounds somewhat like the Cheaters Win argument, but the model is not really the same. Charlie Company was interested in intelligence, but they didn't seem to believe that torture was going to be very productive. As William Calley puts it, "Nothing worked ever" (78). Instead, a desire for revenge drove their behavior.

For reasons that may blend desperation and revenge, soldiers and veterans frequently link deaths in their unit to subsequent torture. According to Martinsen, "There was not much force used—coercion and harassment, yes—but not much physical force until after members of the detachment were killed and death became a reality."[23] Former lieutenant David Rudoi recounts:

We were building this POW compound out at firebase Moore, a brand-new base. A patrol went out in front to a village and settled in. In the middle of the night they all got zapped. The villagers didn't tell them that Charlie was around them. They just let these people go and 11 people died. Eleven guys. Next morning, Americans went out and brought in all the villagers. They also had Vietnamese soldiers with them. . . . And to get information from these people . . . they wired them up, and they did it in one of the buildings that we built. (quoted in Conroy 2005)

Rudoi's unit wanted information, so the Revenge argument is not complete by itself, but feelings of anger and a desire for retribution following the death of brothers in arms pushed the men into a realm in which torture was highly likely.

Sometimes revenge plays a more subtle role in explaining American torture in Vietnam than the preceding examples suggest. In a revealing question-and-answer sequence that relates to the premise of this book, Martinsen explains the content and direction of revenge for some soldiers:

[CARL] OGLESBY [TRIBUNAL MEMBER]: How did you learn to use the field telephone in the interrogation process as an instrument of torture?

MARTINSEN: I heard about it before I went to Vietnam. I asked others, "How do you interrogate people?" . . . They said, "You get a little field telephone, and you ring him up and he always answers." That was an overstatement; it's very untrue, but it's a common belief, that pain can elicit information.

OGLESBY: If that torture doesn't work, can you explain why that technique continues in use?

MARTINSEN: A man is given the order to get information and it is irrelevant *how* he gets the information. In the case of a recalcitrant prisoner one gets angry and the anger can degenerate into a strong wish to torture.

OGLESBY: I understand that, but you said torture isn't really an efficient way of getting information; torture nevertheless continues to be employed. Is there another purpose that the torture begins to serve?

MARTINSEN: I don't know, I can tell you how it is rationalized. There can be a rationalization about torturing to get information that might save lives: torturing that *might* yield information which *might* save lives. The probability of getting information decreases the more you torture a man. Generally, torture doesn't work. . . .

OGLESBY: Do the interrogators begin to use torture as a mechanism of revenge against the people?

MARTINSEN: I don't think it's used to take revenge against the Vietnamese
people. I think it's an expression of revenge for being placed in Vietnam in
the first place. Vietnam is a disagreeable place to Americans; it's hot; the
people are trying to kill you; snakes are trying to kill you, etc. It's really unlike America. A person is bound to be resentful about being in Vietnam.
(Duffett 1968, 453)

Martinsen might be reading into the situation and stretching the word "revenge" to its conceptual limit. But his idea about what we might call displaced
or redirected revenge makes sense, and it apparently comes from introspec-
tion as well as external observation.

Racism was a common theme in soldiers' testimonies. The Winter Soldier
testimony has multiple examples resembling the following exchange with
Corp. Kenneth Campbell:

MODERATOR. The training—What did you consider the Vietnamese? Were
they equal with you?

CAMPBELL. The Vietnamese were gooks. We didn't just call the VC or the
NVA gooks. All Vietnamese were gooks and they were slant eyes. They
were zips. They were Orientals and they were inferior to us. We were
Americans. We were the civilized people.[24]

Campbell's testimony shows that racial slurs weren't limited to enemies, but
extended to all Vietnamese.[25] In certain military units, if a soldier showed
the slightest sympathy for the Vietnamese people, his fellow soldiers accused
him of "loving gooks."[26] In some ways, the greater prevalence of confessions
of racism in the Vietnam War compared to the Philippine-American War
suggests greater consciousness of racism as a problem, and thus represents
slow, ugly progress. But racism clearly played an important role in the dehumanization of the Vietnamese and subsequent torture.

Organizational Culture

The Cheaters Win evidence I've presented in this chapter shows how
participants, overseers, and observers understood that a permanent

intelligence agency would run the risk of being a portal for the government to engage in unsavory business. After all, intelligence agencies, almost by definition, must break other countries' laws in order to function (Goldman 2010, 161–62). Part of the CIA's extralegal character was its approach to interrogation. The subculture that developed around the behavioral control program was defined by attempts at careful control and secrecy, even within the agency (Helms 1953), and the use of science (or pseudoscience),[27] in addition to the kind of semi-lawlessness that would put CIA scientists in touch with someone like George White. The executive branch did have other options for developing interrogation programs, and the fact that presidents empowered the CIA is significant. Still, the CIA's strange brew of secrecy, pseudoscience, and extralegality is an important reason why the Cold War interrogation program took the shape that it did.

Some Vietnam veterans' descriptions of military training are not unlike the first part of Stanley Kubrick's film *Full Metal Jacket*. According to one veteran, "Training is brainwashing. They destroy your identity and supply you with a new one—a uniform identity that every soldier has. That's the reason for the uniform, for everyone having the same haircut and going to dinner together and eating the same thing. . . . They destroyed the street kid from Newark and created the sailor. They destroyed the sailor and created the SEAL" (quoted in Valentine 2000, 204). Such a comprehensive approach to identity formation makes soldiers vulnerable to acceptance of a set of norms that do not correspond to those of the outside world. Donald Duncan's testimony about learning interrogation strikes similar notes:

[GISELE] HALIMI [TRIBUNAL MEMBER]: You described . . . how an effort was made to depersonalize and psychologically break down the recruits to prepare them for antiguerilla fighting, teach them interrogation methods, torture and the manner in which to get rid of prisoners. Would you indicate briefly to the Tribunal what were the methods used from the moment the recruits arrived until the time when they were sent to Vietnam?

DUNCAN: These methods which you discuss are not something peculiar to Special Forces. This is the standard method of training all young soldiers. I don't even believe it's peculiar to the United States Army; it's essentially a method of depersonalization, isolation, and the changing of a value system, the disorganization of the individual, a reorganization of the individual—and finally with a new value system he does become a soldier. . . . The main purpose, of course, is to take a man from civilian life, to give him a new set of values, to make him amenable to do things which normally he would not allow himself to do or would not be willing to do. In other words, it's a means of giving him a different rationale or a philosophy. (quoted in Duffett 1968, 461)

Duncan's thoughts on soldiers acquiring new values are close to my norms-centered argument about the supposed efficacy of nastiness. Organization cultures can reproduce, foster, and disseminate beliefs about the inadequacy of "normal" values and the need for different ones. The acquired philosophy could be martialed to rationalize killing and torture, behaviors that would usually be considered beyond the pale.

Democratic Restraints

Despite the Doolittle Report's words about introducing the American public to the CIA's work, the agency tried very hard to hide its deeds. The extent of the CIA's behavioral control program was known to as few people as possible. Contracted academics typically were not told how their research would be used. The CIA even set up cover foundations to distribute grants to researchers without exposing government interest. Some of the principal characters—Helms and Gottlieb—behind MKULTRA were also the ones who destroyed most of the MKULTRA files in 1972. Perhaps the CIA cared so much about secrecy because they didn't want potential enemies to know in detail what they were doing. However, that is not what the 1963 inspector general's report emphasizes. The report clearly states that the major concern was the ethically questionable nature of the work and the repercussions that wider knowledge of MKULTRA and its predecessors could have for the CIA and its affiliates (Earman 1963, 1–2).

Rejali cites a number of veterans saying that they were restricted to use of clean torture only. It is not always clear whether soldiers anticipated hiding or playing down their acts, and there's no reason that some of them did not plan on both if necessary. Some evidence suggests that soldiers were primarily trying to hide their deeds. One veteran reported, "We would pretty much do anything as long as we didn't leave scars on the people" (quoted in Conroy 2005). Martinsen says something very similar in this interview with Lane (1970, 146):

Q: Were any direct techniques of torture taught?

A: No, not in the curriculum. Now after the courses, you say to the officer or the sergeant teaching the course, "Sarge, really, how do you interrogate under combat conditions?" And they say, "Well, you take a field telephone and attach it to the man's balls and you wire him up. Then you ring him up."

Q: Who said that?

A: A sergeant. I heard this from officers too. "You ring him up, he always answers." And isn't that illegal? "Yes, but it doesn't leave marks." He said the central rule in interrogation is unsaid officially. But it is always there. It's almost palpable in the air, "You do not leave marks."

Because the officers supervising Martinsen conceded that the methods were illegal, they were likely to be more interested in hiding rather than downplaying their actions.

Duncan testified that he received similar instruction not to leave marks. He states that in devising interrogation techniques, "we were encouraged to use our imagination. The specific thing was always suggested that you do not mark a person. In other words, don't leave physical evidence on his body. Use those types of interrogation where if somebody were to see the prisoner immediately afterwards you couldn't tell that he had been abused" (quoted in Duffett 1968, 464). We can surmise that if that same hypothetically "somebody" stuck around, there would be less abuse overall.

Turse argues that the highest levels of the U.S. military worked hard to cover up U.S. atrocities during the war, presumably to keep themselves from getting in trouble and prevent a decline in support for the war effort.[28] Occasionally, Gen. William Westmoreland and other commanders would issue warnings against poor treatment of prisoners, resulting in at least a temporary reduction in torture.[29] With more and wider exposure, abuse would probably have been less common.

While top-level generals may have been complicit in covering up crimes, there is not much evidence that they encouraged abuse. Rejali (2007, 176) explains:

Veteran testimonials about torture rarely look upon the U.S. military and government in a favorable light. So it is surprising that no veteran mentions any figure like General Massu in Algeria, a general who knowingly allowed troops to use torture techniques. Nor do they identify official army manuals, as in Algeria, that authorized torture techniques. None of the soldiers saw written orders to torture. . . . Thus, even if some veterans wanted to conclude that torture was U.S. government policy, the testimonial evidence as a whole does not suggest that torture was an official policy directed from Washington, DC.

Rather, the testimonial evidence suggests some commanders in Vietnam tolerated a subculture of torture among military interrogators. . . . With the possible exception of the CIA, torture techniques appear to have migrated not from the top down, but laterally from unit to unit as the subculture expanded.

Interrogators sometimes felt some pressure from higher-ups to comply with the norm against torture, and worked around the constraints in response to competing pressure from the same superior officers to produce intelligence. For example, Duncan describes a training class on countermeasures to torture. The punchline of the class was that there were no effective countermeasures; the bulk of the class, therefore, was just learning torture methods. When one recruit asked why they couldn't just learn the techniques directly, the sergeant replied, "We cannot teach you that because the mothers of America would not approve" (Duffett 1968, 463). It's unclear who the "mothers of America" are: politicians, the media, or supposedly squeamish members of the public? Perhaps the phrase is meant to be used broadly, in which case it resembles a more misogynistic version of Rejali's "monitors." Without these "mothers," perhaps torture would have been taught directly and used (even) more frequently.

Summary

From its founding, policymakers and bureaucrats inside and outside the CIA understood the agency to be a specialist in extralegal affairs. As such, it was a natural home for a behavioral control program that would have implications for Vietnam War interrogations and beyond. The CIA did not advocate unlimited physical interrogations for its agents, however. Instead, it pushed for what it viewed as a more balanced approach that emphasized psychological techniques. These included unwitting drug testing and especially sensory deprivation. In Vietnam, the U.S. military turned to the use of water and electricity. While some soldiers admitted the severity of these techniques, others insisted that they were tough but limited methods.

My argument doesn't stand on its own, however. Americans felt desperate in the early Cold War; they were very afraid that the Soviets had a leg up on them. U.S. soldiers became vengeful in the disagreeable and scary jungles of Vietnam. Racism was rampant and consequential. The CIA has had a culture of law circumvention since its founding, and some U.S. soldier training emphasized depersonalization and aggression, suggesting a pivotal role for organizational culture in explaining torture. And both the CIA and the U.S. military showed a strong interest in hiding abuses from democratic oversight, and not simply downplaying severity. An explanation of U.S. torture during the Cold War is not complete without these important additions.

In the mid-1970s, when elements of the CIA's "Family Jewels" were making a sizable splash in major newspapers, President Gerald Ford turned to his cabinet to help manage the political crisis. Ford's point men were Chief of Staff Donald Rumsfeld and especially his assistant Richard Cheney (Prados 2013). In his memoir, Cheney writes that "the president was often irate about the congressional committees—and with good cause. At times their sensational proceedings seemed sure to cripple America's intelligence capacity, if not destroy it" (quoted in Savage 2011). For Cheney, more supervision, rules, and enforcement spelled reduced effectiveness. Instead of congressional oversight, Cheney wanted to keep the review within his boss's branch of government, reasoning, "It offers the best prospect for heading off Congressional efforts to further encroach on the executive branch" (quoted in Prados 2013, 30). Cheney would get a chance to empower the presidency, limit legislative control, and realize his vision of an intelligence agency bound by few rules when he served as vice president during the war on terror, the subject of the next chapter.

6

Twenty-First-Century Torture

The War on Terror

In 2009, after her stint as national security advisor and secretary of state under George W. Bush, Condoleezza Rice responded to an activist confronting her on the Bush administration's use of torture: "If you were there in a position of authority and watched Americans jump out of 80 story buildings because these murderous tyrants went after innocent people, then you were determined to do anything that you could, that was legal, to prevent that from happening" (CBS News 2009). By that time, the United States and the world had already learned that "anything you could" meant as coercive as the administration thought it could be without its members facing prosecution. Rice answers as if anyone in charge would have done the same thing, but this is doubtful since more than one experienced, successful interrogator during the war on terror condemned the administration's use of "enhanced interrogation" and refused to participate in it (Soufan 2011; Alexander 2008; Carle 2014). Not everyone would have tortured. Why did the Bush administration do so?

I argue that significant members of the Bush administration were convinced that countering terror required ruthlessness, especially concerning interrogations. To circumvent laws and norms prohibiting torture in the United States, the administration specifically selected some of the world's nastiest regimes as destinations for its detainees. When the administration wanted to develop its own interrogation program, it chose the Central Intelligence Agency, which was short on interrogation experience but long on willingness to push limits. The Bush administration also announced that the Geneva Conventions on detainee treatment would not apply to war on terror captives after key administration lawyers argued that Geneva put too many constraints on interrogators. Much of the detainee abuse that followed, especially by the U.S. military, can be traced to that decision. For administration members, norms and laws prohibiting torture defined, by exclusion or close to it, the set of techniques that they could expect to be effective.

American Torture from the Philippines to Iraq. William L. d'Ambruoso, Oxford University Press. © Oxford University Press 2022. DOI: 10.1093/oso/9780197570326.003.0006

The Bush administration sidestepped normative and legal concerns by dramatically redefining torture. The Office of Legal Counsel (OLC), in coordination with lawyers in the White House and the Pentagon, issued memos that gave interrogators wide latitude to physically and mentally coerce detainees. The OLC sequestered the definition of torture to the most extreme end of the severity spectrum, thereby exempting most behavior from legal and normative opprobrium. Certain interrogators, politicians, and observers in the media also exploited torture's sliding scale by downplaying the severity of "enhanced interrogations" and calling the torture statutes and treaties "vague." The point here is not that these actors were convinced deep down that the United States was not torturing. Rather, what is most important for explaining torture is that these actors thought they could make such justifications. I argue that the torture norm's lack of specificity opened the door.

The War on Terror and the Torture Therein

Though the United States and its Western allies pursued terrorists before the Bush administration, the war on terror was a response to the attack on September 11, 2001. Almost three thousand people died in the attack, making it easily the largest terrorist attack on U.S. soil in history. The American people were initially shocked, and then eager to respond. Bush summed this up in a speech before Congress: "Our grief has turned to anger, and our anger to resolution" (White House 2001a).

That resolution turned into the ill-defined but still useful term "war on terror." I am including under this heading the airstrikes, invasion, and occupation of Afghanistan starting in late 2001; the invasion and occupation of Iraq beginning in 2003; coordination with other countries leading to the arrest and interrogation of suspected terrorists; and the development of detention facilities, including Guantánamo Bay and the CIA's "black sites," where suspects were held and interrogated.

Torture during the war on terror occurred along three separate but interrelated paths. First, the Bush administration via the CIA used extraordinary rendition, which is the extrajudicial transfer of persons from one state to another, often with the aim of circumventing human rights laws. The United States has had a rendition program since at least the Reagan administration (Garcia 2010; Prados 2013), but it was mostly used for "delivering [captives] to a criminal justice system," not for avoiding one (Horton 2009). Only in the mid- to late 1990s was the program used to keep detainees in third-party countries, some of whom were subsequently tortured (Hutchinson et al. 2013, 165). After September 11, the Bush administration expanded the program significantly (Mayer 2005).

States that are parties to the United Nations (1984) Convention against Torture can render their prisoners to other states as long as there are no "substantial grounds for believing" that detainees will be tortured as a result. The subjective nature of that phrase gives leaders "plausible deniability" and the potential to claim, as Secretary of State Rice did in a speech in 2005, that "the United States has not transported anyone, and will not transport anyone, to a country when we believe he will be tortured" (Gilmore 2005). Rice's claim is preposterous. As one official stated bluntly early in the war, "We don't kick the [expletive] out of them. We send them to other countries so they can kick the [expletive] out of them" (Priest and Gellman 2002).[1] A study by *Mother Jones* documented fifty-three cases of extraordinary rendition to third countries, not including black sites and Guantánamo Bay (Bergen and Tiedemann 2008). Among the most well-known of these cases was that of Maher Arar, a Syrian Canadian arrested at JFK Airport in 2002 and sent to Syria. Arar was never charged, and, after being tortured by beatings and electricity in a Syrian prison, he was released a year later (Mayer 2005).

The extraordinary rendition program also set the stage for a second, related pathway to torture. The CIA, with the help of private contractors, developed its own in-house torture program, used primarily at "black sites," secret prisons around the world to which those perceived to be high-value detainees were rendered. Although the Senate Torture Report argues that the CIA exceeded its authority in some cases,[2] we should not exaggerate the CIA's rogue status. Senior Bush administration officials knowingly and eagerly signed off on the interrogation program in detail. The OLC, housed in the Justice Department, declared highly abusive practices to be legal in a series of documents now known as the Torture Memos. If the CIA had stuck strictly to the letter of what the OLC pronounced permissible, it still would have been able to put prisoners in cramped spaces, force them to hold stress positions, keep them awake for days, and, in some select cases, subject them to the waterboard (Bybee 2002b). The more important the detainee, the closer the management and, in most cases, the harsher the treatment. According to the CIA, "the confinement conditions and treatment of high profile detainees . . . were closely scrutinized at all levels of management from the outset" (Central Intelligence Agency 2013). Although there was some pushback from within the Bush administration (Nuñez-Mietz 2013), torture (as I define it in chapter 2) was the administration's official policy.

Third, the military began using torture in its own detention facilities—at Bagram Air Base in Afghanistan, Abu Ghraib in Iraq, and elsewhere. CIA and military torture overlapped at Guantánamo Bay and other sites, and both were influenced by the administration's position on the Geneva Conventions. Military torture also followed a separate track, with Secretary of Defense Donald Rumsfeld authorizing (and then rescinding authorization for, and then reauthorizing with more limitations) the use of certain techniques by military interrogators. While some abuse went beyond what was approved, other techniques were standard operating procedure. The abuse at Abu Ghraib, made famous by photographs, included both (Hutchinson et al. 2013, 399–400). Maj. Gen. George Fay summarizes the connection in his report on abuse at Abu Ghraib:

> The MPs [Military Police] being prosecuted claim their actions came at the direction of MI [Military Intelligence]. Although self-serving, these claims do have some basis in fact. The environment created at Abu Ghraib contributed to the occurrence of such abuse and the fact that it remained undiscovered by higher authority for a long period of time. What started as nakedness and humiliation, stress and physical training (exercise), carried over into sexual and physical assaults by a small group of morally corrupt and unsupervised soldiers and civilians. (Fay 2004, 9–10; quoted in Hutchinson et al. 2013, 106)

Much of the confusion comes from who was authorized to do what to whom. We now know that within the military, forced standing, nudity, and sensory deprivation techniques like hooding and removal of sensory stimuli were approved at the highest levels, though not for every interrogator and every detainee.[3] The 2008 Senate Armed Services Committee report goes further than General Fay, but along similar lines: "The abuse of detainees in U.S. custody cannot simply be attributed to the actions of 'a few bad apples' acting on their own. The fact is that senior officials in the United States government solicited information on how to use aggressive techniques, redefined the law to create the appearance of their legality, and authorized their use against detainees" (U.S. Senate, Armed Services Committee 2008, xii).

Some of the most important sources of evidence for the war on terror case are the Torture Memos, several of which are available to the public (with some redactions). Three extensive reports that draw on these memos and other primary sources fill in much of the story. In addition to the 2008 report, the Senate report released in 2014 and the CIA rebuttal refer to documents that are still classified (U.S. Senate, Select Committee on Intelligence 2014; Central Intelligence Agency 2013).[4] The watchdog group The Constitution Project also released a comprehensive, invaluable report on detainee treatment during the war on terror (Hutchinson et al. 2013). Journalists at the *Washington Post*, the *New York Times*, and the *New Yorker* have contributed significantly to our understanding of the events as well. While gaps remain, the lack of a full picture appears less pronounced for this case than most others in the data-poor world of torture studies.

Evidence

Cheating Meant Winning for the Bush Administration

Almost immediately after the September 11 attacks, the Bush administration imagined a war in which normative (as well as financial) constraints would not bind those charged with winning it. Counterterrorism advisor Richard Clarke (2004, 24) recalls President Bush's exchange with Rumsfeld, which set the tone:

> "I want you all to understand that we are at war and we will stay at war until this is done. Nothing else matters. Everything is available for the pursuit of this war. Any barriers in your way, they're gone . . . " When, later in the discussion, Secretary Rumsfeld noted that international law allowed the use of force only to prevent future attacks and not for retribution, Bush nearly bit his head off. "No," the President yelled in the narrow conference room, "I don't care what the international lawyers say, we are going to kick some ass."[5]

With the war on terror just a few hours old, Bush was already stating his belief that to really "kick ass" in wartime, one had to ignore the constraints of "international lawyers."

A few days later, in a well-known interview with Tim Russert on *Meet the Press*, Vice President Dick Cheney laid out his philosophy for how to fight the war on terror:

VICE PRES. CHENEY: I'm going to be careful here, Tim, because I—clearly it would be inappropriate for me to talk about operational matters, specific options or the kinds of activities we might undertake going forward. . . . We . . . have to work, though, sort of the dark side, if you will. We've got to spend time in the shadows in the intelligence world. A lot of what needs to be done here will have to be done quietly, without any discussion, using sources and methods that are available to our intelligence agencies, if we're going to be successful. That's the world these folks operate in, and so it's going to be vital for us to use any means at our disposal, basically, to achieve our objective.

MR. RUSSERT: There have been restrictions placed on the United States intelligence gathering, reluctance to use unsavory characters, those who violated human rights, to assist in intelligence gathering. Will we lift some of those restrictions?

VICE PRES. CHENEY: Oh, I think so. I think the—one of the by-products, if you will, of this tragic set of circumstances is that we'll see a very thorough sort of reassessment of how we operate and the kinds of people we deal with. There's—if you're going to deal only with sort of officially approved, certified good guys, you're not going to find out what the bad guys are doing. You need to be able to penetrate these organizations. You need to have on the payroll some very unsavory characters if, in fact, you're going to be able to learn all that needs to be learned in order to forestall these kinds of activities. It is a mean, nasty, dangerous dirty business out there, and we have to operate in that arena. I'm convinced we can do it; we can do it successfully. But we need to make certain that we have not tied the hands, if you will, of our intelligence communities in terms of accomplishing their mission.

MR. RUSSERT: These terrorists play by a whole set of different *rules*. It's going to force us, in your words, to get mean, dirty and nasty in order to take them on.

VICE PRES. CHENEY: Right. (NBC News 2001)[6]

Cheney's assertion that the United States must fight "dirty," as the terrorists do, exemplifies the notion that nasty equals effective. Interestingly, Russert uses the phrase "whole set of different rules." His phrasing and Cheney's affirmation imply that for Cheney, terrorists' lawlessness gives them an *advantage*, and so in order to get the upper hand, the United States would have to "get mean."

The day after Cheney's interview with Russert, President Bush authorized the CIA to capture and detain suspects related to the attacks. The memo is still classified, but the authors of the 2014 Senate report have had access. The report says that the memo "provided unprecedented authorities, granting the CIA significant discretion in determining whom to detain, the factual basis for the detention, and the length of the detention" (U.S. Senate, Select Committee on Intelligence 2014, 11). Though the September 17 memo does not discuss interrogation specifically (11), it pushed boundaries in terms of detention and provided an initial basis for the administration's extensive use of the CIA and for the eventual development of the CIA's "black sites."

Why the CIA? It wasn't because the agency had a lot of recent detention or interrogation experience at that point (CIA Inspector General 2004). The CIA was going to need help setting up prisons, and it planned on assistance from the Department of Defense or the Bureau of Prisons (12). It also had less experience with interrogation than the military or the FBI, and it would have to turn to private contractors to create an interrogation program. Rather, the organization's willingness to push boundaries was a key factor in why Bush chose them. "The truth," said one CIA official, "is that the President wanted it. So everyone else wanted to be the most aggressive. A lot of ambitious people played on Cheney and the President's fascination with this" (Mayer 2008, 53).

Some of Cheney's "unsavory characters" turned out to be part of the intelligence agency in Egypt, where the Bush administration, via the CIA, sent one of its earliest (allegedly) high-value detainees. Officials believed that Ibn al-Shaykh al-Libi, whom Pakistani authorities captured and turned over to the United States in the first few days of 2002, was the most senior Al Qaeda official captured to date (Schmitt 2002). At first, the FBI handled much of the questioning, and according to some reports, al-Libi was talking (*Frontline* 2005). But the CIA then forcibly removed al-Libi from Bagram Air Base and FBI access and transferred him to Egypt through extraordinary rendition.

As former CIA officer Vinnie Castrovince explains, "[Al-Libi is] carried off to Egypt, who torture him. And we know that he's going to be tortured. Anyone who's worked on Egypt, has worked on other countries in the Middle East, knows that" (quoted in Kirk 2006). Egypt's primary—perhaps sole—draw was that it did not follow ethical and legal norms of interrogation. In the words of former CIA agent Robert Baer, "If you want a serious interrogation, you send a prisoner to Jordan. If you want them to be tortured, you send them to Syria. If you want someone to disappear—never to see them again—you send them to Egypt" (ACLU 2005).

But the Bush administration would not be able to render all of their detainees to places like Egypt, and may not have wanted to outsource so much intelligence gathering even if it could have done so. So it developed an in-house program. In late 2001, the Defense Department asked the OLC whether detainees in the war on terror were protected by the Geneva Conventions III on the Treatment of Prisoners of War (GPW). John Yoo and Robert Delahunty (2002) of the OLC, in a memo to the general counsel at the Defense Department, argued in early January 2002 that the GPW need not apply to Alqaeda or Taliban detainees, but they remained at least nominally agnostic about whether waiving Geneva guidelines as a matter of policy was a sound idea.[7] On January 18, Bush told members of his administration that GPW would not apply, and Rumsfeld relayed this news to his subordinates the next day. The only additional instructions for detainee treatment contained in Rumsfeld's memo on January 19 sounded notes of restraint, but left a sizable loophole: "The Combatant Commanders shall, in detaining Al Qaida and Taliban individuals under the control of the Department of Defense, treat them humanely and, *to the extent appropriate and consistent with military necessity*, in a manner consistent with the Geneva Conventions of 1949" (Rumsfeld 2002, emphasis added). The fact that the military repeatedly drove through that loophole suggests that they believed following Geneva was often inconsistent with military necessity.

The State Department and some members of the military dissented, and a revealing internal debate ensued. In late January, a memo to Bush bearing White House Counsel Alberto Gonzales's signature, but likely penned in large part by Cheney's lawyer David Addington (Gellman 2008, ch. 7), summed up the policy argument against applying Geneva:

> As you have said, the war against terrorism is a new kind of war. It is not the traditional clash between nations adhering [to] the laws of war that formed the backdrop for GPW. The nature of the new war places a high premium on other factors, such as the ability to quickly obtain information from captured terrorists and their sponsors in order to avoid further atrocities against American civilians. . . . [T]his new paradigm renders

obsolete Geneva's strict limitations on questioning of enemy prisoners."
(Gonzales 2002)

This is strong evidence for the Cheaters Win argument. The memo was not
meant for the public, and captures a real policy debate among Bush administration lawyers. It makes clear the problem of "limitations." The height-
ened need for intelligence meant that American interrogators could not be
fenced in by Geneva, the memo argues. They would need a "new set of rules"
(Yoo 2006, 47). Furthermore, the outcome of the debate was highly consequential: the decision to forgo Geneva, which Bush (2002) confirmed two
weeks later, was instrumental in leading to abuses, especially in the military
(Hutchinson et al. 2013; Phillips 2012).

The CIA also worried about Geneva's constraints, as the 2014 Senate report makes clear:

> A letter drafted for [Director of Central Intelligence George] Tenet to the
> president urged that the CIA be exempt from any application of these
> protections, arguing that application of Geneva would "significantly
> hamper the ability of CIA to obtain critical threat information necessary
> to save American lives." On February 1, 2002—approximately two months
> prior to the detention of the CIA's first detainee—a CIA attorney wrote that
> if CIA detainees were covered by Geneva there would be "few alternatives
> to simply asking questions." The attorney concluded that, if that were the
> case, "then the optic becomes how legally defensible is a particular act that
> probably violates the convention, but ultimately saves lives." (U.S. Senate,
> Select Committee on Intelligence 2014, 20)

The CIA viewed "saving lives" and following Geneva as mutually exclu-
sive realms. The agency wanted "flexibility," in Yoo's (2006, 43) euphemistic
terms: "[T]reating the detainees as unlawful combatants would increase
flexibility in detention and interrogation, potentially yielding actionable intelligence that could prevent future terrorist attacks and locate al Qaeda personnel and assets."

The CIA was beginning to set up a separate interrogation program at that
time. Since the agency had no recent interrogation experience, it sought the
advice of others. The CIA employed two psychologists, James Mitchell and
Bruce Jessen, who had experience with the Survival, Evasion, Resistance, and
Escape (SERE) training endured by U.S. military members most in danger of

capture. The SERE techniques included "stripping students of their clothing, placing them in stress positions, putting hoods over their heads, disrupting their sleep, treating them like animals, subjecting them to loud music and flashing lights, and exposing them to extreme temperatures" (U.S. Senate, Armed Services Committee 2008, xiii). Some SERE schools also used the waterboard, and the Mitchell-Jessen variant that the CIA used was even more brutal than the already rough training version (Mayerfeld 2016, 137). The only "attractive" feature of Mitchell and Jessen's résumé was their knowledge of a kind of science of brutality—there was no other compelling reason for the CIA to hire them. According to the Senate report, "Neither psychologist had experience as an interrogator, nor did either have specialized knowledge of al Qa'ida, a background in terrorism, or any relevant regional, cultural, or linguistic expertise" (U.S. Senate, Select Committee on Intelligence 2014, 21). The CIA partnered with experienced interrogators from the FBI, but the FBI interrogators were subordinate to the less experienced, but more aggressive, contracted psychologists (Soufan 2011). The CIA and the Bush administration may have valued experience, but they valued harsh measures even more.

A back-and-forth between the CIA and Senate investigators about Mitchell and Jessen's experience clarifies the CIA's preferences in the early days of the war on terror:

> The CIA's June 2013 Response states that the Committee Study was "incorrect… in asserting that the contractors selected had no relevant experience." The CIA's June 2013 Response notes [Mitchell] and [Jessen]'s experience at the Department of Defense SERE school, and [Mitchell]'s "academic research" and "research papers" on "such topics as resistance training, captivity familiarization, and learned helplessness—all of which were relevant to the development of the program." The CIA's June 2013 Response does not describe any experience related to actual interrogations or counterterrorism, or any relevant cultural, geographic, or linguistic expertise. The CIA's June 2013 Response provides the following explanation: "Drs. [Mitchell] and [Jessen] had the closest proximate expertise CIA sought at the beginning of the program, specifically in the area of *non-standard means of interrogation*. Experts on traditional interrogation methods did not meet this requirement. Non-standard interrogation methodologies were not an area of expertise of CIA officers or of the U.S. Government generally. We believe their expertise was so unique that we would have been derelict had we not sought them out when it became clear that CIA would

be heading into the uncharted territory of the program." (U.S. Senate, Select Committee on Intelligence 2014, 32, emphasis in original)[8]

Though the Senate report argues at times that the contractors were pivotal in convincing the CIA to move in harsher directions, the CIA leadership was talking to these contractors in the first place for a reason. The agency's initial interest in outside-the-box interrogation meant that they were looking beyond norms prior to the contractors' influence.[9]

Like the CIA of the Cold War, the agency's 2013 response to the Senate makes clear that it was also seeking a scientific approach. In his memoirs and testimony, Mitchell claims that he was drawing on the work of well-known scientists like Ivan Pavlov and Martin Seligman in an effort to "condition" detainees and induce a bounded sense of helplessness that would prompt them to seek relief in the form of answering questions. As with the CIA efforts described in the previous chapter, the value that science added to the program deserves some skepticism.[10] Mitchell explained the process: "[C]ondition [the detainee] so that when he began to resist, he experienced an adverse of consequence, right? And when he started to cooperate, that adverse of consequence went away, which is straight Pavlovian conditioning."[11] Rewarding compliance and punishing resistance is also known as coercion, and it predates Pavlov—and science, for that matter. Still, regardless of how scientific enhanced interrogation actually was, CIA officials may have been drawn to the idea of a controlled, limited, professional coercive interrogation program,[12] a theme I expand on in the next two sections.

The CIA had already begun to test limits by late 2001. The Senate report provides the earliest evidence of CIA brainstorming about what would be allowable in terms of interrogation:

[B]y the end of November 2001, CIA officers had begun researching potential legal defenses for using interrogation techniques that were considered torture by foreign governments and a non-governmental organization. On November 26, 2001, attorneys in the CIA's Office of General Counsel circulated a draft legal memorandum describing the criminal prohibition on torture and a potential "novel" legal defense for CIA officers who engaged in torture. The memorandum stated that the "CIA could argue that the torture was necessary to prevent imminent, significant, physical harm to persons, where there is no other available means to prevent the harm," adding that "states may be very unwilling to call the U.S. to task for torture when it resulted in saving thousands of lives." (U.S. Senate, Select Committee on Intelligence 2014, 19)

It is unclear how the CIA could have believed a standard necessity defense was "novel." Much clearer is the agency's hunch that successful interrogation might require expanding beyond legal bounds. The November 26 memo mentioned "cold torture," "forced positions," "enforced physical exhaustion," "sensory deprivation," "perceptual deprivation," "social deprivation," "threats and humiliation," "conditioning techniques," and "deprivation of sleep" (179). The memo's use of the word "torture," together with a rationalization based on necessity, suggests that it was not yet relying on the not-quite-torture justifications (discussed more at length in the next section) featured so prominently in the OLC memos from August 2002.

There is evidence that the CIA had explored more above-board detention and interrogation options in early November 2001, and it is not obvious what changed in that month (U.S. Senate, Select Committee on Intelligence 2014, 19; Apuzzo and Risen 2014). It may be that the agency's—and the administration's—imaginations simply caught up with their change of mood, and the turning point was September 11 itself. In a statement before Congress in 2002, the CIA's lead counterterrorism official Cofer Black cryptically reported, "All I want to say is that there was 'before' 9/11 and 'after' 9/11. After 9/11 the gloves come off." For Black as well as many others, following norms and rules after 9/11 would have been like wearing gloves in a bareknuckled world. This is why Black concluded his statement by advocating the continuation of a policy of "no limits aggression" (U.S. Congress 2002).

When Abu Zubaydah, a Palestinian national whom U.S. authorities believed to be a trainer for Al Qaeda, was captured in Pakistan in March 2002, he took al-Libi's place as America's most important detainee to date in the war on terror. As with al-Libi, FBI interrogators at first reported success in getting Zubaydah to talk using rapport-building methods (Soufan 2011). But they soon came in conflict with the CIA contractors. The CIA had primary authority over interrogation, and the coercive measures began. "At the end of April 2002, the DETENTION SITE GREEN [where Zubaydah was held] interrogation team provided CIA Headquarters with three interrogation strategies. CIA Headquarters chose the most coercive interrogation option, which was proposed and supported by CIA contractor [Mitchell]" (U.S. Senate, Select Committee on Intelligence 2014, 30). The CIA leadership was convinced that "more coercive" meant "more effective."

The CIA was simultaneously petitioning the OLC for legal clearance regarding a set of techniques to use on Zubaydah. The OLC, in a memo bearing the name of Jay Bybee (2002b) but mostly written by John Yoo, followed up on a few months of verbal assurances with written affirmation of almost all of the requested techniques, including sleep deprivation and use of the waterboard. As Yoo explains, the CIA wanted to know "what the legal limits of interrogation [were]" (quoted in Gellman and Becker 2007). The CIA also seemed to subscribe to a nastier-equals-more-effective calculus among their set of harsh interrogations. In their petitions for approval, the psychologists emphasized that the waterboard, which they viewed as the harshest of the bunch,[13] was an "absolutely convincing technique," and therefore necessary to break Zubaydah (U.S. Senate, Select Committee on Intelligence 2014, 36). The CIA was obviously "convinced": Zubaydah suffered the waterboard eighty-three times in August 2002, according to the CIA inspector general (2004, 90).[14] As Mitchell would later put it, the CIA had decided to "go right up to the line of what was legal, put their toes on it, and lean forward" (Borger 2020).

Later in 2002, military interrogators at Guantánamo Bay asked the Pentagon for approval of harsher measures. The leading line of the request states the perceived problem forthrightly: "The current guidelines for interrogation procedures at GTMO [Guantánamo] limit the ability of interrogators to counter advanced resistance" (Phifer 2002, 1). The Guantánamo soldiers believed they were chafing under the yoke of then-current limits on interrogation methods. After Defense Counsel William J. Haynes trimmed the list, Rumsfeld approved all of Haynes's recommendations, which included forced standing, sensory deprivation, hooding, removal of clothing, and use of dogs to induce fear (2). Other techniques, like exposure to cold, the "wet towel" method (similar to the waterboard), and death threats, were deemed legal but required per-use approval. Regarding forced standing, Rumsfeld (2002) hand-wrote, "I stand for 8–10 hours a day. Why is standing limited to 4 hours?" The implicit message seems to be, when it comes to coercion, more is better.

While Bush did not openly discuss the CIA's coercive interrogation program until 2006, observers were already noticing at least a year earlier that those responsible for designing and approving the torture program did not suffer professionally—if anything, they were promoted:

What happened to higher-up architects and consultants on administration policy? Mr. Rumsfeld revealed last week that he twice offered to resign over the Abu Ghraib scandal and was twice turned down by President Bush. Mr. Bybee, who defined torture as pain equivalent to "organ failure," was nominated by Mr. Bush to the Ninth Circuit Court of Appeals and took his seat there in 2003. Michael Chertoff, who in his capacity as head of the Justice Department's criminal division advised the C.I.A. on the legality of coercive interrogation methods, was selected by President Bush to be the new secretary of homeland security. William J. Haynes II, the Department of Defense's chief legal officer, who helped oversee Pentagon studies on the interrogation of detainees, was twice nominated by President Bush to the Fourth Circuit Court of Appeals. And Mr. Gonzales, who used the words "obsolete" and "quaint" in reference to the Geneva Conventions, was confirmed last week as attorney general, the nation's top legal post. (Kakutani 2005)

Bush went out of his way to reward those who pushed for the harshest measures. While their primary "virtue" may have been loyalty, it is hard to separate loyalty from the vision to which that loyalty adhered, namely, an aggressive approach to detention and interrogation.

Defenders of harsh interrogation, including Bush and Cheney, continued their advocacy of such practices through Bush's two terms and beyond.[15] In a chapter on the administration's use of torture, Holmes (2007, 279, emphasis in original) writes:

One reason the Administration's defenders remain unmoved by the numerous powerful arguments against the utility of coercive interrogation might be that they are not really focused on the information extracted by these methods. . . . They may prize the cruel, inhumane, and degrading treatment of prisoners precisely *because* it violates international norms and the rules of war. Psychologically persuasive evidence that a medicine is effective is that it tastes unbearably foul.

Holmes goes a bit too far here; former administration officials and CIA officers use examples to argue their side, even if the evidence does not always add up. However, their initial intuitions and reading of the evidence about the efficacy of torture may well have been (and continue to be) informed by torture's status as an off-limits practice.

In one of his first public appearances after the end of his second term, Bush described his thought process after capturing 9/11 mastermind Khalid Sheik

Mohammed (KSM): "The first thing you do is ask, what's legal? What do the lawyers say is possible?" (Hamby 2009).[16] In other words, how far would interrogators be able to go in terms of severity?[17] Interestingly, Bush does *not* say that he first asked "Who are the most experienced interrogators? Who has the best record of success?" Degree of severity likely informed estimates of the probability of successful interrogation.

The Bush administration pushed the normative envelope in a number of areas during the war on terror, including indefinite detention, closed trials, preventive war, and targeted killing, in addition to detainee abuse. This suggests that torture was not an act specifically plucked from a pile of war tactics for its stellar record as a means of producing intelligence; rather, torture emerged from a broader set of beliefs about the efficacy of policies that many have considered too harsh or unjust to be an accepted practice.

Playing Down the Damage: The Lack of Specificity Argument

The memos that authorized the CIA to use torture focus on downsizing the definition of torture and portraying the CIA's favored methods as mild, thereby creating distance between the acts and their (correct) label. To be sure, Yoo's memo to Gonzales in August 2002 also tries to include blanket permission for the president to use torture as anyone would define it. The justification for this was a controversial reading of the power that the U.S. Constitution grants to the president during a time of war. Yoo conditions the allowance on the severity of the threat, leading to a legalistic defense based on necessity.[18] While provocative, the thrust of the OLC memos from August 2002 is about why almost all of the CIA's proposed acts did *not* constitute torture. Yoo's memos are a clinic on how to take advantage of the torture norm's lack of specificity, both in redefining torture and in emphasizing the limited nature of the proposed techniques.

As Noah Feldman (2005) explains, "In order to expand the range of coercive tactics that could lawfully be used against suspected terrorists, [government lawyers] pared down the legal definition of torture to the barest minimum." The definition of torture in U.S. Code's Section 2340–2340A under title 18, the one that criminalizes torture outside the United States, echoes the UN's Convention against Torture: torture consists of "severe physical or mental pain or suffering" in both. Yoo calls this the "key statutory phrase." He writes, "Section 2340 makes plain that the infliction of pain or suffering per se, whether it is physical or mental, is insufficient to amount to torture. Instead, the text provides that pain or suffering must be 'severe.' The statute does not, however, define the term 'severe'" (Bybee 2002a, 5). This is Yoo's opening. He asserts that in order to qualify as severe pain, "The victim must experience intense pain or suffering of the kind that is equivalent to the pain that would be associated with serious physical injury so severe that death, organ failure, or permanent damage resulting in a loss of significant body function will likely result." When the statute clarifies "severe mental pain or suffering" as meaning "prolonged" harm, "it must result in significant psychological harm of significant duration, e.g., lasting for months or even years" (Bybee 2002a, 1). The section on torture's definition concludes, "In short, reading the definition of torture as a whole, it is plain that the term encompasses *only* extreme acts" (13, emphasis added). The use of "only" is almost a confession of what Mayerfeld (2016, 123) calls a "vanishingly narrow definition of the word 'torture.'"

Given this approach to torture's definition, it is unsurprising that the OLC approved nearly every technique the CIA requested. The memos that cover the techniques, which draw heavily on the CIA's reassurances, fuss over details in an effort to downplay the negative effects. The memos sound remarkably similar to the court-martial defendants from the Philippine-American War. When a detainee is slammed against a wall, he won't suffer injury because the wall is "flexible." For the facial slap, "the goal . . . is not to inflict physical pain that is severe or lasting. Instead, the purpose of the facial slap is to induce shock, surprise, and/or humiliation." Stress positions are "not designed to produce pain," only "muscle fatigue." The effects of extensive sleep deprivation "will remit after a few good nights of sleep." Even the waterboard will not "result in any physical harm" or have "long-term mental health consequences" (Bybee 2002b, 2–6). These methods would merely "dislocate his [in this case, Zubaydah's] expectations regarding the treatment he believes he will receive" (1–2).

In memos to the OLC, the CIA and its contractors stressed that they would wield the techniques with a regulated and limited hand. Mitchell and Jessen wrote, "[A]ny physical pressure applied to extremes can cause severe mental pain or suffering. Hooding, the use of loud music, sleep deprivation, controlling darkness and light, slapping, walling (slamming a prisoner into a loud, flexible wall), or the use of stress positions taken to extreme[s] can have the same outcome. The safety of any technique lies primarily in how it is applied and monitored" (quoted in U.S. Senate Select Committee on Intelligence 2014, 36). It's difficult to know the extent to which Mitchell and Jessen believed their own rhetoric. In any case, the contractors' view that their techniques could be sold as something less than torture, by describing degrees of severity that their methods would not exceed, underscores the importance of torture's blurry definition in justifying harsh methods before and while they were occurring.

The coercive techniques' origins as part of SERE training, like other "We tried it ourselves" justifications detailed in the previous two chapters, also allowed practitioners and lawyers to portray the methods as acceptable. The OLC memos discuss at length how the SERE training has had little or no long-term adverse consequences for trainees:

> These same techniques, with the exception of the insect in the cramped confined space, have been used and continue to be used on some members of our military personnel during their SERE training. Because of the use of these procedures in training our own military personnel to resist interrogations, you [the CIA and contractors] have consulted with various individuals who have extensive experience in the use of these techniques. You have done so in order to ensure that no prolonged mental harm would result from the use of these proposed procedures. Through your consultation with various individuals responsible for such training, you have learned that these techniques have been used as elements of a course of conduct without any reported incident of prolonged mental harm. (Bybee 2002b, 4)

The memo makes plain that the CIA played up the SERE training roots in order to play down the severity of the techniques. A *New York Times* investigation sums up the CIA's and the administration's thinking on the matter: "The program began with Central Intelligence Agency leaders in the grip of an alluring idea: They could get tough in terrorist interrogations without risking legal trouble by adopting a set of methods used on Americans during military training. How could that be torture?" (Shane and Mazzetti 2009).

After the OLC released the August 2002 memos, military officers in Guantánamo Bay were seeking harsher interrogation methods. In October 2002, CIA lawyer Jonathan Fredman attended a Counter Resistance Strategy Meeting with Guantánamo officials. According to the minutes of that meeting, Fredman assured his military counterparts that most things short of killing a detainee would be allowable:

> Under the Torture Convention, torture has been prohibited by international law, but the language of the statutes is written vaguely. Severe mental and physical pain is prohibited. The mental part is explained as poorly as the physical. Severe physical pain is described as anything causing permanent damage to major organs or body parts. Mental torture is described as anything leading to permanent, profound damage to the senses or personality. *It is basically subject to perception. If the detainee dies, you're doing it wrong.* Any of the techniques that lie on the harshest end of the spectrum must be performed by a highly trained individual. Medical personnel should be present to treat any possible accidents. (U.S. Army 2002, 3, emphasis added)

The death of a detainee, in Fredman's view, would be an absolute, difficult to minimize. But short of causing death, the proposed methods are subjective, open to interpretation. This is the opportunity that Fredman and the Guantánamo interrogators saw in the "vague" language of the statute.

A few years later, Bush would use the same word—"vague"—at a press conference to describe the language in treaties to which the United States was supposed to adhere:

> QUESTION: What do you say to the argument that your proposal is basically seeking support for torture, coerced evidence and secret hearings? . . .
> BUSH: Common Article 3 [of the Geneva Conventions] says that, you know, there will be no outrages upon human dignity. That's like—it's very vague. What does that mean, "outrages upon human dignity"? That's a statement that is wide open to interpretation. And what I am proposing is that there be clarity in the law so that our professionals will have no doubt that that which they are doing is legal. (CQ Transcriptions 2006)

The Bush administration took advantage of what it saw as vagueness to interpret Geneva as it saw fit.

If it had looked, the administration would have found some comfort in its "sliding scale" approach to harsh interrogation from certain members of the press, even some self-described "liberals." In November 2001, Jonathan Alter of *Time* wrote:

In this autumn of anger, even a liberal can find his thoughts turning to . . . torture. OK, not cattle prods or rubber hoses, at least not here in the United States, but *something* to jump-start the stalled investigation of the greatest crime in American history. Couldn't we at least subject them to psychological torture, like tapes of dying rabbits or high-decibel rap? (The military has done that in Panama and elsewhere.) How about truth serum, administered with a mandatory IV? Or deportation to Saudi Arabia, land of beheadings? . . . We can't legalize physical torture; it's contrary to American values. But even as we continue to speak out against human-rights abuses around the world, we need to keep an open mind about certain measures to fight terrorism, like court-sanctioned psychological interrogation. And we'll have to think about transferring some suspects to our less squeamish allies.

Alter wasn't alone in the press in believing that the post-9/11 world called for harsh but limited interrogation. After details began to leak of the Bush administration's torture program, *Atlantic* correspondent Mark Bowden (2003, 76) applauded the administration's approach:

The Bush Administration has adopted exactly the right posture on the matter. Candor and consistency are not always public virtues. Torture is a crime against humanity, but coercion is an issue that is rightly handled with a wink, or even a touch of hypocrisy; it should be banned but also quietly practiced. Those who protest coercive methods will exaggerate their horrors, which is good: it generates a useful climate of fear. It is wise of the President to reiterate U.S. support for international agreements banning torture, and it is wise for American interrogators to employ whatever coercive methods work. It is also smart not to discuss the matter with anyone. If interrogators step over the line from coercion to outright torture, they should be held personally responsible. But no interrogator is ever going to be prosecuted for keeping Khalid Sheikh Mohammed awake, cold, alone, and uncomfortable. Nor should he be.

(Nor has he been to date, we might now add after eighteen years.)

Even when news of Zubaydah suffering the waterboard was made public, Bowden did not back down. He continued to use the same "continuum of coercion" logic to excuse the Bush administration's choices:

> Waterboarding is a process by which a detainee is strapped down and forced to ingest and inhale water until he experiences the terror of drowning. It is not torture in the traditional sense of inflicting pain; it inflicts fear, intense, visceral fear, without doing physical harm. It is a method calculated to straddle the definitions of coercion and torture, and as such merely proves that both methods inhabit the same slippery continuum. There is a difference between gouging out a man's eyes and keeping him awake, and waterboarding falls somewhere in between. (Bowden 2007)

It's unclear whether these journalists had any causal impact on the Bush administration's choices. The quotes do show, however, that when the Bush administration was ready to sell its methods as stopping short of torture, it had some sympathetic audience members.

In the aftermath of the Bush administration's policies, Yoo (2006, 44) suggests that detainees were treated "humanely":

> The White House released a list of the conditions provided to the detainees, including adequate food, clothing, housing, shelter, medical care, and the right to practice their religion. I witnessed these humane standards myself at Gitmo. . . . Some detainees received the first modern medical and dental care of their lives. To be sure, conditions were not those of a hotel. . . . [However,] U.S. armed forces were ordered to treat the al Qaeda and Taliban humanely, and they did so admirably.

Yoo conveniently skips the fact that detainees were denied sleep for as much as a week, or air for as much as forty seconds, in his discussion of what constitutes humane treatment. Meals delivered rectally without medical necessity could hardly count as humane, either.[19]

Yoo's insinuation that the detainees were receiving the best medical care of their lives uses another version of favorable comparison: a contrast with the supposedly squalid conditions of the detainee's life before capture. Gen. Janis Karpinski, commander at Abu Ghraib, said in an interview, "[L]iving conditions now are better in prison than at home. At one point we were concerned that they wouldn't want to leave" (quoted in Otterman 2007, 165). Justifications like these enabled harsher treatment.

Cheney took favorable comparisons to a ridiculous extreme in an interview following the release of the Senate report. When NBC's Chuck Todd asked him to define torture, he said:

Well, torture, to me, Chuck, is an American citizen on a cell phone making a last call to his four young daughters shortly before he burns to death in the upper levels of the Trade Center in New York City on 9/11. There's this notion that somehow there's moral equivalence between what the terrorists do and what we do. And that's absolutely not true. We were very careful to stop short of torture. The Senate has seen fit to label their report torture. But we worked hard to stay short of that definition. (NBC News 2014)

Cheney had obviously given up on producing any legalistic distinction at that point and tried for a sort of shock-effect comparison; the result is absurd. But in a sense, Cheney is right about the Bush administration's efforts: it did try to "stop short of torture," and it did so by defining torture in the narrowest way and showing how almost anything can be justified under such a definition.

The "Enhanced Interrogation" Middle Ground

If the Bush administration did not use the word "torture" to describe its methods, what did it call them? The phrases they picked—"enhanced interrogation," "robust interrogation," "special interrogation" (Mayer 2008, 151)—are telling. They contain my two main explanations simultaneously. Take "enhanced interrogation techniques," the euphemistic term for the CIA's torture program that was used commonly enough to warrant an acronym, EITs. Andrew Sullivan translated the phrase as "torture-that-isn't-somehow-torture."[20] Those in the administration who used the phrase clearly wanted to separate the techniques from the torture label, thus playing down the severity of the acts.[21]

Simultaneously, the euphemism alludes to the effectiveness and the severity of the methods. To "enhance" means to intensify, and also to improve. The enhanced interrogation techniques, then, were more intense and more effective than standard methods, or so the Bush administration would have us believe. But they were not quite torture, the administration claimed. They occupied the idealized middle ground. As one lawyer who wrote the guidelines for a more coercive military interrogation program put it, "We wanted to find a legal way to jack up the pressure.... We wanted a little more freedom than in a U.S. prison, but not torture" (Priest and Stephens 2004).

Bush himself reached for this middle ground when he first acknowledged the CIA program in 2006 and began to sell it to the public. He starts with another euphemistic phrase for the approved torture methods:

> The CIA used an *alternative set of procedures*. These procedures were designed to be safe, to comply with our laws, our Constitution, and our treaty obligations. The Department of Justice reviewed the authorized methods extensively and determined them to be lawful. I cannot describe the specific methods used—I think you understand why—if I did, it would help the terrorists learn how to resist questioning, and to keep information from us that we need to prevent new attacks on our country. But I can say the procedures were *tough*, and they were safe, and lawful, and *necessary*. (Bush 2006, emphasis added)[22]

Taking together the italicized words from the last sentence, the procedures were tough and necessary. That is, it was necessary to be tough. But the CIA was not out of control. The procedures were also limited and legal. (See Figure 6.1 for an illustration.) Yoo (2006, 44) would back up Bush's claims the same year with similar reasoning in his book: "President Bush chose the right policy, one that provided the United States with flexibility to develop the rules that should apply to the new enemy of global terrorism, but which, in treating the enemy humanely, maintained American values."

Cheney (2008) used a similar tactic in defending the CIA program in a speech to the Conservative Political Action Conference:

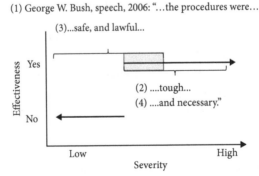

Figure 6.1 Bush seeks a middle ground on the (perceived) severity spectrum.

[A] small number of terrorists, high-value targets, held overseas have gone through an interrogation program run by the CIA. It's a tougher program, for tougher customers. (Applause.) These include Khalid Sheikh Mohammed, the mastermind of 9/11. He and others were questioned at a time when another attack on this country was believed to be imminent. It's a good thing we had them in custody, and it's a good thing we found out what they knew. (Applause.)

The procedures of the CIA program are designed to be safe, and they are in full compliance with the nation's laws and treaty obligations. They've been carefully reviewed by the Department of Justice, and very carefully monitored. The program is run by highly trained professionals who understand their obligations under the law. And the program has uncovered a wealth of information that has foiled attacks against the United States; information that has saved thousands of lives. (Applause.)

The United States is a country that takes human rights seriously. We do not torture—it's against our laws and against our values. We're proud of our country and what it stands for. We expect all of those who serve America to conduct themselves with honor.[23]

The United States needed this "tougher program," according to Cheney. But because of the wiggle room that Cheney saw in coercive interrogation, he believed that he could at least sell the idea that the United States could adopt this set of techniques and still be a country that "takes human rights seriously."

We can find limited support for a richer model of perceived effectiveness. In his memoir, Bush (2010, 169) recalls that "the choice between security and values was real," which may indicate a direct trade-off between severity and effectiveness over the full range of options. It is difficult to determine how Bush felt about the relative utility of methods outside the targeted middle ground, however. He asserts that he would not allow two of the CIA's requested techniques because he believed they went too far, but he does not say whether he was forgoing even more effectiveness in doing so. He holds that even the methods that were deemed too brutal were still legal, giving the administration a kind of buffer of acceptability, while admitting some compromise on values, ostensibly for the greater good. At the limits of his comfort, Bush found waterboarding to be sufficiently "tough" but likely to result in "no lasting harm" (169).[24]

The CIA contractors preferred their middle-ground methods to all other forms for hardened detainees, as shown in Figure 6.2. They praised sleep deprivation and walling as good tools for "conditioning" detainees (Mitchell 2016, 235). Their contention that waterboarding was an "absolutely convincing" technique suggests that they believed there would not be much more to be gained by pushing into the realm of torture that scars and maims. In subsequent statements, they recommended methods "between waterboarding and worse, and what is in the Army Field Manual. There has to be some legal form of coercion" (Altman 2016). They have also indicated some concern that overly harsh or poorly timed coercion could incapacitate the detainee in ways that hurt intelligence gathering. In early 2020, Mitchell testified that he expressed concern to CIA headquarters in August 2002 that Zubaydah's health was "likely to deteriorate to unacceptable levels" if the harshest phase of the program continued (Borger 2020). In his memoir, Mitchell (2016, 231) also expresses disdain for the "stupid and self-indulgent activities" shown in the Abu Ghraib photographs.

The CIA contractors' alleged abhorrence of other abusive behaviors may be more politically convenient than true. It could also be the case that the contractors, like their early Cold War predecessors at the CIA, believed that their "scientific" approach was in all ways superior to more severe interrogations. As part of a deposition for a civil trial filed against the psychologists, Mitchell said that his aim was to introduce some learned helplessness to the detainees, but not so much that memory loss or a dramatic breakdown would result. Although Mitchell complained that some CIA agents wanted to take things too far, Jose Rodriguez (2012, 64),

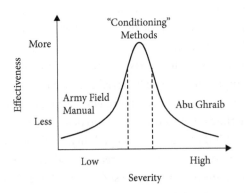

Figure 6.2 CIA contractors' beliefs about interrogation methods during the war on terror.

head of the CIA Counterterrorism Center, sounds a similar note in his memoir: "Detainees were brought to a point of cooperation when they concluded that the hopelessness of their situation could end only by cooperating," which the CIA endeavored to produce "with the least amount of discomfort because gratuitous pain is counterproductive." Mitchell, his partners, and his employers may well have found solace in the belief that their approach was both more ethical and more effective because they thought they were calibrating the force used, even if they were wrong, and even if they disagreed among themselves exactly how far they should push (Salim et al. v. Mitchell et al. 2017, 108, 287–88).

Alternative Explanations

Democratic Restraints and Monitoring

Coming into the office of the vice presidency, Cheney already had strong beliefs about the importance of shifting the balance of power away from the legislature and in favor of the executive branch. As noted in the previous chapter, he viewed congressional oversight during the Ford administration as unwarranted encroachment that threatened to hamper the CIA's intelligence-gathering capabilities. He also railed against congressional overreach both as a member of Congress during the Iran-Contra Affair and afterward (Cheney et al. 1987; Cheney 1989). He brought this conviction back to the executive branch during Bush's two terms: "White House officials said Cheney's long-held constitutional views fit well with Bush's determination to show a strength his father was accused of lacking. This would not be a 'prudent,' compromising White House, and Bush would not disparage, as his father had, 'the vision thing.' A bold presidency called for bold use of power.... [T]he vice president pushed on an open door with Bush" (Gellman 2008, ch. 4).

The September 2001 attacks presented a substantial opportunity for Cheney, and increasingly Bush, to see this vision through. The rally-around-the-flag effect was considerable. Bush was soon enjoying a 90% approval rating after the attacks (Gallup 2016). Congress was not in a strong position, or a mood, to deny the executive branch much in the way of capabilities. It passed several sweeping pieces of legislation with near-unanimity, including authorization of force: "[T]he President is authorized to use all necessary and appropriate force against those nations, organizations, or persons he determines planned, authorized, committed, or aided the terrorist attacks that occurred on September 11, 2001, or harbored such organizations or persons, in order to prevent any future acts of international terrorism against the United States by such nations, organizations or persons" (U.S. Congress 2001). This was the legal language behind the amorphous "war on terror." The OLC also penned a memo in 2001 arguing that the president had "broad constitutional power" to wage war with minimal interference (Yoo 2005).

Congress had little knowledge or oversight of the administration's interrogation programs. The Senate report emphasizes all the ways in which the CIA did not inform Congress; the CIA responds by trumpeting all the ways in which it did. Still, the CIA confesses that it withheld details, especially early on: "We disagree with the [Senate] Study's conclusion that the Agency actively impeded Congressional oversight of the CIA detention and interrogation program. We believe the record demonstrates that CIA leaders made a good faith effort to keep oversight committee leaders fully briefed on the program *within the strict limits on access that had been set by the White House*" (Central Intelligence Agency 2013, emphasis added). More congressional oversight would likely have spelled less torture. This is why CIA legal counsel John Rizzo, in an interview, discussed "scaling the program back and . . . bringing more members of Congress into it" in the same breath (Moughty 2015).

Torturers were not just worried about their own government finding out; they also feared backlash from media and public opinion in other countries in the near term, even if some were resigned to the idea that the news would get out eventually (Moughty 2015). Cofer Black, in a memo to Director Tenet, addressed the risks associated with the CIA maintaining a detention facility: "As captured terrorists may be held days, months, or years, the likelihood of exposure will grow over time. . . . Media exposure could inflame public opinion against a host government and the US, thereby threatening the continued operation of the facility" (U.S. Senate, Select Committee on Intelligence 2014, 12).

Army legal advisor Diane Beaver also feared monitoring by human rights groups at Guantánamo Bay. At the Counter Resistance Strategy Meeting, Beaver explained, "We may need to curb the harsher operations while ICRC [International Committee of the Red Cross] is around. It is better not to expose them to any controversial techniques. . . . The ICRC is a serious concern. They will be in and out, scrutinizing our operations, unless they are displeased and decide to protest and leave. This would draw a lot of negative attention" (U.S. Army 2002, 3). Beaver would go on to write a legal memo for the army arguing that a number of proposed harsh interrogations would be legal. Apparently she doubted whether the ICRC would agree, and she believed that the consequences of ICRC contact would be detrimental and maybe fatal to the continuation of the program. Moreover, the connection Beaver made between the ICRC and "negative attention" implies that she was worried about wider exposure, under the assumption that more attention would be more constraining.

Beaver turned out to be right: wider circles of people with knowledge of the interrogation program led to less torture. For starters, the number of lawyers influencing the interrogation policy grew. When more lawyers from the Departments of Defense and State weighed in, the torture policy began to fade (Nuñez-Mietz 2013). Also consequential were the Abu Ghraib revelations. Christophe Girod, who led Washington's ICRC office, "said that the revelations about Abu Ghraib had an enormous impact, including at Guantánamo. 'After Abu Ghraib, everything changed,' he said. 'It was an awakening, media-wise and political-wise'" (Hutchinson et al. 2013, 55). Monitoring reduced torture.

Neither the Abu Ghraib incident nor the leak of torture memos in 2004 cost Bush the election later that year, however. While elections are about a lot of things, national security played a prominent role at the time, and the public was not sufficiently disgusted with Bush to oust him, despite the revelations. For some voters, the unveiling may have helped build a case that Bush was tough on terrorism. One 2004 exit poll shows that voters who were more concerned about terrorism than any other issue broke for Bush over Kerry, 86 to 14% (CNN.com 2004). U.S. public opinion polls indicate some tolerance for torture, too. Gronke and Rejali (2010) look at public opinion polls from the Bush years and find that support for torture is low, but their measurement conflates the responses "torture is rarely justified" and "torture is never justified" into a single category. Perhaps those who thought torture was rarely justified also believed that detainees like KSM, a key figure in the 9/11 attacks, were just the sort of characters for whom a government's rare right to torture should be preserved. If so, torture of KSM would have received majority support. Thus, while the military, the CIA, and the Bush administration in general certainly did not welcome exposure, politicians did not seem to pay a price for voter knowledge of the torture program.

Desperation

To show the terrorist threat has been overblown since 2001, John Mueller (2006, 2) has collected examples of alarmism over Al Qaeda's next moves following the 9/11 attacks:

> In 2003, a group of 200 senior government officials and business executives, many of them specialists in security and terrorism, pronounced it likely that a terrorist strike more devastating than 9/11—possibly involving weapons of mass destruction—would occur before the end of 2004. In May 2004, Attorney General John Ashcroft warned that al Qaeda could "hit hard" in the next few months and said that 90 percent of the arrangements for an attack on U.S. soil were complete. . . . On the first page of its founding manifesto, the massively funded Department of Homeland Security intones, "Today's terrorists can strike at any place, at any time, and with virtually any weapon."

It's not hard to imagine desperation springing from such scary estimates. Perhaps most surprisingly, Mueller's examples come at least a year after the September 2001 attacks. The mood right after the attacks was, if anything, more desperate.

The first chapter of Jane Mayer's (2008) book on torture during the war on terror is aptly titled "Panic." Directly following September 11, political leaders believed that another attack was likely, and that they were probably the next targets. According to Roger Cressey, who led the Terrorist Threats Sub-Group of the National Security Council, "They thought they were going to get hit again. They convinced themselves that they were facing a ticking time bomb. . . . I firmly expected to get hit again too. It seemed highly probable." Another former administration official called the anthrax incidents of October 2001 "really, really scary. They thought Cheney was already lethally infected." Although Cheney never had the reputation of a cuddly teddy bear, after September 11 a family friend described him as "more steely, as if he was preoccupied by terrible things he couldn't talk about." Lawrence Wilkerson, a critic of much of the war on terror policies, said, "Cheney was traumatized by 9/11. The poor guy became paranoid." Part of the problem was that Cheney and Bush wanted to see raw intelligence reports. The stream of threats that these reports contained made people "paranoid" and sowed the seeds for an extreme response, even though much of it was "garbage," according to

Cressey (all quoted in Mayer 2008, 2–6). The genesis of the torture program, therefore, "was very much in the context of the threat streams that were just eye-popping at the time" (quoted in Shane and Mazzetti 2009).

Tenet (2007, 497), who as CIA director saw plenty of incoming intelligence, was one of several administration officials to make the reflective desperation case:

> We at CIA engaged in such a debate from the beginning, struggling to determine what was required to protect a just society at so much risk. But from where we sat, in the late summer of 2003, preventing the death of American citizens was paramount. It is easy to second-guess us today, but difficult to understand the intensity of our concerns when we made certain decisions and the urgency we felt to protect the country.

Tenet takes for granted a "tension" between "protecting Americans" and "how [the CIA] might be perceived years after the trauma of 9/11 had faded from the nation's memory" (497).

While desperation may have been a necessary ingredient in the creation of a torture program, it was not a sufficient one. For instance, the FBI interrogators, who mostly did not embrace torture, were just as committed to gathering intelligence as CIA officials and other government agents who did. Moreover, desperation for intelligence can drive officials to search high and low for the most experienced interrogators, but the Bush administration chose willingness to push limits as its chief criterion for selecting the agency to lead the interrogations of the most valuable detainees. Without an understanding of key individuals' beliefs, it is unclear where desperation will lead.

Organizational Culture

Michael Hayden, the CIA director when the Bush administration finally acknowledged the agency's coercive interrogation program in 2006, spoke to a group of foreign ambassadors about the program: "This is not CIA's program. This is not the President's program. This is America's program."[25] Was he right? Or was the torture program a narrow product of the CIA's organizational culture, containing a certain attitude toward illicit activities forged at the agency's founding?

Certainly, some of the creative content of the program came from the CIA. John Rizzo claims as much: "I was the first lawyer inside the government to hear about this proposed interrogation program. It was a creature of CIA.... This was something our people came up with, this proposed program" (Moughty 2015). Yet just because CIA agents dreamed up the plan does not mean that torture was embedded in the CIA's culture. It may have felt like a creative venture because the CIA had not done anything of the sort recently. Although the CIA obviously had a history with coercive interrogation, the war on terror led to a definite shift (Blakeley 2011; U.S. Senate, Select Committee on Intelligence 2014, 19). The agency had not had its own program since the Cold War. The only recent connection to torture had been extraordinary rendition, which the Bush administration expanded (as mentioned earlier). As for the in-house program, the CIA was not "torture-ready." It had to seek outside sources. FBI interrogator Ali Soufan (2009a) claims that the contractors were more to blame for harsh interrogations than mid- and lower-level CIA agents.[26] FBI documents from April 2002 suggest a sea change with the arrival of the contracted psychologists at Abu Zubaydah's detention site, comporting with Soufan's recollections (U.S. Senate, Select Committee on Intelligence 2014, 26–27). Even within the sub-department put in charge of interrogation, three CIA agents approached by the leadership refused to be trained in the enhanced techniques (Rejali 2007).[27] The CIA needed personnel changes and outside expertise in order to marry torture to their existing structure and know-how.

Since the details of the CIA's interrogation program were unveiled, several current and former CIA officials have come forward to either condemn the acts, describe a different CIA than the one under the Bush administration, or both. Robert Baer told ABC News that torture is "bad interrogation": "I mean you can get anyone to confess to anything if the torture's bad enough" (Ross and Esposito 2005). Another former CIA officer, Larry Johnson (2005), wrote in the Los Angeles Times after talking with other former CIA members, "What real CIA field officers know firsthand is that it is better to build a relationship of trust—even with a terrorist, even if it's time-consuming—than to extract quick confessions through tactics such as those used by the Nazis and the Soviets, who believed that national security always trumped human rights." Former CIA officer and inspector general Fred Hitz had a similar view of the wider culture of the CIA: "If there is support for this kind of torturous behavior in the Agency, it's not the Agency I remember" (Spannaus 2006). These former agents joined the CIA after most of the early Cold War behavioral control experimentation was over. This is not to say that the CIA did not have defenders of the harsh interrogation program—it did, and it still does—but the evidence casts doubt on the idea that the CIA's culture was a primary factor in determining national policy, because the agency has housed plenty of dissent. In light of this, it is not surprising that many in the agency *opposed* the CIA exemption that the Bush administration pushed into the Military Commissions Act, a law that banned the use of harsh interrogations for other agencies (Hosenball and Isikoff 2006).[28]

If a culture of torture developed in certain corners of the bureaucracy, it was because higher-ups in the administration fostered an atmosphere ripe for transgressions through the creation of new agencies and by promoting certain individuals. CIA contractor Mitchell was given security clearances to go with legal affirmations until he could personally administer the waterboard to high-value detainees (Leopold 2014). Within the military, Rumsfeld created the Special Access Program (SAP) to conduct secret operations and harsh interrogations because he thought the military leadership was too cautious; members of SAP were behind some of the abuses at Abu Ghraib (Hersh 2004a). Given these beginnings, it is hard to imagine a culture developing within SAP that did not condone torture.

The example of Maj. Gen. Geoffrey Miller shows how the development of torture cultures was sometimes rooted in the administration's conviction that cheaters win. Miller, who presided over harsh interrogations at Guantánamo Bay, was transferred to Iraq to "Gitmo-ize" the Abu Ghraib prison (White and Higham 2004)—that is, to bring torture techniques from Guantánamo to Abu Ghraib. He told interrogators in Iraq that they were being too lenient (Hutchinson et al. 2013, 398). Like the Bush administration, Miller derived the effectiveness of techniques in part from their proximity to the laws. Regarding the use of extreme temperatures for interrogation, Miller once declared, "If the Torture Statute says 80 degrees is bad, we will set the thermometer at 79.9 degrees" (quoted in Mayer 2008, 203). For Miller, "bad" was good. Evidently, the Bush administration liked this approach.

Revenge and Racism

Many of the signs that revenge motivated post-9/11 policies like torture do not quite qualify as strong evidence: Bush's announcement in downtown Manhattan that "the people who knocked these buildings down will hear all of us soon," and the resulting roar of the crowd (Walsh 2013); the twinkle in Bush's eye as he declared that some terrorists "are no longer a problem to the United States and our friends and allies" (presumably because they've been killed or "disappeared") (Bush 2003); Cheney's half-smile (or smirk?) as he described the CIA interrogation program to a group of conservatives, followed by enthusiastic applause (Cheney 2008). These examples are suggestive, but not conclusive. It is difficult to measure a twinkle or a smirk and firmly deducing its meaning.

We can find a clearer demonstration of revenge in Cheney's choice of words when he talked about detainee treatment in terms of what they did and did not "deserve": "They don't deserve to be treated as a prisoner of war. They don't deserve the same guarantees and safeguards that would be used for an American citizen going through the normal judicial process." Cheney pushed for military commissions with limited rights for terrorism suspects, explaining, "We think it guarantees that we'll have the kind of treatment of these individuals that we believe they deserve" (Bumiller and Myers 2001).[29] In early 2002, he claimed that Guantánamo detainees were being treated "better than they deserve" (BBC News 2002). Off-the-cuff estimates of what terrorists "deserve" are likely to be characterized by revenge. If intelligence is the primary concern, what a detainee deserves is rather beside the point.

Cofer Black made some exclamations that sounded vengeful bordering on creepy. He told two agents shortly after 9/11, "I want bin Laden's head shipped back in a box filled with dry ice. . . . I want to be able to show bin Laden's head to the president" (Levenson 2007). To convince the White House about the merits of his plan for pursuing Al Qaeda, Black said, "When we're through with them, they will have flies walking across their eyeballs," after which he "became known in Bush's inner circle as 'the flies-on-the-eyeballs guy'" (Woodward 2002, 52). It is difficult to imagine such theatrical utterances without some motivation for revenge.

The actual treatment of detainees suggests that revenge probably played a role. Although such observations mix up dependent and independent variables, the sheer number of times Zubaydah and KSM were subjected to the waterboard makes revenge a likely influence (Mayerfeld 2016, 138). The alternative, in which an interrogation team calmly and coolly administers the waterboard to a single individual 183 times in a month, is less plausible, even if turning up the heat on a detainee is consistent with a more-is-more logic of coercion. A sense of frustration distinct from revenge—perhaps with intelligence yields?—may have played a role as well.[30]

Racism was less blatant in this case than in previous ones, as one might expect. A U.S. military interrogator in Afghanistan, who took up the pseudonym "Chris Mackey" when he returned, feared that he and his fellow interrogators might come to resemble soldiers in previous wars:

> Mackey wondered how [increasing levels of] hostility would affect his work as an interrogator, and how the antagonistic environment would generally alter his troops' outlook and behavior toward their detainees. "It made me wonder sometimes whether we were becoming like the troops in Vietnam who had become so prejudiced against the 'gooks' and 'slopes' and 'Charlie,'" he mused. (Phillips 2012, 36)

Mackey suspected that he and other soldiers were entering a nasty spiral in which hostility bred racism and racism in turn inspired more hostility, with torture as one of the symptoms. But he was even more aware of the dangers of racism than were U.S. soldiers in Vietnam, who in turn were more cognizant of their own racist tendencies than the U.S. Army in the Philippines. Awareness does not nullify racism, but it may be the first step toward its reduction, and it suggests that the feelings may not have been as strong in the later war.

Revenge and racism were probably behind the excesses at Abu Ghraib. According to Sgt. Ken Davis, "People were being told to rough up Iraqis that wouldn't cooperate. We were also told they're nothing but dogs. You start looking at these people as less than human, and you start doing things to them you would never dream of. And that's where it got scary" (Gibney 2007). Interrogations in Iraq and Afghanistan were not initially divorced from a real need for intelligence, but, as with the CIA's repeated use of the waterboard, anger and dehumanization sometimes took a front seat even when they were only lurking at the beginning.

Still, racism and revenge cannot be the whole story. Bush administration members had to be interested in intelligence, too. Even the most uncharitable view of the administration members would still expect them to want to save themselves, and the panic they felt after September 11 reflected their conviction that they could be the next victims. Moreover, the administration's interest in connecting Saddam Hussein to the 9/11 attacks represented intelligence-skewing practices that are not unusual among executives. Robert Jervis (2010) demonstrates with numerous examples that the Bush administration was no less interested in accurate intelligence than its predecessors were. Using the CIA, the Bush administration saved its harshest tactics for those detainees that it thought were guarding the war on terror's most important secrets. Racism and revenge cannot account for the connection between torture and intelligence without help from other theories.

Summary

In an effort to sort through the debate between the CIA and the 2014 Senate report authors, Jervis (2015) has criticism for both sides. Regarding the CIA, he argues, "[A] Goldilocks view of the CIA's interrogations—that they were not so cruel as to constitute torture but just harsh enough to compel hardened terrorists to divulge critical intelligence—seems too convenient to be true." Jervis is right that this belief may not be true, but it was convenient—and consequential.

The desperation that key actors felt, especially in the months and years following September 2001, conditioned responses as well. But desperation did not lead inexorably to torture. Surely the FBI was very interested in intelligence, too, but their interrogators were not as persuaded that nastier meant more effective. Certain elements of the CIA and the military *were* convinced, however, and the Bush administration picked them to lead interrogation efforts, even if it meant choosing away from experience.

From the beginning, the Bush administration looked to take advantage of the antitorture norm's lack of specificity by quibbling over technique details, narrowly defining torture, using euphemisms, self-application, and promises of careful control. This line of defense did not end with Bush's second term. Even after the Senate report revealed that the CIA had used rectal rehydration without medical necessity, Obama's director of central intelligence, John Brennan, who was in the CIA through the Bush years, thought he could still play ignorant on the question of whether the agency's tactics had amounted to torture (Mazzetti and Apuzzo 2014). By contrast, imagine a political leader in the mid-1950s claiming that he was not sure whether the Hiroshima and Nagasaki bombs were really of an atomic character. Some acts are amenable to gray area justifications and pleas of ignorance, either feigned or real, and some are not.

7

Conclusion

Takeaways, Scope, and Torture's Future

When faced with a security problem, political actors usually want to be both tough and ethical. Sometimes they believe that being tough requires not always adhering to what many view as appropriate behavior. But these same actors rarely want to commit blatantly egregious acts. As a result, they shoot for a middle ground, the common area between what they perceive to be widely acceptable and what they believe to be effective. This middle ground might not truly exist, but the promise of a best-of-both-worlds scenario can be hard to resist.

So it was with torture in this book's three cases. In the Philippine-American War, American soldiers claimed that Filipinos would divulge information only if they were "pressured" or "frightened," but they also claimed that the "water cure" and other favored methods did not cause "pain" or "permanent damage." In the early Cold War, some policymakers were convinced that they would have to compromise liberal values at least surreptitiously in order to take on the Communists, who were not similarly bound. CIA agents developed, tested, and, during the Vietnam War, used interrogation practices that they reassured themselves were sufficiently, but not excessively, coercive. Finally, during the war on terror, politicians and bureaucrats were convinced that standard interrogation tactics would not suffice, but they did not want to do something brazenly illegal, either. Accordingly, well-placed lawyers minimized the definition of torture to make room for "enhanced interrogation techniques," which practitioners and supporters touted to be both safe and effective.

My argument does not provide a complete account on its own. Desperation played a key, if indeterminate, role in all three cases, and was especially pronounced in the early Cold War and in the years following September 11, 2001. Racism and dehumanization are important permissive causes in all three cases, most obviously in the Philippines and Vietnam, even if they do not explain the torture-intelligence connection. Organizational (sub)

American Torture from the Philippines to Iraq. William L. d'Ambruoso, Oxford University Press. © Oxford University Press 2022. DOI: 10.1093/oso/9780197570326.003.0007

cultures condoning and even promoting torture developed perhaps most vividly, but not exclusively, in the CIA cases. Anger and revenge probably best explain the U.S. military's use of torture in Vietnam. And surely some of the torture from all three cases was kept stealthy, with the goal of keeping the deeds hidden, not just more widely acceptable. My argument picks up where these accounts leave off, explaining why actors believe torture works, and why the antitorture norm has not driven torture to extinction even when the act is likely to be exposed.

To conclude, I will elaborate on the contributions that this study makes. Then I will examine the generalizability and limits of the central arguments. Finally, I will consider the future of the norm against torture and whether we might expect a continuation of this book's key observations.

Takeaways

This book contains at least four main takeaways. First, the antitorture norm has had persistent lack-of-specificity problems. CIA dissenter Glenn Carle (2014), in response to the Bush administration's redefinition of torture, writes, "I was stunned. This undermined 800 years of Western law, from the Magna Carta to the Geneva Conventions." Perhaps so, but his framing makes it sound like the Bush administration was the first to do such a thing. A similar tone of shock colors the "unthinkable" quotes at the beginning of this book. In reality, actors have been playing a similar game for years. Torture has never been as unthinkable to liberal democracies as we might like to believe. While the Bush administration's approach proved unique in some ways (as I elaborate later), characterizing one's own behavior as less than torture is an old game.

The second takeaway is an implication of the first. One way to lessen the instances of torture is to tackle the specificity problem by going after "cruel, inhuman, [and] degrading treatment" with more vigor (United Nations 1984). Too much of the discussion in the United States has been over whether the "enhanced interrogation techniques" are really torture. The 2016 Republican primary debate boiled down America's torture problem to one question, which was posed to several candidates: "Is waterboarding torture?" While bringing up a specific technique, paired with the "T-word," may make the question more difficult for the candidates to dodge, it gives them far too much wiggle room to continue advocating harsh treatment even if they decide that waterboarding is torture (which more than one did not) (Team Fix 2016). Perhaps future candidates could answer this question: "Some politicians have argued that the Bush-era 'enhanced interrogation techniques' are not severe enough to deserve the word torture. Yet the UN Convention against Torture also prohibits 'cruel, inhuman, or degrading treatment' of detainees, and our own Constitution rules out cruel and unusual punishment. Do you think the United States should be treating detainees in cruel, inhuman, or degrading ways?"

Comparing the European Union and the United States reveals the importance of prohibiting (with enforcement) torture's slightly milder cousins. Jamie Mayerfeld (2016, 93) describes the importance of unequivocal language in the European Convention on Human Rights:

> Beginning in 1951, ratifying states have pledged in Article 3 that "no one shall be subjected to torture or to inhuman or degrading treatment or punishment." The prohibition is stated in absolute terms: unlike most other rights asserted in the Convention, it admits no exceptions. The prohibition may not be suspended even during an emergency "threatening the life of the nation" (art. 15[2]). It also extends beyond torture to include all inhuman or degrading treatment or punishment, thus forbidding brutality in all its forms and removing the temptation to fiddle with the meaning of the word "torture."

This is one reason Mayerfeld finds a better, though not perfect, human rights picture in Europe as compared to the United States. The latter ratified the Convention against Torture but added caveats—"reservations, understandings, and declarations"—that limited the treaty's reach. Subsequent statutes that were supposed to be sufficient to protect human rights ended up narrowing torture's definition, especially regarding mental and psychological torture, in which only acts causing "prolonged mental harm" constituted criminal mental abuse. The U.S. version also forced prosecutors to prove intent on the part of the alleged torturer. The OLC memos sailed right through these loopholes: "With this definition, it became remarkably easy for the OLC lawyers to argue that all manner of psychological torment did not constitute torture as defined by the Torture Statute, because it was not inflicted with the specific intention of causing prolonged mental harm" (Mayerfeld 2016, 156). Because of their commitments to human rights treaties, it would be difficult for parties to the European

Convention on Human Rights to play the same game. Unambiguous laws can succeed where norms fail, as the case of former U.S. president Donald Trump's resistance to human rights norms and peaceful transitions of power illustrates (detailed later).

Third, implicit links between norm-breaking harshness and effectiveness are influential and need reexamination. Equating nastiness and effectiveness can lurk behind the ubiquitous Necessity defense. If an actor says, "We had to get tough with detainees because we desperately needed intelligence" or "We can't afford scruples if our enemies don't have any," some variation on the Cheaters Win argument is probably operating as an underlying assumption. Given the frequency with which torturers use the Necessity defense, the Cheaters Win argument may have wide applicability.

Fighting small wars—fighting insurgents and terrorists—may lead to more Cheaters Win justifications for torture even if the connection is not inevitable. Counterinsurgency victories may require much more coercion, especially in the form of displaced populations and civilian victimization (Hazelton 2021), than much of the recent literature on the topic allows. Expecting busy policymakers to parse which brutal methods are necessary and which are not could be asking too much. Equating harshness and effectiveness can serve as a convenient time-saver. One of the benefits of a more restrained foreign policy could be the improved image that comes with avoiding messy, costly small wars and the temptation to cheat on human rights norms that they often entail (Mearsheimer and Walt 2016).

Fourth, my study shows that norms can have broad influence and can affect even those who seem to ignore them. Norm transgressors constitute hard cases for the impact of norms.[1] If norms can influence even their violators, then the scope of normative impact may be much wider than is commonly understood. For most actors, we would do well to ask not if norms influence their behavior, but how.

Scope

Cheaters Win and Generalizability

Which norms are more likely to be susceptible to the Cheaters Win model? Though the following list is surely incomplete, I offer here a starting point. First, norms will not lead to their own violation if the norm is so robust and deeply internalized that thoughts of violation do not even occur to the actor. For instance, the norm against cannibalism is strong enough in the United States and most other places in the world that politicians and generals would probably never even think to violate the norm, no matter how intimidating to enemies such a policy might prove. But if a person can "think the unthinkable"—as with torture—then the act, of course, is not really unthinkable, despite the dramatic rhetoric. Likewise, wartime violence acts like assassination and civilian victimization have not really been rendered too taboo to mention, inviting initial consideration that may be followed by bad-is-good logic.

Second, norms that prohibit harsh acts whose efficacy is debated may open the door for alternative means of determining effectiveness. The norm against targeted killings is one possible example.[2] Because the effectiveness of targeted killing is not well-established,[3] some may use harshness as an indicator. Importantly, targeted killing may actually be an effective tool of counterterrorism. The Cheaters Win argument does not simply explain blunders, and hunches about the effectiveness of cheating may in fact be correct.

Third, ethical norms preventing acts that are almost guaranteed to harm someone physically,[4] emotionally, psychologically, or in other ways may be more likely to be susceptible to the Cheaters Win explanation. One possible example is civilian victimization. Civilian victimization clearly causes harm, and some may expect such pain to yield gain in difficult circumstances (such as those faced by Churchill, discussed later). By contrast, consider the norm of creating states with similar features.[5] It is more difficult to imagine the founders of a new nation-state believing that those who cheat on the standard form of state-building have an advantage.

This does not mean that we cannot apply the Cheaters Win explanation to standards beyond wartime violence norms, however. Consider the recent backsliding on liberal and/or democratic norms in places like Hungary, Venezuela, and Turkey, and similar threats in Brazil and the United States. What attracts democratic leaders to autocratic rule? It could be that autocrats appear to operate without restraints in passing legislation, bringing the media to heel, and so on.

Trump's autocratic envy is well-documented (Rubin 2018; Stracqualursi 2018). He has long equated autocracy with strength. In a 1989 interview, he said that China's crackdown in Tiananmen Square "shows you the power of strength," whereas the United States "is right now perceived as weak" (quoted in Calamur 2018). More recently he called Russian president Vladimir Putin a "strong leader" even when confronted with Putin's penchant for killing journalists (Kaczynski, Massie, and McDermott 2017). At one meeting with Putin, Trump stated longingly that Russia did not have the problems with "fake news" that the United States did (Phelps 2019; Putin responded that Russia did have problems with "fake news"). He praised the Philippines leader Rodrigo Duterte's extrajudicial killing spree against alleged drug traffickers as an "unbelievable job" (Margon 2018). Trump admiringly pointed out the lack of institutional constraints in Recep Tayyip Erdoğan's Turkey:

> Erdogan was the only allied leader spared from Trump's criticism at the 2018 NATO summit in Brussels. Trump noted that other leaders had to go through their legislatures to get more defense spending. He then turned to Erdogan, who has been stifling democracy and assuming more power in Turkey, and said, "Except for Erdogan over here. He does things the right way." He then [fist-bumped] Erdogan. (National Journal 2019)

For Trump, there is the slog of liberal-democratic norms and processes, or there is the "right way."

Even Saddam Hussein did not escape Trump's praise, specifically for his willingness to blow past human rights norms in the hunt for terrorists. "He killed terrorists. He did that so good. They didn't read them the rights. They didn't talk. They were a terrorist. It was over" (Margon 2018). By implication, when countries that follow the rule of law read detainees their rights or conduct trials, they will not be pursuing terrorists as "good" as Saddam.

As this book implies, Trump need not, and sometimes does not, look outside of U.S. history to find and honor heroes of brutality. Gideon Rachman (2019) explains:

> [O]ne Trumpian remark that has stuck with me is the US president's repeated insistence that, after conquering Iraq, "we should have kept the oil." To the ears of the Washington establishment, this was yet another Trump gaffe. Even Dick Cheney . . . most hawkish of hawks, had never portrayed Iraq as a war of conquest. But Mr Trump's deliberately provocative remark was an insight into both his philosophy and his appeal to voters. When many Americans feel frightened that both US power and their own living standards are in decline, Mr Trump is making an appeal to American ruthlessness. The US president says to voters that the country cannot afford to be "politically correct" any more. The way to Make America Great Again, in the words of his slogan, is to rediscover the ruthless instincts that

made America great in the first place. In a nod to past American ruthless-ness, Mr Trump has hung the portrait of Andrew Jackson, US president from 1829–1837, on the wall of the Oval Office. Jackson was once seen as one of the great builders of the American nation and his statue stands in Lafayette Square, opposite the White House. But a more recent generation of historians has accused Jackson of complicity in genocide for ordering the forced removal of Native Americans from their land—a policy that led to the "trail of tears" in which thousands died. By honouring Jackson, whom he praised as a "very tough person," Mr Trump is honouring the brutal pol-icies that allowed the US to conquer the west.

For Trump, the United States must venture beyond the pale to be sufficiently ruthless and "great again."

Lack of Specificity and Generalizability

A premise behind the Lack of Specificity argument in this book is that tor-ture is particularly susceptible to enabling justifications because it lies on a sliding scale with milder acts. What other norms are susceptible? One problem with identifying such norms is that susceptibility itself is a contin-uous variable: norms may be more or less susceptible. Another problem with identification is that collective understandings about how clear a line is can, within certain limits, change over time. Hugo Dobson (2003) argues that Japanese antimilitarism norms were well-defined until the late 1990s and early 2000s, when the requirements of emerging UN peacekeeping norms began compromising strict understandings of what it meant to adhere to pacifist commitments. Israel's recent use, and subsequent ban, of white phos-phorus shells, which are legal for creating smokescreens on the battlefield but prohibited from direct use against human targets because they cause chem-ical burns, is another possible example. Under heavy criticism from its use of white phosphorus in Gaza in the 2008–9 campaign, Israel decided to shelve the weapons, perhaps clarifying what could have been an emerging gray area between chemical and conventional weapons (Kershner 2013).

While specificity can change, inherent characteristics still matter. Nuclear weapons, for example, are probably much more amenable than torture to an absolute ban. Almost all explosions are either nuclear or nonnuclear, and their status is quickly known to all. Still, nuclear weapons have required agreement to keep them separate, even if they are inherently disposed to being walled off from other types of weapons:

> The "neutron bomb" is illustrative. This is a bomb, or potential bomb, that, because it is very small and because of the materials of which it is constructed, emits "prompt neutrons" that can be lethal at a distance at which blast and thermal radiation are comparatively moderate. As advertised, it kills people without great damage to structures. The issue of producing and deploying this kind of weapon arose during the Carter Administration, evoking an anti-nuclear reaction that caused it to be left on the drawing board. But the same bomb—at least, the same idea—had been the subject of even more intense debate 15 years earlier, and it was there that the argument was honed that was ready to be used again in the 1970s. The argument was simple—and it was surely valid, whether or not it deserved to be decisive. It was that it was important not to blur the distinction—the firebreak, as it was called—between nuclear and conventional weapons, and either because of its low yield or because of its "benign" kind of lethality it was feared, and it was argued, that there would be a strong temptation to use this weapon where nuclear weapons were otherwise not allowed, and that the use of this weapon would erode the threshold, blur the firebreak, and pave the way by incremental steps for nuclear escalation. (Schelling 2006, 6090–91)

Maintaining the nuclear "firebreak" necessitated social forces—criticism and debate—to keep them that way. At the same time, such a firebreak was possible because of inherent characteristics. It is harder to imagine a torture threshold on which most people could consistently agree.

Recent variation in attempts to erode liberal-democratic norms in the United States shows the difference that the Lack of Specificity can make. Liberal democracy has so many facets: free and fair elections, freedom of the press, due process, and so on. With so many moving parts, an overall decline in liberal-democratic values can be hard to discern for the average observer. Moreover, most of these concepts are slippery and up for debate. Republicans have taken advantage of this malleability in recent times by playing "constitutional hardball," a term used to describe "behavior that, while technically legal, uses the letter of the law to subvert its spirit" (Levitsky and Ziblatt 2019).[6] Senate Republicans' refusal to consider Merrick Garland for the U.S. Supreme Court in 2016 is one example of constitutional hardball.

Republicans felt that they could sell this maneuver as a continuation of earlier conventions about election-year judicial nominees. By contrast, the overrunning of the Capitol building in early 2021 by Trump supporters who were trying to stop the certification of electoral college votes in favor of President-Elect Joe Biden was not a gradual shift in tactics and has not (yet) engendered the same kinds of justification attempts.

Other Conditions and Cases

Under which circumstances might the normative effects from my main argument be more likely to occur? I offer here another nonexhaustive list. First, moments that citizens, civilian leaders, or the military determine to be critical to the life of the state might push key individuals to see norms as a fence dividing them from more effective means. Walzer (2000) calls these "supreme emergencies," a phrase used by Winston Churchill in 1939. Walzer argues that the phrase "contains an argument: that there is a fear beyond the ordinary fearfulness . . . of war, and a danger to which that fear corresponds, and that this fear and danger may well require exactly those measures which the war convention bars" (251).

The second set of circumstances bears some similarities to the first. The Cheaters Win explanation becomes more likely if events persuade actors that the world is a more dangerous place than they previously believed. The September 11 attacks were just such an event. The Bush administration justified "new thinking" regarding detainee treatment by arguing that the war on terror was a "new" kind of war and the dangers faced were "unprecedented" (Jackson 2007, 356–57). This change squares with work in political psychology about how surprising events can amplify emotional responses and cause preference shifts and reversals (Mercer 2013). Actors may also go on the hunt for new arguments (or new-to-them arguments) about what constitutes torture in the face of what they consider new dangers. Perhaps what was once unthinkably cruel would suddenly appear not so extreme in the face of a serious nuclear threat (as from the early Cold War) or a group of determined terrorists (from the war on terror). In such times, actors may erode norm specificity to get "tougher" with the opposition.

Third, if an enemy uses unscrupulous means in war, a political actor might be convinced that his or her country is now engaged in a dirty war in which such means are necessary. This is especially true if the enemy lands a punch or two while operating outside of war's laws and norms, causing the newly bruised to consider the possibility that rule-following would put them at a disadvantage. Having an opponent that does not fight fair also weakens the argument that one's side must stick with the laws and norms of war in order to engender the same treatment from the other side.

Unscrupulous enemies also open the door for actors to take advantage of the lack of specificity in a norm. In this case, the enemy supplies real-time examples of egregious behavior that can be used for favorable comparisons. The enemy's behavior can even *become* the definition of torture, as we saw with Cheney in the previous chapter.

Finally, I have focused on the United States in the empirical chapters. To which types of states and actors does my argument apply? Can we generalize beyond liberal democracies? While actors under any regime type may be susceptible to Cheaters Win thinking, democratic actors may be particularly disposed. Surrounded by human rights norms and other standards limiting violence, these actors are more likely to generate a bad-is-good philosophy (as opposed to a "What's the problem?" mindset that may characterize nondemocratic regimes more accustomed to higher levels of violence). Democratic actors might also be especially nervous that their own countries have been 'softened' by liberal norms.

There is also a strong chance that torturers in democracies are more likely to exploit the torture norm's lack of specificity. Just as Rejali (2007) finds that democratic torturers fear being caught, the same set will also want to play down the severity of their acts even if they are caught. Danger of exposure is higher in democracies with a free press as well as human rights laws and enforcement. The gap between democracies and nondemocracies is narrowing, however, as global monitoring, peacekeeping, and international court capabilities (which can raise the costs of human rights abuses) increase.

Limits

Beyond regime type, I am reluctant to specify types of actors that would be more likely to fit the models I have detailed. It might be tempting to associate Cheaters Win believers with hawkish foreign policy beliefs generally. Hawks believe that the international realm can be a brutal place and that dealing with its worst actors requires force. It would not be surprising if hawks extended their thinking to interrogation, in which strict rule-following would curtail coercion.

Yet some hawks categorically reject torture as wrong and are not willing to play any minimization games that take advantage of the torture norm's lack of specificity. Theodore Roosevelt is one. He advocated tough war-fighting measures, but he showed little tolerance for torture. He understood the water cure to be a "mild torture," but he still thought the practice should be abandoned and its users punished. He promoted some generals who were sometimes tolerant of torture, but those generals were more well-known for other characteristics and achievements. To take one example, J. Franklin Bell, a general who sometimes quietly winked at torture, was promoted to Roosevelt's cabinet after the war (Miller 1982, 260). But Bell was highly regarded for his thorough knowledge of counterinsurgent war-making and his successful pacification of northwestern Luzon and the province of Batangas, not his tolerance of torture (Linn 2000, 300). He was celebrated as a tough fighter, not a lawbreaker. The story is more complicated than the straightforward rewarding of torturers.

Like Roosevelt, war-on-terror hawks such as Republican senators John McCain and Lindsey Graham have also pushed for aggressive war-fighting without torture, and therefore are not well-covered by my argument. Perhaps Roosevelt, McCain, and Graham subscribe to a kind of moral absolutism that does not countenance gray-zone thinking when it comes to detainee treatment.[7] If so, then arguments in favor of a comprehensive torture ban may be right at home in some strands of essentially conservative thought.

Neither half of my thesis does particularly well in explaining why torture ended when it did in the war on terror.[8] Most detainee abuses ended after 2005 (Hutchinson et al. 2013, 7). Yet beliefs about the utility or importance of off-limits practices, including torture, did not change. Neither did the conviction that the interrogation methods used could be sold as something short of torture. Bush and Cheney continued to trumpet the efficacy and legality of "enhanced interrogation techniques" after the administration was out of office. This may be the nature of explaining events and behavior that have so many causes (Jervis 1988, 675): one thing can cause a series of events (in this case, resulting in torture) to occur, and something else can end it. Still, the inability to explain this piece of variation in the war on terror shows the limits of my argument's explanatory power.

The Present and Future

While the norm against torture has had some persistent robustness problems that predate the war on terror, the Bush administration may have done some new damage to the norm's prospects. The Constitution Project summarizes the developments:

> In the course of the nation's many previous conflicts, there is little doubt that some U.S. personnel committed brutal acts against captives, as have armies and governments throughout history.
>
> But there is no evidence there had ever before been the kind of considered and detailed discussions that occurred after September 11, directly involving a president and his top advisers on the wisdom, propriety and legality of inflicting pain and torment on some detainees in our custody. (Hutchinson et al. 2013, 1)

Attorney General John Ashcroft, who, along with other top cabinet members, received from the CIA regular requests for approval of particular techniques, reportedly "argued that senior White House advisers should not be involved in the grim details of interrogations. . . . According to a top official, Ashcroft asked aloud after one meeting: 'Why are we talking about this in the White House? History will not judge this kindly'" (Greenburg, Rosenberg, and de Vogue 2008).

Thus far, history has judged the Bush administration all too kindly on this particular topic. Torture, once universally condemned, has become essentially a partisan issue in the United States, not unlike the debate over the death penalty (Mayer 2014). Part of the reason is the continued support for an enhanced interrogation program by former administration officials, including Bush and Cheney themselves. The lack of some kind of bipartisan truth commission to help the country come to terms with war-on-terror abuses may also be a factor.[9]

Another important reason is the willingness of some politicians—importantly, not limited to Trump—to bring American torture into a new era.[10] In fact, 2016 Republican presidential candidates produced talking points very much in line with this book's case studies. Senator Ted Cruz was perhaps the most moderate of the candidates on the issue of torture (Crowley 2016). He seemed to be taking a clear stance against the practice when he said, "Torture is wrong, unambiguously. Period. The end. Civilized nations do not engage in torture and Congress has rightly acted to make absolutely clear that the United States will not engage in torture" (quoted in Crowley 2016). But when asked during a debate whether use of the waterboard was torture, Cruz said, "Well, under the definition of torture, no, it's not. Under the law, torture is excruciating pain that is equivalent to losing organs and systems, so under the definition of torture, it is not. It is enhanced interrogation, it is vigorous interrogation, but it does not meet the generally recognized definition of torture." While saying that he would not bring back enhanced interrogations "in any sort of widespread use," he did promise that "if it were necessary to, say, prevent a city from facing an imminent terrorist attack, you can rest assured that as commander in chief, I would use *whatever enhanced interrogation methods we could* to keep this country safe" (Team Fix 2016, emphasis added). Cruz, like many before him, is seeking a middle ground: he pledges to use "whatever methods" are necessary, but sticks to euphemistic "enhanced interrogation" language.

With his characteristic inconsistency, then-candidate Trump took a similar line, stating, "[W]aterboarding is peanuts compared to what [terrorists like ISIS are] doing to us, what they did to [American journalist] James Foley when they chopped off his head" (ABC News 2015). Trump has apparently been worried that the debate over rule-following was making us appear too weak: "Can you imagine—can you imagine these people, these animals over in the Middle East, that chop off heads, sitting around talking and seeing that we're having a hard problem with waterboarding? We should go for waterboarding and we should go tougher than waterboarding" (Federal News Service 2016). While discussing torture, he railed against President Barack Obama's "weak" response to ISIS, a lawless enemy: "We have to play the game the way they're playing the game. You're not going to win if we're soft and . . . they have no rules" (Diamond 2016). Trump appears to believe that "more ruthless" means "more effective" over the full spectrum of severity, as shown in Figure 7.1. Regarding whether waterboarding was torture, Trump said, "It's so borderline. It's like your minimal, minimal, minimal torture" (Johnson and Del Real 2016). Yet when pushed about whether he would openly endorse lawbreaking, Trump pulled back: "I . . . understand that the United States is bound by laws and treaties and I will not order our military or other officials to violate those laws and will seek their advice on such matters." Thus, after a wild journey, Trump, like Cruz, vowed to "use every *legal* power . . . to stop these terrorist enemies" (McCarthy 2016).[11]

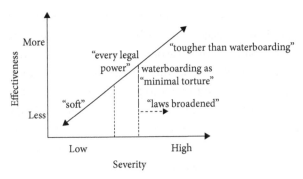

Figure 7.1 Then-candidate Donald Trump's interest in expanding the middle ground.

Other parts of the executive branch under Trump showed little interest in renewing a coercive interrogation program. Jim Mattis, who served as defense secretary under Trump for the administration's first two years, favored a beer-and-cigarettes, rapport-building approach (Fink and Cooper 2017). Michael Hayden, who directed the CIA at the end of George W. Bush's term, said that he believed his former agency would refuse to use coercive methods after the fallout from the war on terror. "Multiple investigations, grand juries, presidential condemnations, and congressional star chambers have a way of doing that to you," Hayden said, adding that if Trump wanted the CIA to use waterboarding, he'd have to "bring [his] own bucket" (Dilanian 2016). The Trump administration was not above abuse, as shown by family-separation policies and inhumane conditions in its immigration detention facilities (Romero et al. 2019). But shifting organizational preferences and newer, clearer, more stringent laws kept Trump from restarting an interrogational torture program. Trump was already feeling the pinch of the new legal landscape in 2016, claiming, "We're going to stay within the laws. But you know what we're going to do? We're going to have those laws broadened" (Diamond and Scott 2016).

While there are more legal and bureaucratic barriers to torture now than there were in 2001, coercive interrogation still has well-placed advocates, including members of Congress. For instance, Representative Liz Cheney, daughter of Richard, is carrying on the family tradition of supporting harsh interrogation. In response to McCain's criticism of the war-on-terror program, the younger Cheney (2018) wrote on Twitter: "The Enhanced Interrogation Program saved lives, prevented attacks, & produced intel that led to Osama bin Laden. The techniques were the same as those used on our own people in the SERE program. No one should slander the brave men & women who carried out this crucial program." Some of the pieces remain in place for the next generation of leaders to use euphemisms and claims of self-application to play down the severity of abusive interrogation programs while still insisting that they are essential.

Notes

Chapter 1

1. The quotes in this paragraph are from Dershowitz (2002, 13), McCarthy (2004), Jacoby (2005), and Friedersdorf (2013).
2. For an example of the former, see Bagaric and Clarke's (2007) *Torture: When the Unthinkable Is Morally Permissable*. One movie about counterterrorism torture is simply titled *Unthinkable* (Jordan 2010).
3. For one example among many, see Hathaway 2002.
4. See also Foot 2006; McKeown 2009.
5. See, for instance, Krasner 1999.
6. This argument is as old as Aristotle, runs through Cicero, St. Augustine, and Beccaria, and continues to be made today. For historical recounts, see Holmes 2007; Langbein 2004. For a recent example, see Soufan 2009b.
7. For one example of this argument, see Alexander 2008. It is possible that torture, if sufficiently widespread, could deter potential recruits from joining the enemy's cause. Torture may well be a successful tool of intimidation—see Rejali 2007—but this is not a stand-alone reason for adopting *interrogational* torture.
8. U.S. Marine Corps publications (e.g., 2005) make this argument.
9. See, for instance, McCoy 2006.
10. The titles of these CIA's programs are code names with no deeper meaning.
11. The programs sound like science fiction or the product of conspiracy theorizing, but they were quite real, and they became the subject of a congressional investigation in the 1970s. In hindsight, MKULTRA and other brainwashing attempts resemble the cruel folly of amateurs rather than the clever designs of evil geniuses.

Chapter 2

1. See also Fukuyama 1992; Rummel 1994; Poe and Tate 1994.
2. In one of the foundational constructivist texts in international relations, Wendt (1992) draws on shifting relations between the United States and the Soviet Union at end of the Cold War to demonstrate how different worlds with greater levels of cooperation are possible.
3. See, for instance, Mearsheimer 1990.
4. See especially Pinker 2011.

5. For a project that both highlighted and furthered the dominance of constructivism and rationalism, see Katzenstein, Keohane, and Krasner 1999.

6. There has been some discussion as to how authentic this demonstration truly was. Hitchens's (2008) more detailed account may be more compelling for some, although it does not have the benefit of coming from a previous defender of the practice.

7. Keelhauling was a practice in which a "sailor was tied to a rope and pulled around the bottom of the ship's hull. If he didn't drown, he would be slashed to ribbons by the encrusted barnacles" (Pinker 2011, 146).

8. Einolf (2007) argues that the historical record suggests a "fall [in the nineteenth century] and rise [in the twentieth] of torture," but the frequency of torture in the 1800s is not sufficiently known to permit firm conclusions. Awareness of abuse certainly grew in the 1900s, however.

9. Rejali (2007) claims that sweeping explanations like the National Security model are usually too broad to account for torture. Instead, "Hell is in the details."

10. Wallace (2015) also argues that severe fighting and wars of attrition may make leaders—including democratic ones—desperate, leading to more prisoner abuse. I address this in the next section.

11. See also Davenport, Moore, and Armstrong 2007; Davenport 2007; Gleditsch and Ward 1997.

12. See also Tsebelis 2002.

13. See, for instance, Lichtblau 2009. Conrad and Moore (2010) also argue that violent domestic dissent can lead to the suspension of liberal democratic institutions, which can then lead to human rights abuses, including torture.

14. This is, in fact, what Rejali (2007, 487) argues about Merom's featured case, the French-Algerian War. Along similar lines, Rejali writes that the Phoenix Program in South Vietnam was effective as a "death squad," not as a fount of accurate information (472).

15. Because of its closeness to the desperation argument, I do not consider intuition as a separate explanation in the cases.

Chapter 3

1. It should be noted that Cobalt was not actually safe by any definition. Many detainees suffered there and at least one died of hypothermia. See Central Intelligence Agency 2003, 1.

2. See also Rejali 2007.

3. The belief may be the result of socialization in a Hobbesian international environment. See Wendt 1999, ch. 6.

4. See, for instance, Schelling 1960.

5. See also Kier and Mercer 1996, 86.

6. For further discussion on the "heroism" of morally problematic choices such as torture, see d'Ambruoso 2015.

7. Experiments resembling these examples follow the original statement of the theory in Brehm 1966.
8. See also Einolf 2014.
9. The idea of favorable comparisons corresponds with psychologists' observations that people are more willing to excuse the actions of a member of their own group. See Mercer 1995.
10. In this sense, my argument bears some resemblance to that of Michelle Bentley (2016), who argues that the Obama administration's emphasis on and strategic use of the chemical weapons taboo kept it from developing a more comprehensive foreign policy regarding Syria.
11. My discussion from the previous chapter of Christopher Hitchens's explanation of the difference between his own treatment on the waterboard and torture victims in U.S. custody is relevant here.
12. This treatment of norms bears some resemblance to subcultural theory, a branch of sociology and criminology that emphasizes alternative sets of norms from those of the wider society. The usual subject of subcultural theory is deviant youth. For a review of this literature, see Williams 2011. I thank Alexander Kamprad for showing me this connection.
13. The latter two are from Jervis 2006, 645.
14. Using the same conceptualization, the norm may have become more robust in Europe in recent years. I discuss this further in the concluding chapter.
15. For some evidence for the claim that the Bush administration did not know the extent to which it was repeating previous patterns, see Shane and Mazzetti 2009.

Chapter 4

1. Thayer (2016) and Krider (2018) provide short biographies.
2. In these notes, I refer to court-martial files by the last name of the defendant followed by the General Court-Martial (GCM) case number. The most comprehensive overviews of these files and the other investigations comes from Einolf 2014 and Vestal 2017.
3. This summary draws especially from Linn 2000; Miller 1982; Jones 2012; and Kramer 2006.
4. See the testimony of Joveniano [Tobeniano] Ealdama in Glenn GCM 30755.
5. Ryan GCM 31443.
6. Bell's statement is in Morris C. Foote, "Report of an Investigation of Outrages by American Soldiers in Batangas Province," February 1902, 5–6, Adjutant General's Office Document Number 476653, Record Group 94, National Archives, Washington, D.C.
7. James Franklin Bell to "My Dear Colonel" William Bisbee, March 30, 1900, Letter Sent No. 69, Book 1, Entry 2206, Record Group 395, National Archives, Washington, D.C. Much of this is quoted in Linn 2000, 224, emphasis added.

8. Ryan GCM 31443; Lieber 1863, art. 5.

9. Davis's letter in Glenn GCM 30755.

10. Glenn and Russell's written statement in Glenn GCM 30755.

11. Glenn GCM 34401, 18.

12. Glenn GCM 30755, 90–93.

13. Ryan GCM 31443, 9.

14. Ibid., 5.

15. Glenn's written statement in GCM 30755, 1, 6–7.

16. See Boughton's letter in Hickman GCM 33367, 4.

17. Einolf (2014, 183–86) argues that some U.S. soldiers in the Philippines underwent a kind of "moral inversion" in which they came "to see evil actions as good." I am arguing along similar lines here.

18. Linn (2000, 300) also argues that Bell was "respected enough to check officers . . . from engaging in indiscriminate counterterrorism." However, Bell does not give one the impression that he regularly restrained himself. "[T]he innocent must generally suffer with the guilty," he claimed, and it was impossible to tell "the actively bad from only the passively so" (quoted in Miller 1982, 208).

19. Funston, "Exhibit A," in U.S. Senate 1902, 951.

20. Ibid.

21. Glenn and Russell's statement in Glenn GCM 30755, 3.

22. Ibid., 4.

23. Glenn GCM 30755.

24. Glenn and Russell's statement in ibid., 4.

25. Thomas GCM 16870, 68.

26. Ibid., 7.

27. Brandle GCM 19802, 13–15.

28. Glenn GCM 30755, 99–100, 120–21.

29. Glenn and Russell's statement in Glenn GCM 30755, 3.

30. GCM 31443, 179–80.

31. "Proceedings of a Board of Officers . . . to Inquire into Allegations Made by Maj. Cornelius Gardener, 13th Infantry . . . ," April 20, 1902, 76–77, Adjutant General's Office Document Number 421607, Record Group 94, National Archives, Washington, D.C.

32. Ibid., 78.

33. Glenn's written statement in GCM 30755, 6–8. The verbose Glenn takes advantage of the lack of specificity with another slippery slope argument: he suggests that other methods that have traditionally garnered approval might count as torture if the water cure does: "I have never been taught that I could not produce in [the] enemy's mind a state of fright or fear although this may sometimes constitute mental anguish and mental anguish is sometimes called torture. There is no doubt that to arrest and confine a man produces a state of fear or fright yet, in time of war, many people actually are and must necessarily be arrested and confined. Are we to cease arrests and confinements during war simply because doing so produces mental anguish and so-called torture?" (6–8).

34. Ryan GCM 31443, 34, 41.

35. Glenn's statement in GCM 30755, 6. And again, what's wrong with a little fear, Glenn wants to know? "I have always understood that it was one of the first principles of war to inculcate into the minds of your enemy both collectively and individually a wholesome fear and respect for you both collectively and individually" (6).

36. Glenn GCM 30755, 75–76.

37. Ibid., 92.

38. See also Hickman GCM 33367.

39. See the court's verdict in Glenn GCM 30755.

40. Glenn and Russell's written statement in Glenn GCM 30755, 4–5.

41. Glenn's written statement in Glenn GCM 30755, 5–6.

42. Glenn GCM 30755.

43. Diary, October 8, 1901, Frederic M. Presher Papers, U.S. Army Heritage and Education Center, Carlisle, PA.

44. The quoted text forms part of the title of chapter 4 in Einolf 2014.

45. Thomas GCM 16870, 68.

46. Glenn GCM 30755, 80–89.

47. Russell and Glenn's statement in Glenn GCM 30755, 19, emphasis in original.

48. Glenn's written statement in Glenn GCM 30755, 4.

49. Letter to wife, January 13, 1901, Samuel Lyon Papers, U.S. Army Heritage and Education Center, Carlisle, PA. Miller (1982, 184) misquotes this passage. See d'Ambruoso (2016) for a scanned copy of the original letter.

50. It is unclear whether Hagedorn believes that more severe measures would be more effective, and not just justified.

51. See Miller 1982, especially chapter 10, for several examples.

52. Exhibit #31 in Glenn GCM 34401, 10.

53. Ryan GCM 31443.

54. Judge Advocate General Davis's letter in Gaujot GCM 30756, 5. See also Einolf 2007, 90.

55. Glenn made a similar argument through a series of questions when he was serving as his own lawyer. See Glenn GCM 30755, 90–93.

56. Ryan GCM 31443, 129.

57. Glenn GCM 30755.

58. See also Gates 1973, 161–63.

59. Glenn GCM 30755.

60. Theodore Roosevelt to Hermann Speck von Sternburg, July 19, 1902, Theodore Roosevelt Digital Library, Dickinson State University, Library of Congress Manuscript Division, http://www.theodorerooseveltcenter.org/Research/Digital-Library/Record.aspx?libID=o182813.

61. For an example from the civilian side, see Root 2016.

62. Samuel Young, "'Our Soldiers in the Philippines': An Address Delivered before the Men's Club of the Church of the Epiphany of Washington, D.C.," November 13, 1902, 6, U.S. Army Heritage and Education Center, Carlisle, PA.

63. Ibid., 4.

64. Ibid., 6.
65. Bell, J. Franklin, "To All Station Commanders," Telegraphic Circular No. 3, December 9, 1901. Reprinted in Ramsey III 2007, 46.
66. Glenn and Russell's written statement in Glenn GCM 30755.
67. "Exhibit 1" in Glenn GCM 34401.
68. Glenn's written statement in Glenn GCM 30755, 10.
69. Under a photograph showing American soldiers and their allies applying the water cure to a Filipino detainee, Kramer (2006, 142) notes the "complacency" with which the soldiers watch the procedure, possibly indicating that the practice had become commonplace in that particular company.

Chapter 5

1. See, for instance, Janis 1949, quoted in McCoy 2006, 22–23.
2. Note that the Communists were trying to intimidate prisoners and elicit confessions, not gather accurate intelligence. The CIA was more interested in behavioral control and intelligence-producing interrogation, but agency members either did not make this distinction or believed that they could appropriate the enemy's methods to their ends.
3. See also Marks 1979, 145–46.
4. Lane's book has come under serious criticism. See especially Sheehan 1970.
5. The proceedings of the Russell Tribunal are reprinted in Duffett 1968.
6. Testimony of Peter Martinsen, in Duffett 1968, 432.
7. Ibid., 428, emphasis in original.
8. Ibid., 430, emphasis added.
9. Ibid., 428.
10. Given the number of informal conversations that Eisenhower had with the Dulles brothers, he almost certainly knew about some of the details of MKULTRA. He once reassured a congressman, "There is a very great aggressiveness on our side that you have not known about and I guess that is on the theory of why put burdens on people that they don't need to know about." He confessed that he "knew so many things that I am almost afraid to speak to my wife" (quoted in Thomas 2012, ch. 10). Henry Kissinger testified that Nixon knew about and approved of every covert action, and Kissinger was "nearly certain" that this rule held for previous administrations as well (quoted in U.S. Senate 1976, 46).
11. The Church Committee Report bluntly explains, "The concept of 'plausible denial' is intended not only to hide the hand of the United States Government, but to protect the President from the embarrassment of a 'blown' covert operation" (U.S. Senate 1976, 46).
12. The NSC-68 authors do argue that free societies have some advantages in the struggle, however. For instance, they emphasize the greater appeal of free societies which they hope will attract a wider set of allies.

13. Note the use of the euphemism "revolutionary."
14. I discuss Snepp's case further later in the chapter.
15. ARTICHOKE/BLUEBIRD Document #136, 1952.
16. Ibid.
17. The following story draws on Marks 1979, 67–74.
18. MKULTRA document #352, 1955, 4.
19. Interestingly for the Cheater's Win explanation, Colby recalls superiors saying, essentially, that it may become necessary to be more ruthless than the enemy in order to be more effective.
20. McCoy (2006) finds a similar contrast.
21. See also Pincus 2006.
22. See also Rejali 2007, 582.
23. Testimony of Peter Martinsen, in Duffett 1968, 434.
24. Campbell's testimony in Winter Soldier Investigation 1971. For similar examples, see also Camile's, Eckert's, and Sachs's responses.
25. Sachs also describes a scenario in which an officer told him not to risk his skin for "gook marines," members of the Vietnamese military. See Sachs's testimony in Winter Soldier Investigation 1971.
26. See Roberson's and Worrell's interviews in Lane 1970, 63, 121.
27. For more on why there can never be a true science of torture, see Rejali 2007, especially chapter 21.
28. See Turse's interview in Denvir 2013.
29. For one example, see Lane 1970, 159.

Chapter 6

1. Censored in the original. The next section provides more evidence that the Bush administration knew that transferred captives would be tortured. Some officials have claimed that they had no control over what other states did, but this too is preposterous.
2. U.S. Senate, Select Committee on Intelligence 2014, "Findings and Conclusions," 12. See also Blakeley 2011.
3. See Rumsfeld 2002. Though Rumsfeld retracted this memo soon afterward, he continued to approve harsh methods on a case-by-case basis. See, for instance, U.S. Senate, Armed Services Committee 2008, 137–38.
4. The CIA responded to the first draft of the Senate report, and then the Senate report was updated in response to the CIA; hence the backward chronology.
5. Bush's response may be an example of psychological reactance theory—he does not want international law to encroach on his behavioral freedom. See Brehm 1966.
6. The video recording slightly corrects the transcript released by the administration. See White House 2001b.
7. Yoo would later applaud Bush's policy choices. See Yoo 2006, 44.

8. See also Central Intelligence Agency 2013, 49.

9. Mitchell's (2016) retelling matches this sequence.

10. For his part, Martin Seligman did not see a clear link between learned helplessness, which he researched extensively, and the production of accurate intelligence. See Konnikova 2015.

11. Mitchell's testimony, in Salim et al. v. Mitchell et al. 2017, 279.

12. Mitchell casts some doubt on the CIA's preference for a limited program. He asserts that officials at CIA headquarters wanted him to continue to subject Abu Zubaydah to the waterboard when he and Jessen were ready to move to less harsh treatment (ibid., 287). If true, Mitchell's story does not mean that the CIA wanted an *unlimited* program, just that the agency was more interested in raw coercion than Mitchell's and Jessen's attempts to let scientific calibration inform the choice of methods.

13. For evidence that the contractors saw the waterboard as the harshest of the techniques, see the reference to them in Bybee 2002b, 2.

14. By counting sessions that include multiple "pours," others arrive at a different total. See Mitchell 2016.

15. Administration officials continued to push for harsh interrogation even after the program was discontinued. I discuss the implications of this at the end of the chapter.

16. Philip Zelikow, an intelligence advisor, remembers Bush asking George Tenet if the CIA's proposed techniques would work: "The director of the CIA tells him that these techniques will be effective, and he makes that point strongly" (Kirk 2015). We're still left to wonder (a) why Tenet was so confident and (b) why Bush so willingly believed Tenet, even though he knew that Tenet had no firsthand experience with such matters. In his memoir, Tenet (2007, 241) actually echoes the legal focus when discussing the CIA's early effort to find methods for interrogating Zubaydah: "Despite what Hollywood might have you believe, in situations like this you don't call in the tough guys; you call in the lawyers."

17. KSM received treatment similar to Zubaydah: he endured 183 applications of the waterboard in March 2003. See CIA Inspector General 2004, 91; Bradbury 2005.

18. See Bybee 2002b, especially pts. V and VI.

19. The 2014 Senate report said that the CIA used "rectal rehydration" against at least five detainees. See U.S. Senate, Select Committee on Intelligence 2014, "Findings and Conclusions," 4.

20. Sullivan (2007) shows a parallel with the German "Verschärfte Vernehmung," a phrase used by the Nazis to describe similar techniques. I have not seen any evidence that the CIA or any other Bush administration members learned of the term from Nazi documents, trials, or stories, however.

21. Much of the media started using the term "enhanced interrogation" after the Bush administration went public with it, and there was a debate as to whether simply using the term (rather than "torture") validated the administration's position. See the NPR Ombudsman's discussion of the matter in Shepard 2009.

22. Bush (2010, 169) writes specifically of use of the waterboard, "No doubt the procedure was tough, but medical experts assured the CIA that it did no lasting harm."

23. See also Frey 2008.

24. The extent to which Bush himself was involved in the finer details of the interrogation methods in the summer of 2002 is debated. See Peralta 2014 for a summary.
25. Quoted in U.S. Senate, Select Committee on Intelligence 2014, "Findings and Conclusions," 6.
26. For a dissenting view, see Thiessen 2012.
27. For an account of another CIA agent who rejected the use of harsh interrogations, see Carle 2014.
28. See also Spannaus 2006.
29. Eventually, the Bush administration came to believe that even military commissions were too generous for some prisoners, opting instead for indefinite detention without trial.
30. I thank an anonymous reviewer for suggesting these points.

Chapter 7

1. As such, this book heeds the call from some scholars for more constructivist work on hard cases, especially those dealing with security. See Garcia 2011. See also Johnston 1996.
2. Nils Melzer (2008, 5) defines targeted killing as "the use of lethal force attributable to a subject of international law with the intent, premeditation, and deliberation to kill individually selected persons who are not in the physical custody of those targeting them."
3. For a summary of the scholarly debate, see Price 2012. For an example of think-tank analysts debating the effectiveness of targeted killing, see Masters 2013. Policymakers and military strategists have debated this as well; see quotes from John Brennan and Gen. Stanley McChrystal in Worth, Mazzetti, and Shane 2013.
4. This may be especially surprising since some scholars argue that norms prohibiting acts that inflict bodily harm are more likely to have standard regulatory and constitutive effects. See Price 1998; Keck and Sikkink 1998.
5. See Meyer et al. 1997.
6. Mark Tushnet (2003) coined the term "constitutional hardball." Levitsky and Ziblatt (2019) do not argue that Republican behavior is unusual, but rather what we might expect when a party is worried about the consequences of losing (due to polarization) and long-term electoral prospects.
7. Roosevelt was known for his rigidity on law-and-order matters. See Morris 2002.
8. See Conrad and Moore 2010.
9. For a more thorough examination of the impact of the U.S. violation on the state of the global antitorture norm, see Schmidt and Sikkink 2019.
10. Though it does not count as interrogational torture, the Trump administration's detention of migrants in squalid conditions suggests no lack of willingness to be brutal toward defenseless people. For a summary, see Kanno-Youngs 2019.
11. Trump also sounds vengeful. He said of the waterboard, "Believe me, it works. And you know what? If it doesn't work, they deserve it anyway, for what they're doing" (Johnson 2015).

References

Archive Collections

General Court-Martial (GCM) transcripts are from the National Archives and Records Administration, Washington, D.C., Record Group 153: Records of the Judge Advocate General's Office. Citations are by folder name and GCM number.

MKULTRA, BLUEBIRD, and ARTICHOKE documents are from the National Security Archives, Washington, D.C. Citations are by document number.

Published Sources

ABC News. 2015. "'This Week' Transcript: Donald Trump and Ben Carson." November 22. http://abcnews.go.com/Politics/week-transcript-donald-trump-ben-carson/story?id=35336008.

ACLU (American Civil Liberties Union). 2005. "Fact Sheet: Extraordinary Rendition." https://www.aclu.org/national-security/fact-sheet-extraordinary-rendition.

Adams, Guy B., Danny L. Balfour, and George E. Reed. 2006. "Abu Ghraib, Administrative Evil, and Moral Inversion: The Value of 'Putting Cruelty First.'" *Public Administration Review* 66, no. 5: 680–93.

Alexander, Matthew. 2008. "I'm Still Tortured by What I Saw in Iraq." *Washington Post*, November 30, sec. Opinions. http://www.washingtonpost.com/wp-dyn/content/article/2008/11/28/AR2008112802242.html.

Alter, Jonathan. 2001. "Time to Think about Torture." *Newsweek*, November 4. http://www.newsweek.com/time-think-about-torture-149445.

Altman, Howard. 2016. "Q&A: Pasco Psychologist behind Waterboarding Calls for Soul-Searching on Security." *Tampa Bay Times*, December 26. https://www.tampabay.com/news/military/war/qa-pasco-psychologist-behind-waterboarding-calls-for-soul-searching-on/2307482/.

Ambrose, Stephen E. 1983. *Eisenhower*. Vol. 2. New York: Simon and Schuster.

Apuzzo, Matt, and James Risen. 2014. "C.I.A. First Planned Jails Abiding by U.S. Standards." *New York Times*, December 10. http://www.nytimes.com/2014/12/11/us/politics/cia-first-planned-jails-abiding-by-us-standards-.html.

Apuzzo, Matt, Sheri Fink, and James Risen. 2016. "How U.S. Torture Left a Legacy of Damaged Minds." *New York Times*, October 8, sec. World. https://www.nytimes.com/2016/10/09/world/cia-torture-guantanamo-bay.html.

Aronson, Elliot, ed. 2003. *Readings about the Social Animal*. New York: Macmillan.

Bagaric, Mirko, and Julie Clarke. 2007. *Torture: When the Unthinkable Is Morally Permissable*. Albany: SUNY Press.

BBC News. 2002. "No POW Rights for Cuba Prisoners." January 27, sec. Americas. http://news.bbc.co.uk/2/hi/americas/1784700.stm.

Begala, Paul. 2009. "Yes, National Review, We Did Execute Japanese for Waterboarding." *Huffington Post* (blog), May 25. https://www.huffingtonpost.com/paul-begala/yes-inational-reviewi-we_b_191153.html.

Bennett, Andrew. 2004. "Case Study Methods: Design, Use, and Comparative Advantages." In *Models, Numbers, and Cases*, edited by Yael Nahmias-Wolinsky, 19–55. Ann Arbor: University of Michigan Press.

Bentley, Michelle. 2016. *Syria and the Chemical Weapons Taboo: Exploiting the Forbidden.* Manchester: Manchester University Press.

Bergen, Peter, and Katherine Tiedemann. 2008. "Disappearing Act: Rendition by the Numbers." *Mother Jones*, March 3. http://www.motherjones.com/politics/2008/03/disappearing-act-rendition-numbers.

Birtle, Andrew James. 1998. *US Army Counterinsurgency and Contingency Operations Doctrine, 1860–1941.* Washington, D.C.: U.S. Army, Center of Military History.

Blakeley, Ruth. 2007. "Why Torture?" *Review of International Studies* 33, no. 3: 373–94.

Blakeley, Ruth. 2011. "Dirty Hands, Clean Conscience? The CIA Inspector General's Investigation of 'Enhanced Interrogation Techniques' in the War on Terror and the Torture Debate." *Journal of Human Rights* 10, no. 4: 544–61.

Borger, Julian. 2020. "Guantánamo: Psychologist Tells of 'Abusive Drift' in Treatment of Terror Suspects." *Guardian*, January 22. https://www.theguardian.com/us-news/2020/jan/22/guantanamo-psychologist-tells-of-abusive-drift-in-treatment-of-terror-suspects.

Bowden, Mark. 2003. "The Dark Art of Interrogation." *Atlantic*, October. http://www.theatlantic.com/magazine/archive/2003/10/the-dark-art-of-interrogation/302791/.

Bowden, Mark. 2007. "In Defense of Waterboarding." *Philadelphia Inquirer*, December 23. http://www.freerepublic.com/focus/f-news/1946468/posts.

Bradbury, Steven G. 2005. "Memorandum for John A. Rizzo, Senior Deputy General Counsel, Central Intelligence Agency, Re: Application of United States Obligations Under Article 16 of the Convention Against Torture to Certain Techniques That May Be Used in the Interrogation of High Value Al Qaeda Detainees." May 30. Rendition Project. http://www.therenditionproject.org.uk/pdf/PDF%2018%20%5BBradbury%20Memo%20to%20Rizzo%2030%20May%202005%5D.pdf.

Branche, Raphaëlle. 2007. "Torture of Terrorists? Use of Torture in a 'War against Terrorism': Justifications, Methods and Effects: The Case of France in Algeria, 1954–1962." *International Review of the Red Cross* 89, no. 867: 543–60.

Brehm, Jack Williams. 1966. *A Theory of Psychological Reactance.* New York: Academic Press.

Brundage, W. Fitzhugh. 2018. *Civilizing Torture: An American Tradition.* Cambridge, MA: The Belknap Press of Harvard University Press.

Bumiller, Elisabeth, and Steven Lee Myers. 2001. "A Nation Challenged: The Presidential Order; Senior Administration Officials Defend Military Tribunals for Terrorist Suspects." *New York Times*, November 15, sec. U.S. http://www.nytimes.com/2001/11/15/us/nation-challenged-presidential-order-senior-administration-officials-defend.html.

Bush, George W. 2002. "Memorandum for the Vice President et al.; Subject: Humane Treatment of al Qaeda and Taliban Detainees." February 7. Rendition Project. http://www.therenditionproject.org.uk/pdf/PDF%206%20%5BBush%20Memo%207%20Feb%202002%20on%20Geneva%20Conventions%5D.pdf.

Bush, George W. 2003. "President Bush's 2003 State of the Union Address." *Washington Post*, January 28. http://www.washingtonpost.com/wp-srv/onpolitics/transcripts/bush text_012803.html.

Bush, George W. 2006. "President Bush Delivers Remarks on Terrorism." *Washington Post*, September 6, sec. Politics. http://www.washingtonpost.com/wp-dyn/content/arti cle/2006/09/06/AR2006090601425.html.

Bush, George W. 2010. *Decision Points*. New York: Crown.

Bybee, Jay S. 2002a. "Memorandum for Alberto R. Gonzales, Counsel to the President, Re: Standards of Conduct for Interrogation under 18 USC §§ 2340-2340A." U.S. Department of Justice, Office of Legal Counsel, August 1. https://nsarchive2.gwu.edu// NSAEBB/NSAEBB127/02.08.01.pdf.

Bybee, Jay S. 2002b. "Memorandum for John Rizzo, Acting General Counsel of the Central Intelligence Agency: Interrogation of al Qaeda Operative." U.S. Department of Justice, Office of Legal Counsel, August 1. https://www.justice.gov/sites/default/files/ olc/legacy/2010/08/05/memo-bybee2002.pdf.

Calamur, Krishnadev. 2018. "Nine Notorious Dictators, Nine Shout-Outs from Donald Trump." *Atlantic*, March 4. https://www.theatlantic.com/international/archive/2018/ 03/trump-xi-jinping-dictators/554810/.

Calley, William L. 1971. *Lieutenant Calley: His Own Story*. New York: Viking Press.

Carle, Glenn L. 2014. "Torture Is Wrong." *Boston Globe*, October 6, sec. Opinion. http://www.bostonglobe.com/opinion/2014/10/06/torture-wrong/D9uUPipS5yV am4YlTQxelL/story.html.

Carpenter, R. Charli. 2003. "'Women and Children First': Gender, Norms, and Humanitarian Evacuation in the Balkans 1991–95." *International Organization* 57, no. 4: 661–94.

CBS News. 2009. "Stanford Student Assails Rice on Torture." May 1. http://www.cbsnews. com/news/stanford-student-assails-rice-on-torture/.

Central Intelligence Agency. 1963. "KUBARK Counterintelligence Interrogation." July. National Security Archive. http://nsarchive.gwu.edu/NSAEBB/NSAEBB122/.

Central Intelligence Agency. 2003. "Memorandum for: Deputy Director of Operations; Subject: Death Investigation—Gul Rahman." January 28. Torture Database. https:// www.thetorturedatabase.org/files/foia_subsite/cia_17_29.m_0.pdf.

Central Intelligence Agency. 2008. "A Look Back . . . Truman Appoints First DCI, 1946." CIA News and Information, January 17. https://www.cia.gov/news-information/featu red-story-archive/2008-featured-story-archive/truman-appoints-first-dci.html.

Central Intelligence Agency. 2013. "Memorandum for: The Honorable Diane Feinstein; The Honorable Saxby Chambliss; Subject: CIA Comments on the Senate Select Committee on Intelligence Report on the Rendition, Detention, and Interrogation Program." Washington, DC, June 27. https://irp.fas.org/congress/2014_rpt/cia-ssci.pdf.

Cheney, Liz. 2018. "The Enhanced Interrogation Program Saved Lives . . ." Tweet. @liz_cheney (blog), March 13. https://twitter.com/liz_cheney/status/9736734 12785827840?lang=en.

Cheney, Richard. 1989. "Congressional Overreach in Foreign Policy." Draft. Paper presented at Foreign Policy and the Constitution conference, American Enterprise Institute, March 14–15. https://assets.documentcloud.org/documents/339579/congre ssional-overreaching-cheney.pdf.

Cheney, Richard. 2008. "Speech at the 35th Annual Meeting of the Conservative Political Action Conference." C-SPAN, February 7. http://www.c-span.org/video/?203995-7/vice-president-cheney-speech.

Cheney, Richard, William S. Broomfield, Henry J. Hyde, Jim Courter, Bill McCollum, Michael DeWine, James A. McClure, and Orrin G. Hatch. 1987. "Reports of the Iran-Contra Committees: Excerpts from the Minority View." New York Times, November 17, sec. World. http://www.nytimes.com/1987/11/17/world/reports-of-the-iran-con tra-committees-excerpts-from-the-minority-view.html.

CIA Inspector General. 2004. "Special Review: Counterterrorism Detention and Interrogation Activities, September 2001–October 2003." May 7. Rendition Project. http://www.therenditionproject.org.uk/pdf/PDF%2020%20%5BCIA%20IG%20In vestigation%20EITs%202004%5D.pdf.

Clarke, Richard A. 2004. Against All Enemies: Inside America's War on Terror. New York: Free Press.

CNN.com. 2004. "U.S. President / National / Exit Poll." https://www.cnn.com/ELECT ION/2004/pages/results/states/US/P/00/epolls.0.html.

Cockburn, Alexander, and Jeffrey St. Clair. 1998. Whiteout: The CIA, Drugs, and the Press. New York: Verso.

Colby, William E. 1978. Honorable Men: My Life in the CIA. New York: Simon and Schuster.

Conrad, Courtenay Ryals, and Will H. Moore. 2010. "What Stops the Torture?" American Journal of Political Science 54, no. 2: 459–76.

Conroy, John. 2005. "Tools of Torture." Chicago Reader, February 3. http://www.chicag oreader.com/chicago/tools-of-torture/Content?oid=917876.

CQ Transcriptions. 2006. "President Bush's News Conference." New York Times, September 15, sec. Washington. http://www.nytimes.com/2006/09/15/washington/15bush_transcript.html.

Crowley, Michael. 2016. "On Torture, Cruz Stands Alone." Politico, January 21. https://www.politico.com/story/2016/01/ted-cruz-republicans-torture-217976.

d'Ambruoso, William L. 2015. "Norms, Perverse Effects, and Torture." International Theory 7, no. 1: 33–60.

d'Ambruoso, William L. 2016. "Sources." https://sites.google.com/site/williamdambru oso/sources.

Davenport, Christian. 2007. State Repression and the Domestic Democratic Peace. Cambridge Studies in Comparative Politics. New York: Cambridge University Press.

Davenport, Christian, Will H. Moore, and Dave Armstrong. 2007. "The Puzzle of Abu Ghraib: Are Democratic Institutions a Palliative or Panacea?" Abstract. SSRN, December 8. http://ssrn.com/abstract=1022367.

Denvir, Daniel. 2013. "The Secret History of the Vietnam War." Vice, April 17. http://www.vice.com/read/vietnam-and-the-mere-gook-rule.

Dershowitz, Alan M. 2002. Why Terrorism Works: Understanding the Threat, Responding to the Challenge. New Haven, CT: Yale University Press.

Diamond, Jeremy. 2016. "Trump on Torture: 'We Have to Beat the Savages.'" CNN Digital, March 6. https://www.cnn.com/2016/03/06/politics/donald-trump-torture/index.html.

Diamond, Jeremy, and Eugene Scott. 2016. "Trump Asks Backers to Swear Their Support, Vows to Broaden Torture Laws." CNN Digital, March 5. https://www.cnn.com/2016/03/05/politics/donald-trump-florida-pledge-torture/index.html.

Dilanian, Ken. 2016. "Trump Needs 'Own Damn Bucket' If He Wants to Waterboard: Ex-CIA Chief." NBC News, February 22. https://www.nbcnews.com/news/us-news/trump-needs-his-own-damn-bucket-waterboard-ex-cia-chief-n523576.

Dobson, Hugo. 2003. *Japan and United Nations Peacekeeping: New Pressures, New Responses.* New York: Routledge.

Doolittle, James H. 1954. "Report on the Covert Activities of the CIA." September 30. Cryptome. http://cryptome.org/cia-doolittle.pdf.

Downes, Alexander B. 2008. *Targeting Civilians in War.* Ithaca, NY: Cornell University Press.

Duffett, John. 1968. *Against the Crime of Silence: Proceedings of the Russell International War Crimes Tribunal.* Flanders, NJ: O'Hare Books.

Dulles, Allan W. 1953. "'Brain Warfare': Summary of Remarks at the National Alumni Conference of the Graduate Council of Princeton University, Hot Springs, VA." Central Intelligence Agency, April 10. https://www.cia.gov/library/readingroom/docs/CIA-RDP80R01731R001700030015-9.pdf.

Earman, John S. 1963. "Memorandum for Director of Central Intelligence; Subject: Report of Inspection of MKULTRA." CIA Inspector General. Central Intelligence Agency, July 26. https://info.publicintelligence.net/CIA-MKULTRA-IG.pdf.

Eggen, Dan. 2006. "Cheney's Remarks Fuel Torture Debate." *Washington Post*, October 27. http://www.washingtonpost.com/wp-dyn/content/article/2006/10/26/AR2006102601521.html.

Einolf, Christopher J. 2007. "The Fall and Rise of Torture: A Comparative and Historical Analysis." *Sociological Theory* 25, no. 2: 101–21.

Einolf, Christopher J. 2014. *America in the Philippines, 1899–1902: The First Torture Scandal.* New York: Palgrave Macmillan.

Einolf, Christopher J. 2018. "US Torture of Prisoners of War in Historical Perspective: The Role of Delegitimization." In *Confronting Torture: Essays on the Ethics, Legality, History, and Psychology of Torture Today,* edited by Scott A. Anderson and Martha C. Nussbaum, 120–45. Chicago: University of Chicago Press.

Fay, George R. 2004. "Investigation of 205th Military Intelligence Brigade's Activities in Abu Ghraib Detention Facility." August 25. Torture Database. https://www.thetorturedatabase.org/document/fay-report-investigation-205th-military-intelligence-brigades-activites-abu-ghraib.

Federal News Service. 2016. "Transcript of the Republican Presidential Debate in Detroit." *New York Times*, March 4. http://www.nytimes.com/2016/03/04/us/politics/transcript-of-the-republican-presidential-debate-in-detroit.html.

Feldman, Noah. 2005. "Ugly Americans: The Laws of a War against Evil. (Book Review)." *New Republic*, May 30. https://business.highbeam.com/4776/article-1G1-132766662/ugly-americans-laws-war-against-evil.

Fink, Sheri, and Helene Cooper. 2017. "Inside Trump Defense Secretary Pick's Efforts to Halt Torture." *New York Times*, January 2, sec. U.S. https://www.nytimes.com/2017/01/02/us/politics/james-mattis-defense-secretary-trump.html.

Fiske, Alan Page, and Philip E. Tetlock. 1997. "Taboo Trade-Offs: Reactions to Transactions That Transgress the Spheres of Justice." *Political Psychology* 18, no. 2: 255–97.

Foot, Rosemary. 2006. "Torture: The Struggle over a Peremptory Norm in a Counter-Terrorist Era." *International Relations* 20, no. 2: 131–51.

Foucault, Michel. 1977. *Discipline and Punish: The Birth of the Prison.* New York: Pantheon Books.

Frey, John Patrick. 2008. "Tim Rutten Lies about Cheney's CPAC Speech." *Patterico's Pontifications* (blog), February 10. http://patterico.com/2008/02/10/tim-rutten-lies-about-cheneys-cpac-speech/.

Friedersdorf, Conor. 2013. "Remember When Torture Was Only Going to Be Used to Stop Ticking Nukes?" *Atlantic*, April 17. https://www.theatlantic.com/politics/archive/2013/04/remember-when-torture-was-only-going-to-be-used-to-stop-ticking-nukes/275054/.

Frontline. 2005. "Interview: Jack Cloonan." PBS, October 18. http://www.pbs.org/wgbh/pages/frontline/torture/interviews/cloonan.html.

Fukuyama, Francis. 1989. "The End of History?" *National Interest* 16: 3–18.

Fukuyama, Francis. 1992. *The End of History and the Last Man*. New York: Simon and Schuster.

Gaddis, John Lewis. 1986. "The Long Peace: Elements of Stability in the Postwar International System." *International Security* 10, no. 4: 99–142.

Gallup. 2016. "Presidential Approval Ratings: George W. Bush." http://www.gallup.com/poll/116500/Presidential-Approval-Ratings-George-Bush.aspx.

Garcia, Denise. 2011. *Disarmament Diplomacy and Human Security: Regimes, Norms, and Moral Progress in International Relations*. New York: Routledge.

Garcia, Michael John. 2010. *Renditions: Constraints Imposed by Laws on Torture*. Darby, PA: Diane Publishing.

Gates, John M. 2002. *The US Army and Irregular Warfare*. Wooster, OH: College of Wooster. http://discover.wooster.edu/jgates/the-us-army-and-irregular-warfare/.

Gates, John Morgan. 1973. *Schoolbooks and Krags: The United States Army in the Philippines, 1898–1902*. Westport, CT: Greenwood Press.

Gellman, Barton. 2008. *Angler: The Cheney Vice Presidency*. New York: Penguin Press.

Gellman, Barton, and Jo Becker. 2007. "Pushing the Envelope on Presidential Power." *Angler: The Cheney Vice Presidency* (blog), June 25. http://voices.washingtonpost.com/cheney/chapters/pushing_the_envelope_on_presi/.

George, Alexander L., and Andrew Bennett. 2005. *Case Studies and Theory Development in the Social Sciences*. Cambridge, MA: MIT Press.

Gibney, Alex. 2007. *Taxi to the Dark Side*. Documentary. ThinkFilm.

Gilmore, Gerry J. 2005. "U.S. Doesn't Condone Torture of Captive Terrorists, Rice Says." DoD News, December 5. http://archive.defense.gov/news/newsarticle.aspx?id=18638.

Gleason, S. Everett. 1953. "Memorandum of Discussion at the 165th Meeting of the National Security Council." In *Foreign Relations of the United States 1952–1954*, Volume 2, Part 1: *National Security Affairs*. Washington, D.C., October 7. https://history.state.gov/historicaldocuments/frus1952-54v02p1/d92.

Gleditsch, Kristian S., and Michael D. Ward. 1997. "Double Take: A Reexamination of Democracy and Autocracy in Modern Polities." *Journal of Conflict Resolution* 41, no. 3: 361–83.

Goldman, Jan. 2010. *Ethics of Spying: A Reader for the Intelligence Professional*. Lanham, MD: Scarecrow Press.

Gonzales, Alberto. 2002. "Memorandum for the President; Subject: Decision Re: Application of the Geneva Convention on Prisoners of War to the Conflict with Al Qaeda and the Taliban." January 25. National Security Archive. http://www.gwu.edu/~nsarchiv/NSAEBB/NSAEBB127/02.01.25.pdf.

Goodman, Barak. 2010. "My Lai." *American Experience*, PBS, April 26. http://www.pbs.org/wgbh/americanexperience/films/mylai/player.

Greenburg, Jan Crawford, Howard L. Rosenberg, and Ariane de Vogue. 2008. "Sources: Top Bush Advisors Approved 'Enhanced Interrogation.'" ABC News, April 9. http://abcnews.go.com/print?id=4583256.

Gronke, Paul, and Darius Rejali. 2010. "U.S. Public Opinion on Torture, 2001–2009." PS: Political Science & Politics 43, no. 3: 437–44.

Hamby, Peter. 2009. "Bush Defends Interrogation Program in Michigan Speech." CNN, May 29. http://www.cnn.com/2009/POLITICS/05/29/george.bush.speech/index.html.

Haslam, Nick. 2006. "Dehumanization: An Integrative Review." Personality and Social Psychology Review 10, no. 3: 252–64.

Haslam, Nick, and Steve Loughnan. 2014. "Dehumanization and Infrahumanization." Annual Review of Psychology 65: 399–423.

Hathaway, Oona A. 2002. "Do Human Rights Treaties Make a Difference?" Yale Law Journal 111, no. 8: 1935–2042.

Hazelton, Jacqueline L. 2021. Bullets Not Ballots: Success in Counterinsurgency Warfare. Ithaca, NY: Cornell University Press.

Helms, Richard. 1953. "Memorandum for Director, Central Intelligence; Subject: Two Extremely Sensitive Research Programs." April 3. https://ronaldtammen.com/wp-content/uploads/2019/04/April-3-1953-Helms-memo.pdf.

Hersh, Seymour M. 2004a. Chain of Command: The Road from 9/11 to Abu Ghraib. New York: HarperCollins.

Hersh, Seymour M. 2004b. "Torture at Abu Ghraib." New Yorker, May 10. http://www.newyorker.com/magazine/2004/05/10/torture-at-abu-ghraib.

Hinkle, Lawrence E., and Harold G. Wolff. 1957. "Communist Interrogation and Indoctrination of Enemies of the States: Analysis of Methods Used by the Communist State Police (A Special Report)." AMA Archives of Neurology & Psychiatry 76, no. 2: 115–74.

Hitchens, Christopher. 2008. "Believe Me, It's Torture." Vanity Fair, July 2. https://www.vanityfair.com/news/2008/08/hitchens200808.

Holmes, Stephen. 2007. The Matador's Cape: America's Reckless Response to Terror. Cambridge: Cambridge University Press.

Holzman, Michael Howard. 2008. James Jesus Angleton, the CIA, and the Craft of Counterintelligence. Amherst: University of Massachusetts Press.

Horton, Scott. 2009. "Renditions Buffoonery." The Stream (blog), February 2. http://harpers.org/blog/2009/02/renditions-buffonery/.

Hosenball, Mark, and Michael Isikoff. 2006. "Out from the Shadows." Newsweek, September 18.

Hutchinson, Asa, James R. Jones, Talbot D'Alemberte, David P. Gushee, Azizah Y. al-Hibri, David R. Irvine, Claudia Kennedy, Thomas R. Pickering, William S. Sessions, and Gerald E. Thomson. 2013. Report of the Constitution Project's Task Force on Detainee Treatment. Washington, D.C.: The Constitution Project. http://detaineetaskforce.org/report/.

Jackson, Richard. 2007. "Language, Policy and the Construction of a Torture Culture in the War on Terrorism." Review of International Studies 33, no. 3: 353–71.

Jacobsen, Annie. 2014. Operation Paperclip: The Secret Intelligence Program That Brought Nazi Scientists to America. New York: Little, Brown.

Jacobson, Adam. 2017. "Could the United States Reinstitute an Official Torture Policy?" Journal of Strategic Security 10, no. 2: 97–118.

Jacoby, Jeff. 2005. "Why Not Torture Terrorists?" *Boston Globe*, March 20. http://archive. boston.com/news/globe/editorial_opinion/oped/articles/2005/03/20/why_not_tor ture_terrorists/.

Janis, Irving Lester. 1949. "Are the Cominform Countries Using Hypnotic Techniques to Elicit Confessions in Public Trials?" Research Memorandum #161. Santa Monica, CA: RAND Corporation, April 25.

https://www.rand.org/content/dam/rand/pubs/research_memoranda/2006/RM161.pdf.

Jeffreys-Jones, Rhodri. 1989. *The CIA and American Democracy*. New Haven, CT: Yale University Press.

Jervis, Robert. 1988. "War and Misperception." *Journal of Interdisciplinary History* 18, no. 4: 675–700.

Jervis, Robert. 2006. "Understanding Beliefs." *Political Psychology* 27, no. 5: 641–63.

Jervis, Robert. 2010. "Why Intelligence and Policymakers Clash." *Political Science Quarterly* 125, no. 2: 185–204.

Jervis, Robert. 2015. "The Torture Blame Game: The Botched Senate Report on the CIA's Misdeeds." *Foreign Affairs* 94, no. 3. https://www.foreignaffairs.com/reviews/2015-04-20/torture-blame-game.

Johnson, Jenna. 2015. "Donald Trump on Waterboarding: 'If It Doesn't Work, They Deserve It Anyway.'" *Washington Post*, November 23. https://www.washingtonpost. com/news/post-politics/wp/2015/11/23/donald-trump-on-waterboarding-if-it-doe snt-work-they-deserve-it-anyway/.

Johnson, Jenna, and Jose A. Del Real. 2016. "Trump Tells Story about Killing Terrorists with Bullets Dipped in Pigs' Blood, though There's No Proof of It." *Washington Post*, February 20. https://www.washingtonpost.com/news/post-politics/wp/2016/02/20/ trumps-story-about-killing-terrorists-with-bullets-dipped-in-pigs-blood-is-likely-not-true/.

Johnson, Larry C. 2005. "I Think Dick Cheney Has Been Watching Too Many . . ." *Los Angeles Times*, November 11. http://articles.latimes.com/2005/nov/11/news/OE-JOHNSON11.

Johnston, Alastair Iain. 1996. "Cultural Realism and Strategy in Maoist China." In *The Culture of National Security: Norms and Identity in World Politics*, edited by Peter J. Katzenstein, 216–68. New York: Columbia University Press.

Jones, Gregg. 2012. *Honor in the Dust: Theodore Roosevelt, War in the Philippines, and the Rise and Fall of America's Imperial Dream*. New York: New American Library.

Jordan, Gregor. 2012. *Unthinkable*. Drama. Sony Pictures.

Kaczynski, Andrew, Chris Massie, and Nathan McDermott. 2017. "80 Times Trump Talked about Putin." CNN, March. https://www.cnn.com/interactive/2017/03/politics/ trump-putin-russia-timeline/.

Kakutani, Michiko. 2005. "Following a Paper Trail to the Roots of Torture." *New York Times*, February 8. http://www.nytimes.com/2005/02/08/books/following-a-paper-trail-to-the-roots-of-torture.html.

Kanno-Youngs, Zolan. 2019. "Squalid Conditions at Border Detention Centers, Government Report Finds." *New York Times*, July 2, sec. U.S. https://www.nytimes. com/2019/07/02/us/politics/border-center-migrant-detention.html.

Karnow, Stanley. 1989. *In Our Image: America's Empire in the Philippines*. New York: Random House.

Katzenstein, Peter J., ed. 1996. *The Culture of National Security: Norms and Identity in World Politics*. New York: Columbia University Press.

Katzenstein, Peter J., Robert Owen Keohane, and Stephen D. Krasner. 1999. *Exploration and Contestation in the Study of World Politics*. Cambridge, MA: MIT Press.

Keck, Margaret E., and Kathryn Sikkink. 1998. *Activists beyond Borders: Advocacy Networks in International Politics*. Ithaca, NY: Cornell University Press.

Keith, Linda Camp. 2002. "Constitutional Provisions for Individual Human Rights (1977–1996): Are They More Than Mere 'Window Dressing?'" *Political Research Quarterly* 55, no. 1: 111–43.

Kelman, Herbert C. 1973. "Violence without Moral Restraint: Reflections on the Dehumanization of Victims and Victimizers." *Journal of Social Issues* 29, no. 4: 25–61.

Kennan, George F. 1947. "The Sources of Soviet Conduct." *Foreign Affairs* 25, no. 4: 566–82.

Kershner, Isabel. 2013. "Israel: Military to Stop Using Shells Containing Phosphorus." *New York Times*, April 26. http://www.nytimes.com/2013/04/27/world/middleeast/israel-military-to-stop-using-shells-containing-phosphorus.html.

Keynes, John Maynard. 1936. *The General Theory of Employment, Interest, and Money*. University of Adelaide eBooks. https://ebooks.adelaide.edu.au/k/keynes/john_maynard/k44g/.

Kier, Elizabeth. 1997. *Imagining War: British and French Military Doctrine between the Wars*. Princeton, NJ: Princeton University Press.

Kier, Elizabeth, and Jonathan Mercer. 1996. "Setting Precedents in Anarchy: Military Intervention and Weapons of Mass Destruction." *International Security* 20, no. 4: 77–106.

Kinzer, Stephen. 2019. *Poisoner in Chief: Sidney Gottlieb and the CIA Search for Mind Control*. New York: Henry Holt.

Kirk, Michael. 2006. "The Dark Side." *Frontline*, PBS. https://www.pbs.org/wgbh/pages/frontline/darkside/etc/script.html.

Kirk, Michael. 2015. "Secrets, Politics and Torture." *Frontline*, PBS. https://www.pbs.org/wgbh/frontline/film/secrets-politics-and-torture/transcript/.

Klein, Joe. 2009. "The Bush Administration's Most Despicable Act." *Time*, January 8. http://content.time.com/time/magazine/article/0,9171,1870503,00.html.

Konnikova, Maria. 2015. "Trying to Cure Depression, but Inspiring Torture." *New Yorker*, January 14. https://www.newyorker.com/science/maria-konnikova/theory-psychology-justified-torture.

Kramer, Paul A. 2006. *Blood of Government: Race, Empire, the United States, and the Philippines: Race, Empire, the United States, and the Philippines*. Chapel Hill: University of North Carolina Press.

Kramer, Paul. 2008. "The Water Cure." *New Yorker*, February 25. https://www.newyorker.com/magazine/2008/02/25/the-water-cure.

Krasner, Stephen D. 1999. *Sovereignty: Organized Hypocrisy*. Princeton, NJ: Princeton University Press.

Krider, Fred. 2018. "Remember When: The Complicated Life, Career of Edwin F. Glenn, Camp Sherman Commander." *Chillicothe Gazette*, July 6. https://www.chillicothegazette.com/story/news/local/2018/07/06/remember-when-complicated-life-career-edwin-f-glenn-camp-sherman-commander/735328002/.

Kristof, Nicholas D. 1995. "Unmasking Horror—A Special Report; Japan Confronting Gruesome War Atrocity." *New York Times*, March 17. http://www.nytimes.com/1995/03/17/world/unmasking-horror-a-special-report-japan-confronting-gruesome-war-atrocity.html.

Kronisch v. United States. 1998. U.S. Court of Appeals, Second Circuit. July 9.

Krugman, Paul. 2010. "The Seductiveness of Demands for Pain." *The Conscience of a Liberal* (blog), June 9. https://krugman.blogs.nytimes.com/2010/06/09/the-seductiveness-of-demands-for-pain/.

Lane, Mark. 1970. *Conversations with Americans*. New York: Simon and Schuster.

Langbein, John H. 2004. "The Legal History of Torture." In *Torture: A Collection*, edited by Sanford Levinson, 95–103. Oxford: Oxford University Press.

Lebow, Richard Ned. 1983. "Miscalculation in the South Atlantic: The Origins of the Falkland War." *Journal of Strategic Studies* 6, no. 1: 5–35.

Legro, Jeffrey W. 1997. "Which Norms Matter? Revisiting the 'Failure' of Internationalism." *International Organization* 51, no. 1: 31–63.

Leopold, Jason. 2014. "CIA Torture Architect Breaks Silence to Defend 'Enhanced Interrogation.'" *Guardian*, April 18. http://www.theguardian.com/world/2014/apr/18/cia-torture-architect-enhanced-interrogation.

Levenson, Michael. 2007. "Romney Adviser at Home in the Spy World Fray." *New York Times*, November 2. http://www.nytimes.com/2007/11/02/world/americas/02iht-02romney.8160855.html.

Levitsky, Steven, and Daniel Ziblatt. 2019. "Why Republicans Play Dirty." *New York Times*, September 20, sec. Opinion. https://www.nytimes.com/2019/09/20/opinion/republicans-democracy-play-dirty.html.

Lewy, Guenter. 1978. *America in Vietnam*. New York: Oxford University Press.

Lichtblau, Eric. 2009. *Bush's Law: The Remaking of American Justice*. New York: Anchor Books.

Lieber, Franz. 1863. "Instructions for the Government of Armies of the United States in the Field [General Orders No. 100 : The Lieber Code]." Avalon Project, Yale University. http://avalon.law.yale.edu/19th_century/lieber.asp.

Linklater, Andrew. 2007. "Torture and Civilisation." *International Relations* 21, no. 1: 111–18.

Linn, Brian McAllister. 1989. *The US Army and Counterinsurgency in the Philippine War, 1899–1902*. Chapel Hill: University of North Carolina Press.

Linn, Brian McAllister. 2000. *The Philippine War, 1899–1902*. Lawrence: University Press of Kansas.

Luban, David. 2007. *Liberalism, Torture, and the Ticking Bomb*. New York: Springer.

Lukes, Steven. 2005. "Liberal Democratic Torture." *British Journal of Political Science* 36, no. 1: 1–16.

Machiavelli, Niccolò. (1513) 1882. *Discourses on the First Ten Books of Titus Livius*. Translated by Christian E. Detmold. Boston: James R. Osgood.

Macy, Christy, and Susan Kaplan. 1980. *Documents*. New York: Penguin Books.

Magruder, John. Undated. "Report of the Director, Strategic Services Unit, Department of War to the Assistant Secretary of War for Air." In *Foreign Relations of the United States 1945–1950: Emergence of the Intelligence Establishment*. Washington, D.C. https://history.state.gov/historicaldocuments/frus1945-50Intel/d34.

Marchetti, Victor. 1974. *The CIA and the Cult of Intelligence*. New York: Knopf.

Margon, Sarah. 2018. "Giving Up the High Ground." *Foreign Affairs* 97, no. 2 (March 27). https://www.foreignaffairs.com/articles/united-states/2018-02-13/giving-high-ground.

Marks, John. 1979. *The Search for the Manchurian Candidate: The CIA and Mind Control*. New York: Times Books. https://archive.org/stream/pdfy-JSKQIeR_oYTgzSjl/John+

Marks+-+The+Search+for+the+Manchurian+Candidate+-+The+CIA+and+Mind+Control_djvu.txt.

Masters, Jonathan. 2013. "Targeted Killings." Council on Foreign Relations. https://www.cfr.org/backgrounder/targeted-killings.

Mayer, Jane. 2005. "Outsourcing Torture." *New Yorker*, February 14. http://www.newyorker.com/magazine/2005/02/14/outsourcing-torture.

Mayer, Jane. 2008. *The Dark Side: The Inside Story of How the War on Terror Turned into a War on American Ideals*. New York: Doubleday.

Mayer, Jane. 2014. "Torture and the Truth." *New Yorker*, December 22. http://www.newyorker.com/magazine/2014/12/22/torture-truth.

Mayerfeld, Jamie. 2008. "In Defense of the Absolute Prohibition of Torture." *Public Affairs Quarterly* 22, no. 2: 109–28.

Mayerfeld, Jamie. 2016. *The Promise of Human Rights: Constitutional Government, Democratic Legitimacy, and International Law*. Philadelphia: University of Pennsylvania Press.

Mazzetti, Mark, and Matt Apuzzo. 2014. "C.I.A. Director Defends Use of Interrogation Tactics, Avoiding Issue of Torture." *New York Times*, December 11. http://www.nytimes.com/2014/12/12/us/politics/cia-director-brennan-torture-report.html.

McCain, John. 2005. "Torture's Terrible Toll." *Newsweek*, November 20. http://www.newsweek.com/tortures-terrible-toll-115193.

McCarthy, Andrew C. 2004. "Torture: Thinking about the Unthinkable." *Commentary*, July 1. https://www.commentarymagazine.com/articles/torture-thinking-about-the-unthinkable/.

McCarthy, Tom. 2016. "Donald Trump Reverses Position on Torture, Saying He Would Abide by Law." *Guardian*, March 4. http://www.theguardian.com/us-news/2016/mar/04/donald-trump-torture-position-statement-military-law.

McCoy, Alfred. 2006. *A Question of Torture: CIA Interrogation, from the Cold War to the War on Terror*. New York: Macmillan.

McKeown, Ryder. 2009. "Norm Regress: US Revisionism and the Slow Death of the Torture Norm." *International Relations* 23, no. 1: 5–25.

Mearsheimer, John J. 1990. "Why We Will Soon Miss the Cold War." *Atlantic Monthly* 266, no. 2: 35–50.

Mearsheimer, John J., and Stephen M. Walt. 2016. "The Case for Offshore Balancing: A Superior U.S. Grand Strategy." *Foreign Affairs* 95, no. 4: 70–83.

Melzer, Nils. 2008. *Targeted Killing in International Law*. Oxford: Oxford University Press.

Melton, H. Keith, and Robert Wallace. 2009. *The Official CIA Manual of Trickery and Deception*. New York: Harper Collins.

Mercer, Jonathan. 1995. "Anarchy and Identity." *International Organization* 49, no. 2: 229–52.

Mercer, Jonathan. 2005. "Rationality and Psychology in International Politics." *International Organization* 59, no. 1: 77–106.

Mercer, Jonathan. 2013. "Emotion and Strategy in the Korean War." *International Organization* 67, no. 2: 221–52.

Merom, Gil. 2003. *How Democracies Lose Small Wars: State, Society, and the Failures of France in Algeria, Israel in Lebanon, and the United States in Vietnam*. Cambridge: Cambridge University Press.

Mettraux, Guénaël. 2003. "US Courts-Martial and the Armed Conflict in the Philippines (1899–1902): Their Contribution to National Case Law on War Crimes." *Journal of International Criminal Justice* 1, no. 1: 135–50.

Meyer, John W., John Boli, George M. Thomas, and Francisco O. Ramirez. 1997. "World Society and the Nation-State." *American Journal of Sociology* 103, no. 1: 144–81.

Miller, Stuart Creighton. 1982. *Benevolent Assimilation: The American Conquest of the Philippines, 1899–1903.* New Haven, CT: Yale University Press.

Mitchell, James E. 2016. *Enhanced Interrogation: Inside the Minds and Motives of the Islamic Terrorists Trying to Destroy America.* New York: Crown.

Morgan, David. 2018. "Trump Fist-Bumped Turkish Leader Erdogan, Said He 'Does Things the Right Way.'" CBS News, July 16. https://www.cbsnews.com/news/trump-fist-bumped-turkish-leader-erdogan-said-he-does-things-the-right-way/.

Morgenthau, Hans J. 1978. *Politics among Nations: The Struggle for Power and Peace.* 5th ed. New York: Knopf.

Morris, Edmund. 2002. *Theodore Rex.* Reprint. New York: Random House.

Moughty, Sarah. 2015. "John Rizzo: The Legal Case for 'Enhanced Interrogation.'" *Frontline*, PBS. http://www.pbs.org/wgbh/frontline/article/john-rizzo-the-legal-case-for-enhanced-interrogation/.

Moyar, Mark. 1997. *Phoenix and the Birds of Prey: The CIA's Secret Campaign to Destroy the Viet Cong.* Annapolis, MD: Naval Institute Press.

Mueller, John E. 1970. "Presidential Popularity from Truman to Johnson." *American Political Science Review* 64, no. 1: 18–34.

Mueller, John E. 2006. "Is There Still a Terrorist Threat?" *Foreign Affairs* 85, no. 5: 2–8.

National Journal. 2019. "The Authoritarians Trump Loves . . . and Envies." Tribune Content Agency, May 21. https://tribunecontentagency.com/article/the-authoritarians-trump-loves-and-envies/.

NBC News. 2001. "9/11 Meet the Press with Dick Cheney." September 16. YouTube. https://www.youtube.com/watch?v=KQBsCIaxMuM.

NBC News. 2014. "Meet the Press Transcript—December 14, 2014." http://www.nbcnews.com/meet-the-press/meet-press-transcript-december-14-2014-n268181.

New York Times. 1977. "Mind-Control Studies Had Origins in Trial of Mindszenty." August 2.

Nizza, Mike. 2008. "A Window into Waterboarding." *The Lede* (blog), July 2. http://thelede.blogs.nytimes.com/2008/07/02/a-window-into-waterboarding/.

Nuñez-Mietz, Fernando Gabriel. 2013. "Lawyering Compliance with International Law: Legal Advisors and the Legalization of International Politics." PhD dissertation, Ohio State University. https://etd.ohiolink.edu/pg_10?0::NO:10:P10_ACCESSION_NUM:osu1370528559.

Otterman, Michael. 2007. *American Torture: From the Cold War to Abu Ghraib and Beyond.* Ann Arbor, MI: Pluto Press.

Peralta, Eyder. 2014. "'Torture Report': A Closer Look at When and What President Bush Knew." NPR, December 16. https://www.npr.org/sections/thetwo-way/2014/12/16/369876047/torture-report-a-closer-look-at-when-and-what-president-bush-knew.

Phelps, Jordyn. 2019. "Trump Blasts 'Fake News' in Front of Putin at G-20 Summit." ABC News, June 28. https://abcnews.go.com/Politics/trump-blasts-fake-news-front-putin-20-summit/story?id=64018038.

Phifer, Jerald. 2002. "Memorandum for Commander, Joint Task Force 170; Subject: Request for Approval of Counter-Resistance Strategies." October 11. National Security Archive. http://nsarchive.gwu.edu/NSAEBB/NSAEBB127/02.12.02.pdf.

Phillips, Joshua E. S. 2012. *None of Us Were Like This Before: American Soldiers and Torture.* London: Verso.

Pincus, Walter. 2006. "Waterboarding Historically Controversial." *Washington Post,* October 5, sec. Politics. http://www.washingtonpost.com/wp-dyn/content/article/2006/10/04/AR2006100402005.html.

Pinker, Steven. 2011. *The Better Angels of Our Nature: Why Violence Has Declined.* New York: Viking.

Poe, Steven C., and C. Neal Tate. 1994. "Repression of Human Rights to Personal Integrity in the 1980s: A Global Analysis." *American Political Science Review* 88, no. 4: 853–72.

Pollyea, Ryan. 2009. "Mancow Waterboarded, Admits It's Torture." NBC4 Washington, July 28. http://www.nbcwashington.com/news/archive/Mancow-Takes-on-Waterboarding-and-Loses.html.

Powell, Emilia Justyna, and Jeffrey K. Staton. 2009. "Domestic Judicial Institutions and Human Rights Treaty Violation." *International Studies Quarterly* 53, no. 1: 149–74.

Prados, John. 2013. *The Family Jewels: The CIA, Secrecy, and Presidential Power.* Austin: University of Texas Press.

Pribbenow, Merle. 2007. "The Man in the Snow White Cell." *Studies in Intelligence: A Central Intelligence Agency Journal* 48, no. 1. https://www.cia.gov/library/center-for-the-study-of-intelligence/csi-publications/csi-studies/studies/vol48no1/article06.html.

Price, Bryan C. 2012. "Targeting Top Terrorists: How Leadership Decapitation Contributes to Counterterrorism." *International Security* 36, no. 4: 9–46.

Price, Richard. 1998. "Reversing the Gun Sights: Transnational Civil Society Targets Land Mines." *International Organization* 52, no. 3: 613–44.

Price, Richard, and Nina Tannenwald. 1996. "Norms and Deterrence: The Nuclear and Chemical Weapons Taboos." In *The Culture of National Security,* edited by Peter J. Katzenstein, 114–52. New York: Columbia University Press.

Priest, Dana, and Barton Gellman. 2002. "U.S. Decries Abuse but Defends Interrogations." *Washington Post,* December 26, sec. Nation. http://www.washingtonpost.com/wp-dyn/content/article/2006/06/09/AR2006060901356.html.

Priest, Dana, and Joe Stephens. 2004. "Pentagon Approved Tougher Interrogations." *Washington Post,* May 9, sec. World. http://www.washingtonpost.com/wp-dyn/content/article/2004/05/09/AR2005040206867.html.

Rachman, Gideon. 2019. "Donald Trump Is Updating America's Historic Ruthlessness." *Financial Times,* May 6. https://www.ft.com/content/c0f92d52-6db3-11e9-a9a5-351eeaef6d84.

Ramsey, Robert D., III. 2007. *A Masterpiece of Counterguerrilla Warfare: BG J. Franklin Bell in the Philippines, 1901–1902.* Fort Leavenworth, KS: Combat Studies Institute Press.

Rejali, Darius. 2007. *Torture and Democracy.* Princeton, NJ: Princeton University Press.

Risen, James. 2014. *Pay Any Price: Greed, Power, and Endless War.* Boston: Houghton Mifflin Harcourt.

Risjord, Norman K. 2002. *Representative Americans: The Civil War Generation.* Lanham, MD: Rowman & Littlefield.

Rodriguez, Jose A., Jr. 2012. *Hard Measures: How Aggressive CIA Actions after 9/11 Saved American Lives.* New York: Threshold Editions.

Romero, Simon, Zolan Kanno-Youngs, Manny Fernandez, Daniel Borunda, Aaron Montes, and Caitlin Dickerson. 2019. "Hungry, Scared and Sick: Inside the Migrant Detention Center in Clint, Tex." *New York Times*, July 6, sec. U.S. https://www.nytimes.com/interactive/2019/07/06/us/migrants-border-patrol-clint.html.

Ron, James. 1997. "Varying Methods of State Violence." *International Organization* 51, no. 2: 275–300.

Root, Elihu. 1902. "Reprint of Cable to General Chaffee." *News and Observer,* April 16.

Root, Elihu. 1916. *The Military and Colonial Policy of the United States: Addresses and Reports by Elihu Root*. Cambridge, MA: Harvard University Press.

Ross, Brian, and Richard Esposito. 2005. "CIA's Harsh Interrogation Techniques Described." ABC News, November 18. http://abcnews.go.com/Blotter/Investigation/story?id=1322866.

Rubin, Trudy. 2018. "Trump Is Suffering from a Bad Case of Autocrat Envy." *Philadelphia Inquirer*, March 30, sec. Opinion. https://www.inquirer.com/philly/columnists/trudy_rubin/trump-putin-xi-jinping-rodrigo-duterte-viktor-orban-autocrats-opinion-20180330.html.

Rummel, Rudolph J. 1994. *Death by Government*. New Brunswick, NJ: Transaction.

Rumsfeld, Donald. 2002. "For: Secretary of Defense; Subject: Counter-Resistance Techniques." November 27. National Security Archive. http://nsarchive.gwu.edu/NSAEBB/NSAEBB127/02.12.02.pdf.

Sagan, Scott D. 1994. "The Perils of Proliferation: Organization Theory, Deterrence Theory, and the Spread of Nuclear Weapons." *International Security* 18, no. 4: 66–107.

Salim et al. v. Mitchell et al. 2017. No. 2:15-CV-286-JLQ. U.S. Court of Appeals, Ninth District. August 7.

Sartre, Jean-Paul. 1963. "Preface." In *The Wretched of the Earth*, by Frantz Fanon, translated by Constance Farrington, 7–41. New York: Grove Press.

Savage, Charlie. 2011. "In Memoir, Cheney Addresses Controversies." *New York Times*, August 25. http://www.nytimes.com/interactive/2011/08/26/us/politics/20110826_CHENEY_MEMOIR.html.

Schelling, Thomas C. 1960. *The Strategy of Conflict*. Cambridge, MA: Harvard University Press.

Schelling, Thomas C. 2006. "An Astonishing 60 Years: The Legacy of Hiroshima." *Proceedings of the National Academy of Sciences* 103, no. 16: 6089–93.

Schmidt, Averell, and Kathryn Sikkink. 2019. "Breaking the Ban? The Heterogeneous Impact of US Contestation of the Torture Norm." *Journal of Global Security Studies* 4, no. 1: 105–22.

Schmitt, Eric. 2002. "U.S. Captures a Top Trainer for Al Qaeda." *New York Times*, January 6, sec. International Style/Asia Pacific. http://www.nytimes.com/2002/01/06/international/asia/06DETA.html.

Shane, Scott, and Mark Mazzetti. 2009. "In Adopting Harsh Tactics, No Look at Past Use." *New York Times*, April 21. http://www.nytimes.com/2009/04/22/us/politics/22detain.html.

Sheehan, Neil. 1970. "Review of Conversations with Americans by Mark Lane." *New York Times Book Review*, December 27. http://mcadams.posc.mu.edu/smearing.htm.

Shepard, Alicia C. 2009. "Harsh Interrogation Techniques or Torture?" National Public Radio, June 21. http://www.npr.org/sections/ombudsman/2009/06/harsh_interrogation_techniques.html.

Shilling, Donovan A. 2003. *Rochester's Transportation Heritage*. Mount Pleasant, SC: Arcadia.

Shue, Henry. 1978. "Torture." *Philosophy & Public Affairs* 7, no. 2: 124–43.

Siems, Larry. 2017. "Inside the CIA's Black Site Torture Room." *Guardian*, October 9. https://www.theguardian.com/us-news/ng-interactive/2017/oct/09/cia-torture-black-site-enhanced-interrogation.

Sikkink, Kathryn. 2013. "The United States and Torture: Does the Spiral Model Work?" In *The Persistent Power of Human Rights: From Commitment to Compliance*, edited by Thomas Risse, Stephen C. Ropp, and Kathryn Sikkink, 145–63. New York: Cambridge University Press.

Smith, W. Thomas. 2003. *Encyclopedia of the Central Intelligence Agency*. New York: Facts on File.

Snepp, Frank. 1977. *Decent Interval: An Insider's Account of Saigon's Indecent End*. New York: Random House.

Snepp, Frank. 2009. "Tortured by the Past." *Los Angeles Times*, April 27. http://articles.latimes.com/2009/apr/27/opinion/oe-snepp27.

Soufan, Ali H. 2009a. "My Tortured Decision." *New York Times*, April 22. http://www.nytimes.com/2009/04/23/opinion/23soufan.html.

Soufan, Ali H. 2009b. "What Torture Never Told Us." *New York Times*, September 6.

Soufan, Ali H. 2011. *The Black Banners: The Inside Story of 9/11 and the War against al-Qaeda*. New York: Norton.

Spannaus, Edward. 2006. "The CIA Is Not Demanding the Right to Torture Prisoners." *Executive Intelligence Review*, October 27. http://www.larouchepub.com/other/interviews/2006/3343frederick_hitz_cia.html.

Steindl, Christina, Eva Jonas, Sandra Sittenthaler, Eva Traut-Mattausch, and Jeff Greenberg. 2015. "Understanding Psychological Reactance." *Zeitschrift für Psychologie* 223, no. 4: 205–14.

Stout, David, and Scott Shane. 2008. "Cheney Defends Use of Harsh Interrogations." *New York Times*, February 7. http://www.nytimes.com/2008/02/07/washington/07cnd-intel.html.

Stracqualursi, Veronica. 2018. "Ex-CIA Director: Trump Has 'Autocratic Envy' toward Putin." CNN, March 2. https://www.cnn.com/2018/03/02/politics/michael-hayden-donald-trump-vladimir-putin-cnntv/index.html.

Sullivan, Andrew. 2007. "Verschärfte Vernehmung." *Daily Dish* (blog), May 29. http://www.theatlantic.com/daily-dish/archive/2007/05/-versch-auml-rfte-vernehmung/228158/.

Talbot, David. 2015. *The Devil's Chessboard: Allen Dulles, the CIA, and the Rise of America's Secret Government*. New York: HarperCollins.

Tannenwald, Nina. 1999. "The Nuclear Taboo: The United States and the Normative Basis of Nuclear Non-Use." *International Organization* 53, no. 3: 433–68.

Tannenwald, Nina. 2007. *The Nuclear Taboo: The United States and the Non-Use of Nuclear Weapons since 1945*. Cambridge: Cambridge University Press.

Team Fix. 2016. "Transcript of the New Hampshire GOP Debate, Annotated." *Washington Post*, February 6. https://www.washingtonpost.com/news/the-fix/wp/2016/02/06/transcript-of-the-feb-6-gop-debate-annotated/.

Tenet, George. 2007. *At the Center of the Storm: My Years at the CIA*. New York: HarperCollins.

Thayer, William. 2016. "Edwin F. Glenn, Cullum's Register, 2698." Reprint of George W. Cullum's Biographical Register of the Officers and Graduates of the United States Military Academy. http://penelope.uchicago.edu/Thayer/E/Gazetteer/Places/America/United_States/Army/USMA/Cullums_Register/2698*.html.

Thiessen, Marc. 2012. "When the Good Cop Was Bad." *National Review Online*, June 25. https://www.nationalreview.com/nrd/articles/302121/when-good-cop-was-bad.

Thomas, Evan. 2012. *Ike's Bluff: President Eisenhower's Secret Battle to Save the World.* New York: Little, Brown.

Thomas, Ward. 2001. *The Ethics of Destruction: Norms and Force in International Relations.* Cornell Studies in Security Affairs. Ithaca, NY: Cornell University Press.

Tickner, J. Ann. 1988. "Hans Morgenthau's Principles of Political Realism: A Feminist Reformulation." *Millennium* 17, no. 3: 429–40.

Truman, Harry S. 1963. "Limit CIA Role to Intelligence." *Washington Post*, December 22, sec. A.

Trump, Donald J. 2016. "I Will Do Whatever It Takes, Trump Says." *USA Today*, April 11. http://www.usatoday.com/story/opinion/2016/02/15/donald-trump-torture-enhanced-interrogation-techniques-editorials-debates/80418458/.

Tsebelis, George. 2002. *Veto Players: How Political Institutions Work.* Princeton, NJ: Princeton University Press.

Turse, Nick. 2013. *Kill Anything That Moves: The Real American War in Vietnam.* New York: Picador.

Tushnet, Mark V. 2003. "Constitutional Hardball." *John Marshall Law Review* 37: 523–53. https://doi.org/10.2139/ssrn.451960.

United Nations. 1984. Convention against Torture and Other Cruel, Inhuman or Degrading Treatment or Punishment. Pub. L. No. A/RES/39/46. http://www.un.org/documents/ga/res/39/a39r046.htm.

U.S. Army. 2002. "Counter Resistance Strategy Meeting Minutes." October 2. http://nsarchive.gwu.edu/torturingdemocracy/documents/20021002.pdf.

U.S. Army. 2006. "Field Manual 3-24: Counterinsurgency." Washington, DC: Headquarters, Department of the Army. https://irp.fas.org/doddir/army/fm3-24fd.pdf.

U.S. Congress. 2001. Authorization for Use of Military Force. Pub. L. No. S.J.Res.23.ENR. http://thomas.loc.gov/cgi-bin/query/z?c107:S.J.RES.23.ENR:

U.S. Congress. 2002. "Statement of Cofer Black." Joint Investigation into September 11. September 26. https://fas.org/irp/congress/2002_hr/092602black.html.

U.S. House of Representatives. 1978. "Hearings before the Select Committee on Assassinations, 95th Congress, 2nd Session." September 15. http://www.history-matters.com/archive/jfk/hsca/reportvols/vol2/html/HSCA_Vol2_0001a.htm.

U.S. Marine Corps. 2005. "War Crimes." MCRP 4-11.8B. September 6. http://fas.org/irp/doddir/usmc/mcrp4-11-8b.pdf.

U.S. National Security Council. 1950. "NSC 68: United States Objectives and Programs for National Security." April 7. http://fas.org/irp/offdocs/nsc-hst/nsc-68.htm.

U.S. Senate. 1902. *Affairs in the Philippine Islands: Hearings before the Committee on the Philippines of the United States Senate.* Washington, D.C.: Government Printing Office.

U.S. Senate. 1976. "Final Report of the Select Committee to Study Governmental Operations with Respect to Intelligence Activities [Church Committee]." http://www.intelligence.senate.gov/resources/intelligence-related-commissions.

U.S. Senate. 1977. "Project MKULTRA: The CIA's Program of Research in Behavioral Modification. Joint Hearing before the Select Committee on Intelligence and the Subcommittee on Health and Scientific Research of the Committee on Human Resources." Washington, D.C., August 3. http://www.nytimes.com/packages/pdf/national/13inmate_ProjectMKULTRA.pdf.

U.S. Senate, Armed Services Committee. 2008. "Inquiry into the Treatment of Detainees in US Custody." November 30. https://www.armed-services.senate.gov/imo/media/doc/Detainee-Report-Final_April-22-2009.pdf.

U.S. Senate, Select Committee on Intelligence. 2014. "Committee Study of the Central Intelligence Agency's Detention and Interrogation Program." https://www.intelligence.senate.gov/sites/default/files/publications/CRPT-113srpt288.pdf.

Valentine, Douglas. 2000. *The Phoenix Program*. Lincoln, NE: iUniverse. https://ia600608.us.archive.org/1/items/THEPHOENIXPROGRAMValentine_201707/THE%20PHOENIX%20PROGRAM%20Valentine.pdf.

Valentino, Benjamin, Paul Huth, and Sarah Croco. 2006. "Covenants without the Sword: International Law and the Protection of Civilians in Times of War." *World Politics* 58, no. 3: 339–77.

Vestal, Allan W. 2017. "The First Wartime Water Torture by Americans." *Maine Law Review* 69, no. 1: 2–66.

Wahl, Rachel. 2013. "Policing, Values, and Violence: Human Rights Education with Law Enforcers in India." *Oxford Journal of Human Rights Practice* 5, no. 2: 220–42.

Wallace, Geoffrey P. R. 2015. *Life and Death in Captivity: The Abuse of Prisoners during War*. New York: Cornell University Press.

Wallach, Evan. 2007. "Drop by Drop: Forgetting the History of Water Torture in US Courts." *Columbia Journal of Transnational Law* 45: 468–506.

Walsh, Kenneth T. 2013. "George W. Bush's 'Bullhorn' Moment." *US News & World Report*, April 25. http://www.usnews.com/news/blogs/ken-walshs-washington/2013/04/25/george-w-bushs-bullhorn-moment.

Walt, Stephen M. 2009. "On the Torture Memos." *Foreign Policy* (blog), April 20. http://foreignpolicy.com/2009/04/20/on-the-torture-memos/.

Waltz, Kenneth N. 1959. *Man, the State, and War: A Theoretical Analysis*. New York: Columbia University Press.

Waltz, Kenneth N. 1975. "Theory of International Relations." In *Handbook of Political Science*, edited by Fred I. Greenstein and Nelson W. Polsby, 8:1–86. Reading, MA: Addison-Wesley.

Walzer, Michael. 2000. *Just and Unjust Wars: A Moral Argument with Historical Illustrations*. 3rd ed. New York: Basic Books.

Wantchekon, Leonard, and Andrew Healy. 1999. "The 'Game' of Torture." *Journal of Conflict Resolution* 43, no. 5: 596–609.

Washington Post. 1968. "Interrogation." January 21.

Weiner, Tim. 2007. *Legacy of Ashes: The History of the CIA*. New York: Doubleday Broadway.

Wendt, Alexander. 1992. "Anarchy Is What States Make of It: The Social Construction of Power Politics." *International Organization* 46, no. 2: 391–425.

Wendt, Alexander. 1999. *Social Theory of International Politics*. New York: Cambridge University Press.

White House. 2001a. "Address to a Joint Session of Congress and the American People." September 20. http://georgewbush-whitehouse.archives.gov/news/releases/2001/09/20010920-8.html.

White House. 2001b. "The Vice President Appears on Meet the Press with Tim Russert." September 16. https://georgewbush-whitehouse.archives.gov/vicepresident/news-speeches/speeches/vp20010916.html.

White, Josh, and Scott Higham. 2004. "Sergeant Says Intelligence Directed Abuse." *Washington Post*, May 20.

Williams, J. Patrick. 2011. *Subcultural Theory: Traditions and Concepts*. Malden, MA: Polity Press.

Winter Soldier Investigation. 1971. First Marine Division Panel Testimony. http://www2. iath.virginia.edu/sixties/HTML_docs/Resources/Primary/Winter_Soldier/WS_03_1Marine.html.

Wilson, James Q. 1989. *Bureaucracy: What Government Agencies Do and Why They Do It*. New York: Basic Books.

Woodward, Bob. 2002. *Bush at War*. New York: Simon & Schuster.

The World. 1902. "The Public and the Philippines." April 16. https://newspaperarchive. com/world-apr-16-1902-p-6/.

Worth, Robert F., Mark Mazzetti, and Scott Shane. 2013. "With Brennan Pick, a Light on Drone Strikes' Hazards." *New York Times*, February 5. http://www.nytimes.com/2013/02/06/world/middleeast/with-brennan-pick-a-light-on-drone-strikes-hazards.html.

Yoo, John. 2005. "Memorandum Opinion for Timothy Flanigan, the Deputy Counsel to the President." In *The Torture Papers: The Road to Abu Ghraib*, edited by Karen J. Greenberg and Joshua L. Dratel, 3–24. New York: Cambridge University Press.

Yoo, John. 2006. *War by Other Means: An Insider's Account of the War on Terror*. New York: Atlantic Monthly Press.

Yoo, John, and Robert J. Delahunty. 2002. "Memorandum for William J. Haynes II, General Counsel, Department of Defense; Re: Application of Treaties and Laws to al Qaeda and Taliban Detainees." January 9. National Security Archive. http://nsarchive. gwu.edu/torturingdemocracy/documents/20020109.pdf.

Index

For the benefit of digital users, indexed terms that span two pages (e.g., 52–53) may, on occasion, appear on only one of those pages.

Tables and figures are indicated by t and f following the page number